LOVE & DEATH

The Murder of Kurt Cobain

LOVE & DEATH

The Murder of Kurt Cobain

Max Wallace and Ian Halperin

ATRIA BOOKS

NEW YORK   LONDON

TORONTO   SYDNEY

ATRIA BOOKS

1230 Avenue of the Americas
New York, NY 10020

ISBN: 978-0-7434-8484-8

First Atria Books trade paperback edition March 2005

10   9   8   7   6   5   4   3   2   1

ATRIA BOOKS is a trademark of Simon & Schuster, Inc.

Credits for the photo insert: page 1 (top) courtesy of Kris Parker;
page 2 (bottom), page 4 (bottom), pages 7 and 8 courtesy of the authors;
page 2 (top) courtesy of Sestini/Gamma; page 2 (bottom), page 3
courtesy of Tom Grant; page 4 (top) courtesy of Brian Garrity;
pages 5 and 6 courtesy of Keystone Agency.

Manufactured in the United States of America

For information regarding special discounts for bulk purchases,
please contact Simon & Schuster Special Sales at 1-800-456-6798
or business@simonandschuster.com

In memory of

KRISTEN PFAFF

INTRODUCTION

Within days of the release of our first book, *Who Killed Kurt Cobain?*, in April 1998, the letters, calls, and e-mails began to pour in. Most of them demanded to know the same thing: Why hadn't we answered the question posed by the book's title?

The seeds of our initial investigation had been planted in 1994, shortly after Cobain's death, when Ian Halperin was on a West Coast tour with his band, State of Emergency. A former member of the band had moved to Seattle a year earlier and formed relationships with a number of people in Cobain's circle, including one of Kurt's drug dealers and his best friend, Dylan Carlson.

When Ian arrived in Seattle, his old bandmate introduced him to a number of Seattle scenesters, including friends of Kurt, each of whom related their doubts about the official story. Even then, soon after the apparent suicide, there was a feeling in Seattle that Kurt's death may not have come at his own hand.

Ian, who had met Kurt in 1990, before a Nirvana gig in Montreal, didn't give much thought to the claims until he heard that a private detective hired by Courtney Love was claiming that Kurt had been murdered and that Courtney may have been involved. When he returned to Canada, Ian contacted his old writing partner, Max Wallace, who was then station manager of North

America's oldest alternative radio station, CKCU-FM, and had solid connections in alternative music circles. A decade earlier, we had shared a *Rolling Stone* magazine award for investigative journalism. We decided to embark on our own minor investigation into the circumstances of Cobain's death, and came out with a somewhat skeptical treatment in the June 1995 issue of *Canadian Disk* magazine. On the strength of the article, we were commissioned to produce a video documentary about the murder theory, and a few months later, we traveled to Seattle and California to investigate the case.

But while we were conducting our own probe, the murder theory was taking on an unstoppable momentum of its own. Courtney Love's private detective, Tom Grant, had gone public with his murder theory in numerous national and international media forums, including a major U.S. network television show. Before long, our documentary had turned into a hastily assembled book, published on the fourth anniversary of Kurt's death.

Instead of taking a stand on Grant's charges, our book examined the facts on both sides and in the end simply called on police to reopen the investigation. Some reviewers mocked the conspiracy theory at the core of our book, but most praised its objectivity. The *New Yorker* issued us an imprimatur of credibility when it labeled the book a "judicious presentation of explosive material." Some readers, however, seemed to believe we had been a little *too* judicious.

Among the myriad of letters we received following the book's release were a number from forensic and law enforcement specialists who told us that we had missed the boat; the details we reported clearly demonstrated that Kurt Cobain had been murdered. But by then, the case was over for us. Max wrote two more books on unrelated subjects, appeared as a guest columnist for the *Sunday New York Times*, and produced two documentary films. Ian wrote three books, was hired as a correspondent for *Court TV,* and embarked on an acting career that landed him a role as Howard Hughes's friend in Martin Scorcese's upcoming film *The Aviator.*

Meanwhile, another high-profile case was making its way back into the headlines. A month after the publication of *Who Killed Kurt Cobain?*, former LAPD detective Mark Fuhrman published *Murder in Greenwich* exploring the 1975 murder of fifteen-year-old Martha Moxley—a book that regularly jockeyed for first place with ours on Ingram's True Crime bestseller list. Fuhrman had pointed to Kennedy cousin Michael Skakel as the likely killer and, when the case was reopened after twenty-seven years, *Murder in Greenwich* was credited. On June 7, 2002, Skakel was convicted of the crime.

For Fuhrman, a crucial piece of new evidence had surfaced two decades after Martha Moxley's death. Nearly a decade after Kurt Cobain's, we came into some damning new evidence of our own.

1

It is a typically rainy day in Montesano, Washington, when we arrive for our interview with Kurt's paternal grandfather, Leland Cobain, in June 2003. Leland and his late wife, Iris, were said to have been closer to Kurt than even his own parents, and there were reports that, shortly before his death, Kurt had made plans to go on a fishing trip with his grandfather. Although we had contacted him while we were researching our first book, Leland—like most of Kurt's immediate family—was reluctant to be interviewed. Now, more than nine years after Kurt's death, we had heard that Leland was finally ready to talk about his famous grandson.

Most biographical accounts of Kurt's early years describe his family living in a trailer park, conjuring up images of a "trailer trash" upbringing. Indeed, the small Montesano lot where Leland resides, and where Kurt had lived on and off during his youth, is officially given this designation in the town directory, and perhaps it once served this purpose. But when we arrive, we are surprised to find that the dwellings aren't trailers at all, but rather small, prefab, bungalow-style units with well-groomed lawns and beautiful trees. Boats and golf carts are parked in many of the driveways, suggesting a more affluent community than what we had been led to expect by the condescending biographies and press accounts.

2 Leland greets us warmly at the door of his slightly cramped two-bedroom house. He and Iris had moved in more than thirty years earlier, when Kurt was just a young child, and Leland had continued living here alone after Iris's death in 1997. Just a stone's throw away is the house where Kurt himself had lived briefly with his father after his parents' divorce. When the going got rough, however, it was his grandparents' house where he sought refuge. It wouldn't be entirely accurate to describe the house as a shrine to Kurt, but from the moment we walk in the door, his presence can be seen and felt everywhere. The first sight that catches one's eye is a framed gold record presented to Nirvana in 1993. Underneath it is a kitschy black velvet portrait of Kurt given to Leland a few years ago by a fan. The rest of the walls and bookshelves are crammed with photos of Kurt and the other grandchildren, sandwiched in between plaques and trophies commemorating Leland's achievements as a champion golfer and dartsman. More Kurt-related memorabilia is crammed in the basement, including hundreds of photos and letters sent to Leland and Iris by Nirvana fans from all over the world.

"I'm very proud of him," says Leland, tearing up slightly as he pauses in front of a photo of a cherubic three-year-old Kurt. "He was a good kid. I miss him." He takes us on a tour of the house, pointing out the many artifacts associated with his grandson and telling stories about the boy who had spent a lot of time within these walls. Leland is a spry seventy-nine-year-old, who wears hearing aids in both ears to remedy a deafness acquired while fighting at Guadalcanal as a young marine during the Second World War and then exacerbated by rolling asphalt for a living years later. After his discharge from the marines, he developed a serious alcohol problem, which he admits made him a "different person." By most accounts, his problems started after his father—a local county sheriff—was killed when his gun went off accidentally. However, his heaviest drinking reportedly started after his third son, a severely retarded boy named Michael, died in an institution at the age of six. Leland, though, soon conquered his personal demons, found religion and gave up alcohol completely. "I became a changed man," he recalls. By the time Kurt was born in 1967, he had become a respected citizen of Montesano, a regular church-goer and, by most accounts, a pretty good father and grandfather, frequently babysitting for Kurt and his younger sister, Kim. But it was Iris, not Leland, with whom Kurt most closely bonded.

"They were so much alike," Leland recalls, pointing to a photo of a strikingly beautiful brunette taken just after the couple were married. "Kurt loved his grandmother so much. I think she was the only member of the family who he could confide in. I think he was closer to Iris than he was to his own mother. He got his artistic side from Iris, that's for sure."

Leland takes out a box of drawings Kurt did as a child. One of them, signed "Kurt Cobain, age 6," depicts Donald Duck and shows undeniable artistic talent for one so young. "When I saw that one, I said to Kurt, 'You traced that, you didn't draw it,' and he got mad; he said to me, 'I did too draw it.' "

After Kurt left his hometown for good in 1987, he kept in touch with his grandparents only sporadically. Leland takes out a Christmas card they received after Kurt moved away:

Dear long lost grandparents: I miss you very much. Which is no excuse for my not visiting. . . . We put out a single just recently and it has sold-out already. . . . I'm happier than I ever have been. It would be nice to hear from you as well. Merry Christmas

love Kurt

Leland hadn't read our first book, and we had yet to tell him the subject of this new one. After a tour of the house, and an hour's worth of anecdotes about Kurt and his family while sitting around the dining room table, we are at last prepared to broach the topic

4 | we thought would be the most difficult to bring up. Two of Leland's brothers had killed themselves years earlier, fueling the most common of all the clichés about Kurt's own fate—that he had somehow inherited the "suicide gene." It is obviously a sensitive subject, and Leland's voice chokes when he talks about the family tragedies. Finally, we ask him how he and Iris felt when they learned their own grandson had killed himself.

His response is not at all what we expected: "Kurt didn't commit suicide," he declares matter-of-factly. "He was murdered. I'm sure of it."

* * *

In the days and weeks following Kurt Cobain's 1994 death, journalists and biographers descended on his hometown of Aberdeen, Washington, seeking clues to help make sense of the suicide of the town's most famous descendant—a town Kurt had constantly scorned in his music, his interviews and his journals. So glaring was Aberdeen's sense of hopelessness that many came away feeling Kurt's eventual fate was hardly surprising, was perhaps even inevitable. The suicide rate in Aberdeen is twice the national average, and the unemployment rate staggering, since the near collapse of the logging industry years before. Drugs and other symptoms of despair were all-pervading.

"It's as if the town were being held accountable for Cobain's ruin—which is not entirely unfathomable," wrote Mikal Gilmore, who visited Aberdeen a week after Kurt's death. "When you are confronted with the tragic loss of a suicide, you can't help sorting backward through the dead person's life, looking for those crucial episodes of dissolution that would lead him to such an awful finish. Look far enough into Kurt Cobain's life, and you inevitably end up back in Aberdeen—the homeland that he fled."

Now we had come to Aberdeen nine years later seeking a different set of clues.

Three hours after our interview with Leland, we stumble upon an unexpectedly rich source of Cobain lore a few miles down the highway: two women in their early twenties, a stringy-haired boy of seventeen, and a baby. They are loitering outside the bus station when we stop to ask for directions, and we quickly strike up a conversation about Aberdeen's most famous native son.

They are too young to have really known Kurt, but we ask them whether they ever listen to his music. "Nobody around here listens to that stuff anymore," replies the boy, who could pass for a teenage Kurt, minus the distinctive blazing blue eyes. Today, he says, hip-hop and death metal rule in Aberdeen. They make us an offer we can't pass up: "You want to see his house?" and then proceed to cram themselves in the car. The baby, wedged between his mother and a skateboard, squirms contentedly in anticipation of whatever adventure lies ahead. "Later, we'll bring you to meet one of Kurt's old friends if you want," says Autumn, the twenty-three-year-old mother. She tells us she has two more children at home, and then ventures, "You're not narcs, are you?"

As we cruise through the streets of this grim town, passing churches and bars and not much else, it calls forth the description of Kurt's Aberdeen friend Dale Crover, who once said, "There's nothing to do here but smoke dope and worship Satan." Is that true? we ask our impromptu tour guides. "Pretty much," says the guy. "Oh yeah, and also skateboarding. There's always that."

The carload of us arrive at a small, impeccably manicured house at 101 East First Street in a section of town the locals call "the flats." Kurt's family moved here shortly after his birth from their rented house in nearby Hoquiam. His father, Don, worked as a mechanic at the local Chevron station to support the family while his mother, Wendy, took care of Kurt, born February 20, 1967, and his sister, Kim, born three years later. Wendy had scrimped and

6 | saved Don's earnings to buy the house—a badge of respectability heralding arrival into the middle class, and a decided step-up from her own working-class roots. She was determined that her children would make something of themselves and eventually escape the dead end that Aberdeen represented for most of the kids who grew up here.

And yet Don's father, Leland, never really approved of Wendy or what he called her "social-climbing ways."

"I think she thought she was better than our family," he recalls. "She was always criticizing Don because he wasn't enough of a muckety-muck. She wanted him to be making more money and she was never satisfied."

Aberdeen does not celebrate its status as a cradle of the musical movement called grunge. Indeed, the first thing you notice when you drive through the town looking for indications that a superstar grew up here is that there are none, even in the museum devoted to preserving local history. There's plenty in the museum about the fact that Aberdeen once boasted more than fifty brothels servicing the loggers and sailors, until a wave of morality shut them down in the 1950s. But it's almost as if the locals are embarrassed to claim Cobain as one of their own.

We ask the museum's curator, Dan Sears, Is the fact that there is not a single mention of Cobain in the Aberdeen Museum of History due to the continuous scorn Kurt heaped on the town— a town whose population he once described as "highly bigoted, redneck, snoose-chewing, deer-shooting, faggot-killing, logger types"?

"Not at all," Sears replies. "It's because my predecessor said he didn't want a bunch of long-haired hippies coming in all the time." He notes that we are the third set of visitors that day asking about Cobain. Just a few minutes earlier, he had fielded a query from a forty-year-old man and his son who had come a thousand miles to visit Kurt's hometown.

Sears does recommend one Kurt-related attraction in Aberdeen that we might want to visit, but even this homage seems to have been treated with a kind of pained embarrassment. Some years earlier, a local truck driver–turned–sculptor named Randi Hubbard had constructed a 600-pound, life-size concrete statue of Cobain in the garage of her husband's muffler shop. "I think we all have a little Kurt Cobain in us," explains Hubbard, who knew Kurt when their families lived a block away from one another in Aberdeen. "He was a precious little kid when I knew him. As Kurt said, the townspeople of Aberdeen didn't like change or culture. I wanted to put something in the entrance to the town to show the world that some of us loved Kurt."

Initially, the Aberdeen City Council had approved her offer to erect the statue in a park at the east entrance of town. But then the angry letters and phone calls from local residents started to pour in, and the town councillors quickly backpedaled. A local chamber of commerce president summed up the general feeling: "There are lots of people who deserve to be honored. . . . [But] there's a difference between being famous and being infamous."

Today the statue sits tucked in among auto parts and greasy rags. Just as well; Kurt would never have approved. He didn't want to have anything to do with Aberdeen or its residents, as his bandmate Krist Novoselic made clear when he publicly threatened to smash the statue to pieces if it was ever unveiled. "If anybody puts up a statue of Kurt, I'll kick it down," Novoselic said in 1994. "He would not have wanted it. That's not what Kurt was about." (A few years later, Hubbard constructed the first sculpture—a statue of a firefighter—to be erected at Ground Zero after September 11.)

But if the town has failed to brag about its most famous native son, it seems that everybody here has some Cobain connection and is quite willing to talk about it, as we discovered when the desk clerk of our hotel told us that she attended kindergarten with Kurt.

"He was a quiet guy," recalls Bobbi Fowler. "Kids used to tease

8 | him 'cause he was from a poor family. He didn't have the popular stuff other kids had. He struggled 'cause of his mom—that was well known. She didn't treat him good. They didn't have a lot of money, Kurt's family." This didn't quite mesh with the description Kurt gave his official biographer, Michael Azerrad, in 1993. "I was an extremely happy child," he recalled. "I was constantly screaming and singing. I didn't know when to quit. I'd eventually get beaten up by kids because I'd get so excited about wanting to play. I took play very seriously. I was just really happy."

From an early age, Kurt had an imaginary friend named Boddah, whom he introduced to his family and for whom he made them set an extra place at the table. When five-year-old Kurt was fingered by Aberdeen police as the prime suspect in the torture of a neighbor's cat, Boddah was blamed. But, other than a brief period on Ritalin to control his hyperactivity—a condition that was to diminish naturally when his parents restricted his sugar intake—by most accounts, Kurt was a typical little boy.

The story goes that the clue to explain what brought this happy childhood to an abrupt crash can be found on a wall inside this house on East First Street—where our newfound friends have taken us on the first stop of our Cobain tour of Aberdeen. Here a young Kurt had allegedly scrawled on his bedroom wall, "I hate Mom, I hate Dad, it really makes me feel so sad," after his parents' relationship started to deteriorate and he heard them fighting almost constantly. The story, like many told by his mother in later years, may be apocryphal, but it has been constantly repeated by chroniclers attempting to explain his self-destructive path, each of whom traces his downward spiral to his parents' 1975 divorce when Kurt was eight. It is the first of a long string of clichés that get trotted out, almost like a mantra, by those seeking pat answers for his eventual fate.

"Of course his parents' divorce had an effect on Kurt," says his grandfather. "What kid isn't affected when their parents split up?

But I think the real impact, which I guess you can blame on the divorce, didn't come until a little later."

Like almost everybody we talked to in Aberdeen, Leland paints a troubling picture of Kurt's relationship with his mother. "She didn't really have much use for him until he became famous. She didn't want anything to do with him. Maybe she couldn't handle him or something, although he wasn't really that much trouble."

When Don finally moved out of the house shortly after Kurt's ninth birthday, Wendy invited her new boyfriend to move in, a man Kurt would later describe as a "mean, huge wife beater." Taking on what he perceived to be the father role, the boyfriend would frequently smack Kurt for the smallest transgression. His mother's failure to protect him caused the boy to withdraw into his own little world. Wendy later admitted that the man was "nuts—a paranoid schizophrenic." At her new boyfriend's suggestion, she soon let Kurt go live with his father, who had taken a small house across the lot from Leland and Iris in Montesano.

If Leland has harsh words for his daughter-in-law's treatment of Kurt, he doesn't spare his own son some of the blame. At first, he recalls, Kurt was extremely happy living with Don. "They used to go fishing and they were together all the time. They did all kinds of father-and-son things. Kurt was thriving. I don't think I'm the only one who noticed that he was ecstatic to get away from his mother. And I think Kurt was about the happiest he'd ever been."

That soon changed when Don met and married a woman who had two children of her own. Kurt's new stepmother did everything she could to win his affection. But she wasn't the problem.

"One thing I noticed early on after Donny married this woman was the way he treated Kurt different than her kids," says Leland. "They could get away with just about anything, but if Kurt did something wrong, his father would give him a hard time. Donny never did want the divorce from Wendy, and I think he was afraid that the new one was going to leave him, so he bent over backwards to please her. She had a boy and a girl, and there could have been an apple sitting on a table and one of her kids could pick up the apple and take a bite out of it and put it back on the table, but if Kurt did that, Donny would hit him in the head or something. I told Donny, 'You're going to lose that kid.' I said, 'Goddamit, you've got to treat him the same as you do hers,' but he denied it, and he said, 'Bull, I don't treat him any different.' I know Kurt resented that, and I think that's when a lot of his problems really began."

When Kurt was young, the kids in Aberdeen and Montesano usually fell into three categories—the jocks, the rockers and the misfits. Kurt fell somewhere between the latter two. Today, explain our young companions, there are still three distinct groups, only the qualifications are now different: you're either a "screecher" (pothead), a "tweaker" (crystal meth addict) or a junkie (heroin or crack addict).

We realize Donnie Collier is definitely a screecher when the first thing he asks us is whether we have any of that "good Canadian weed." Our new friends have brought us to meet Collier at his little house in North Aberdeen because he was supposedly "real tight with Kurt." It soon becomes apparent that it wasn't so much Collier who was friends with Kurt but rather his uncle Dale Crover, a member of a local band called the Melvins, and later a Nirvana drummer.

Kurt had developed a love for pop music at an early age through listening to his favorite bands, the Beatles, the Mamas and the Papas, and the Monkees, on his aunt Mary's old hi-fi. Despite, or because of, his constant drum banging, none of his relatives had ever thought young Kurt had much musical affinity. Everybody just assumed he was going to be an artist after one of his drawings made it into the school paper when he was six. But as he became increasingly alienated from his father's new family, music—not art—became his refuge. Don was into rock and roll in a big way, and he had joined the Columbia House Music Club ("Get twelve records for only a cent"). When the records began to arrive, Kurt discovered a heavier sound than the bubblegum pop he had always loved. It soon brought him into contact with a new circle of friends—a group of much older heavy metal potheads who would come over to listen to and exchange records by the likes of Kiss, Aerosmith and Black Sabbath. "After they turned me on to that music," Kurt later recalled, "I started turning into this little stoner kid."

By the time he got his first guitar from his uncle Chuck on his fourteenth birthday, Kurt had already decided he was going to be a rock star. When he began taking guitar lessons, he wanted to play only Led Zeppelin, recalls Warren Mason, the guitarist in Wendy's brother Chuck's band, who remembers "the little blond kid watching when we jammed." Mason still runs ads all over Aberdeen inviting locals to study with "the man who taught Kurt Cobain to play guitar."

Chuck paid Mason $125 for an old Gibson Explorer and gave it to Kurt as a present. "The first lesson, I asked Kurt if he could play anything and he said yes," recalls Mason. "He played 'Louie, Louie' on one string. Kurt later admitted that a lot of his songs were based on 'Louie, Louie,' which has a one-four-five chord progression. When I asked him his goal, he said he wanted to master 'Stairway to Heaven.' His favorite band at the time was ELO." Years later, Kurt was furious when he read an interview with Mason in *Rolling Stone* revealing Kurt's early love for Led Zeppelin and other mainstream bands. "He was also pissed off that I said he was a nice kid," recalls Mason. Although bands like the Sex Pistols and the Ramones had already pioneered a musical revolution that would one day change his life, punk rock still had not permeated the Aberdeen scene.

By the age of fifteen, unable to get along with Don's wife and his stepsiblings, Kurt was shuttling back and forth between his parents' houses. But his mother's patience with his increasingly rebellious behavior grew thin, especially after Kurt was arrested for spray-painting "Homosexual Sex Rules" on the side of a local bank—an act more reflective of his penchant for pissing off the locals than of his sexual orientation. Wendy sent him to stay with a long series of relatives, including his grandparents, who brought him to church with them every Sunday. He didn't have much use for the sermons, recalls Leland, but he loved the music, and for a time Kurt even joined the choir, where he may have honed his soon-to-be distinct vocal abilities.

And then, at the age of sixteen, Kurt Cobain discovered punk, courtesy of a friend named Matt Lukin, whom Kurt had met in the most unlikely of places. They were on the same Little League baseball team that Kurt had joined to please his father (or so he later claimed, lest anybody accuse him of being a jock). Matt was the bassist for a local band mockingly named after a mentally handicapped Thriftway employee called Melvin who liked to climb on roofs. The year before, Kurt had been in the same high school art class as the Melvins' leader Buzz Osborne, when the band had still been a Jimi Hendrix/The Who cover band. But in the interval, the band had been turned on to the angry, rebellious sounds of punk, just the right music to say "Fuck off!" to all those they had grown to detest—the local rednecks, the jocks, the stoners and, most of all, their parents. Lukin and Osborne began to lend Kurt their precious cache of punk and new-wave tapes, along with their most prized possession, a Sex Pistols photo book. Before long, he joined the other "cling-ons"—the nickname for the assortment of local misfits who congregated around the Melvins—at the Aberdeen rehearsal space where the band pounded out the music that would transform Kurt's world.

"This is what I was looking for," Kurt wrote in his journal after he saw the band play for the first time behind the local Thriftway. "I came to the promised land of a grocery store parking lot and I found my special purpose."

Twenty years later, Donnie Collier, nephew of Dale Crover, the

Melvins' drummer, takes a long hit off his pipe and proceeds to share his memories of Kurt, whom he met at the Melvins' sessions. "There was a bunch of us who'd go over after school while the band rehearsed and just hang out. Sometimes he'd jam with the band, but he still wasn't very good. They didn't pay very much attention to him, I don't think. But they were the coolest guys in town and anybody who hung around with them was automatically considered cool. At least we thought so. I think it's about the only place where Kurt really fit in. You always read that Kurt was really quiet, but I never really noticed that. There was this nerdy guy, Scottie Karate, who would come over and hang out all the time. Kurt would sort of pick on him, just rag on him constantly; he could be a bit of a bully. He was pretty nice to me though, maybe because my uncle was in the band. He used to sell me pot. Kurt wasn't a big-time dealer or anything, but he'd always have a little extra that he'd sell to make some money."

Collier has run out of the homegrown he has been using to fill the pipe that has been going around the room for the past twenty minutes. He offers to take the lot of us to "Kurt Cobain Bridge," so nicknamed because Kurt immortalized it in the heartbreaking song "Something in the Way," and would later claim to have slept under it when his mother threw him out of the house. Recent accounts, fueled by the denials of Kurt's sister, Kim, have suggested the stories are a myth, that Kurt never really slept under the bridge at all, but that he had embellished the stories to make his youth seem more unhappy.

"Nah, the only myth is that it was the Wishkah Bridge he slept under," explains Collier, referring to the massive bridge you have to cross to enter Aberdeen. "You can't sleep under that bridge. The tide would wash you away."

Instead, Collier takes us to a much smaller structure known as the North Aberdeen Bridge, and we climb down a path to the fetid Wishkah River through thorny brambles and bushes, to emerge on a spacious rocky slope sheltered by the span. "Here's where he slept," says Collier, his words occasionally drowned out by the rumbling of the cars overhead. "Just about every kid around Aberdeen ends up sleeping here at one time or another. Anybody who says Kurt didn't sleep here doesn't know what they're talking about. It's dry, it's pretty warm and you can pitch a tent. Kurt would sometimes spend a couple of nights at a time under here whenever his mother threw him out. Then, if it got too damp or miserable, he'd end up sleeping on somebody's floor. But it's a good place to play guitar. The acoustics are perfect." One of the girls, Angela, who's been with us all afternoon, tells us she slept under this bridge for five days in 1995 after her own parents banished her from the house. "It was dry, but it wasn't very warm," she remembers. "I froze my ass off." The remnants of a small cooking fire and an abandoned sleeping bag suggest that somebody has indeed been sleeping here in the not-too-distant past. But it isn't the only sign of human activity. Judging by the graffiti adorning every available inch of the concrete columns, walls and ceiling, we aren't the first to make the pilgrimage under this bridge in search of Kurt's ghost by the banks of the Wishkah.

"Everything I ever knew, I learned from Nirvana. Thank you Kurt!" scribbled one fan. "Kurt Lives!" another had spray-painted. Among the hundreds of sentiments paying homage to their musical hero, we immediately notice the same three-word graffito—"Who Killed Kurt?"—sprayed, painted and scrawled like a nagging whisper from at least ten different locations. Donnie Collier, however, doesn't give much credence to the murder theories. "When I knew him, he certainly didn't seem like the kind of guy who would end up killing himself, but who knows what happened after he left here?" He shrugs. "Nothing would surprise me about that world, but I doubt if he was murdered. I guess he just couldn't take it anymore."

Autumn, the young mother, weighs in: "Who wouldn't want to

kill themselves growing up here? It rains all the time and there's nothing to do. He was a junkie, and junkies die here practically every day. It's so common, the paper doesn't even bother reporting it anymore." She is holding the baby in her arms so that he doesn't accidentally step on a dirty syringe, she says, but we don't see any needles, just a lot of cigarette butts and a few beer bottles.

Why do you stay here? we ask. Do you ever dream of escaping? She looks incredulous before responding meekly, "Where would I go?"

As we emerge from under the bridge, the kids ask us if we want to meet Kurt's daughter. This is an odd question, since Kurt's daughter, Frances Bean, is eleven years old and is known to live in Los Angeles. "No, he has an illegitimate daughter by a local girl that he slept with when he still lived here," Angela claims. "She looks just like him, and she used to say all the time that Kurt was her dad. Most people think it's true." Skeptical, we decline the invitation. After we drop them off downtown and shell out some cash so the kids can each "get a forty" (a 40-ounce can of beer, the drink of choice in these parts), we head to a local bar where we had been told we could hook up with the one person left in Aberdeen who might be able to shed light on how Kurt himself eventually escaped from this sad, seemingly dead-end existence.

* * *

Six nights a week, each evening in a different location, Dave Reed organizes what appears to be the chief source of entertainment in these parts—karaoke. We arrive at Trio's Bar, where the night's program is already well under way. As lowbrow as the surroundings appear, one thing strikes us immediately: the people here are having fun, the first indication since we arrived that not everybody in this town considers it a redneck backwater devoid of culture. As an

16 overweight, middle-aged woman finishes screeching an out-of-tune version of "Brown Eyed Girl," the room erupts with cheers and encouragement.

A fifty-something man sporting a purple tie-dyed T-shirt and a long beaded braid almost to his waist adjusts the mike. This is Dave Reed, the man who was said to have been like a father to Kurt Cobain during his latter teenage years. By 1984, when he was seventeen, Kurt had already experienced frequent and extended bouts of homelessness, living for months at a time in alleys, under bridges and in friends' garages. His mother had taken up with a new boyfriend—a heavy-drinking, womanizing, hot-tempered longshoreman named Pat O'Connor, whom Kurt despised—and she didn't want anything to do with her son. He tried living with his father for a few months, but things were no better than before.

Kurt had recently made friends with a boy named Jesse Reed, the teenage son of evangelical Christians, and began a period of his life that he would not be anxious to discuss in later years. One would be hard-pressed to find any evidence in his soul-baring lyrics or soon-to-be frequent interviews about his Aberdeen youth that Kurt Cobain had found Jesus, become a born-again Christian and had even been baptized at the age of seventeen. Among the chroniclers dissecting the evolution of his drug use, few noted that he spent a portion of his teenage years lecturing friends about the evils of drugs as an abomination against Christ. It was during this period that Dave Reed and his wife, Ethel, invited Kurt to live with their family at the Reeds' large home a few miles outside Aberdeen.

"His family life was a mess," recalls Reed, who was a Christian youth counselor at the time. "He had big problems with his mother, and he was going through a really bad time. He and my son were always together, so I asked him if he wanted to stay with us. He jumped at the chance. I think Kurt saw me as a Ned Flanders–type guy, although I don't think *The Simpsons* were even airing yet. I was with the South Aberdeen Baptist Church. Kurt became a born-again Christian through my son, Jesse, and our family environment. He went to church almost every time the door was open. I was a youth group leader, and Kurt would always come to church with Jesse. For a while, he took Christian life very seriously. But mostly he was into art, horses and music."

By this time, Kurt had dropped out of high school and entered what he would later call his "aimless years." For hours on end, he would sit in the local library reading voraciously or writing the poems that would eventually form the lyrics to many familiar Nirvana songs. Hilary Richrod, the reference librarian at Aberdeen's Timberland Library, recalls Kurt coming every day and reading for hours at a time: "It was hard to miss him. He usually had multicolored hair, and that kind of stuck out in a town like Aberdeen."

The most significant by-product of his churchgoing period was Kurt's burgeoning friendship with a gawky teenage giant named Krist Novoselic, who attended the same church as the Reeds. Kurt and Krist had met in high school, but it was while attending the Baptist church—which Krist joined because he was dating a Christian girl at the time—that they actually bonded, says Reed.

Jesse Reed, who was also a musician, invited Krist over one day to jam with him and Kurt. "You could say that the roots of Nirvana began in our house," says the elder Reed, himself a former musician who had played in a group called the Beachcombers with Kurt's uncle Chuck. "Kurt was really into his music; he practiced all the time and he was writing a lot of songs. He wanted to be a star. He said it all the time." A former member of the Beachcombers had gone on to become a promo man for Capitol Records in Seattle, and after Kurt learned of Reed's connection, he became obsessed with meeting the executive and launching a music career.

Before long, Kurt's flirtation with Christianity waned, he resumed smoking pot and an indignant Dave Reed eventually threw him out when Kurt broke a window one night after he had lost his key. But a small miracle had happened while he was there. Kurt be-

18   gan to believe that he could get out of Aberdeen and that his escape route might be rock and roll. Before long, he and Krist had formed a band with a drummer friend named Aaron Burckhard, rehearsing constantly in a room above the downtown beauty salon operated by Krist's mother.

By the end of our weekend in Kurt's hometown, we had come no closer to determining whether the rejection and alienation of his dysfunctional youth had led inexorably to his self-demise. To each person we interviewed who had known him when he was young, we posed the question. Each in turn said they saw no real signs of self-destruction but blamed whatever happened after he left, perhaps unwilling or unable to indict the community to which they still clung. With the exception of Kurt's first guitar teacher, Warren Mason, who said he "just couldn't see himself doing that at that point in his life," none doubted that he had killed himself. Dave Reed tells us to look elsewhere if we ever hope to make sense of Kurt's death, saying, "It was his fame that killed him."

* * *

Kurt Cobain had always wanted to be famous. That was the one thing virtually everybody we talked to in his hometown agreed on. When he finally got his wish in 1991, it was and wasn't what he'd expected.

He finally escaped Aberdeen for good in 1987, shortly after his twentieth birthday. He had moved to the state capital, Olympia, thirty miles up the road, to live with his first serious girlfriend, Tracy Marander, and discovered what would later be described as his "spiritual mecca"—the ultrahip college town where the bohemians actually outnumbered the rednecks. By the time Kurt moved to Olympia, the band he and Krist had formed in Aberdeen had already played a few gigs under a number of incarnations, including "Skid Row," "Ted Ed Fred" and "Fecal Matter." They were beginning to attract a small following.

When he wasn't practicing his music, Kurt continued to dabble in art, creating surreal landscapes covered with fetuses and mangled animals or, memorably, a collage of photos of diseased vaginas that he'd found in medical textbooks.

With money Kurt saved from a part-time janitorial job, the band was able to record a demo at the studio of a former navy engineer named Jack Endino, who was impressed by Kurt's distinctive vocals and the band's hard-edged sound. Endino passed the demo to a friend named Jonathan Poneman, the head of a new Seattle indie label called Sub Pop. Around this time, the band finally settled on a permanent name. The story goes that Kurt had discovered Buddhism after watching a TV show about Eastern religions and was enchanted by the idea of transcending the cycle of human suffering. He especially liked the name the Buddhists gave to the concept of ultimate enlightenment: Nirvana.

By this time, he had also discovered a new drug. Since he was a teenager, Kurt had experienced intermittent stomach pains that would send him into paroxysms of agony without any warning. He saw an endless series of medical specialists, but doctors were at a loss to explain what was causing the problem, which he later described to *Details* magazine: "Imagine the worst stomach flu you've ever had, every single day. And it was worse when I ate, because once the meal would touch that red area, I would hyperventilate, my arms would turn numb, and I would vomit." He had been offered heroin on a number of occasions, but he had always refused, in part because he was afraid of needles. For the most part, he still confined his drug use to pot, Percodan and magic mushrooms.

By the time he moved to Olympia, the stomach pain was unbearable. A local heroin dealer called Grunt told him that opiates were the ultimate painkiller. Krist Novoselic, who was himself battling alcoholism at the time, later recalled telling Kurt he was "playing with dynamite" after Kurt called to tell him he had just done heroin for the first time.

"Yeah, he did it a few times back then, because he said it was the only thing that could get rid of the pain," confirms Kurt's best friend, Dylan Carlson, whom he first met in Olympia and who was himself a junkie. "But it wasn't a habit or anything, at least not back then."

Things were looking up. When Kurt heard that Sub Pop had agreed to record the band's first single, "Love Buzz," he ran into the streets yelling, "I'm going to be a rock star! Nirvana rules!" An album followed, titled *Bleach*, after the substance junkies employ to clean their needles so they can be reused. *Bleach* was recorded for a grand total of $606.17 at Endino's studio. By this time, the struggling Sub Pop cofounders, Jonathan Poneman and Bruce Pavitt, already deep in debt, had decided that if the Seattle Sound, or "grunge" as it would soon be known, was going to find a wider audience, it would be necessary first to create a buzz in the UK. That's how Seattle's most famous rock-and-roll descendant, Jimi Hendrix, had first made a name for himself two decades earlier.

In the United States, alternative music was still a fringe movement, confined to college radio stations and seedy clubs. The Sub Pop founders were determined to change that, borrowing money to fly in Everett True of the influential London music magazine *Melody Maker* to showcase their label's talent. They couldn't possibly have imagined how much this gambit would pay off. True would later become known as the "godfather of grunge" for his series of articles profiling Sub Pop and the burgeoning Seattle music scene. It may even have been True's seal of approval that started the train rolling for Nirvana, which he described in an article as "the real thing. No rock star contrivance, no intellectual perspective, no master plan for world domination. . . . Kurdt [*sic*] Cobain is a great tunesmith, although still a relatively young songwriter. He wields a riff with *passion*." The music press descended on the city to see what all the fuss was about, and grunge, as the local music paper *The Rocket* described it, had soon "surpassed the status of a happening regional scene to become a worldwide fashion craze."

The mainstream music industry began to pay attention. A & R reps swept through town, cash and contracts in hand, looking to capitalize on what everyone was sure was the next wave in music. Although a number of critics were decidedly unimpressed with *Bleach*—*Rolling Stone* described it as "undistinguished . . . relying on warmed over 70's riffs"—others declared Cobain a genius. Kurt was loving every second of it, recalls his best friend, Dylan, himself a struggling musician: "He kept saying they were going to be bigger than the Beatles. Everybody knew they were getting signed, and believe me, they were getting off on it. When you dream of being a rock star and it finally happens, I guess nothing really beats it."

*   *   *

When *Nevermind*, Nirvana's second album, vaulted past Michael Jackson's *Dangerous* in December 1991 to occupy number one on the *Billboard* charts, music journalists scrambled for an explanation. How could a supposedly alternative band sell three million albums in four months? A year earlier, the band had signed an unprecedented deal with Geffen Records that gave Nirvana complete creative control. It wasn't the million-dollar advance that other labels were offering, but Kurt and his bandmates were ecstatic. They had been spared the noose of corporate rock they all feared when the majors came courting following the explosion of the Seattle music scene during the late 1980s. They would be able to make the kind of album they wanted to make, not the overproduced commercial "crap" they had so often scorned—at least in the company of their indie rock friends. They could hand in a sixty-minute tape of the band defecating and Geffen would have to release it, Kurt

22 | joked. What they actually did instead was go into the studio and record an inspired punk ode to the band's pop roots, an album that would soon be recognized as a masterpiece. It still sounded like noise to most people over thirty, the feedback and hard-driving guitar drowning out the catchy musical bridges unless you listened closely enough.

"We got more attention [than other alternative bands] because our songs have hooks and they kind of stick in people's minds," said Kurt, attempting to explain the album's success. Indeed, each member of Nirvana claimed the Beatles as his favorite group, and it showed. But it was the lyrics—on topics as daring and diverse as rape and religious zealotry—that tapped into the angst of an American youth alienated by a decade of Republicans in the White House and the recently fought Gulf War, which some theorize readied a generation for the rebellion of alternative music. The angry, culture-shifting single "Smells Like Teen Spirit," played ad nauseam on rock radio and MTV, was instantly hailed as the anthem of Generation X, and Cobain its voice. "This was music by, for, and about a whole new group of young people who had been overlooked, ignored or condescended to," wrote Michael Azerrad.

Still, this kind of success wasn't supposed to happen. Had Nirvana sold out? It was a question being asked by many of Kurt's old punk rock friends, and he was acutely sensitive to it. He had a simple explanation: "We didn't go to the mainstream, the mainstream came to us." Later he would tell interviewers that he hated the album, that it was the kind of album he himself would never listen to and that it was "too slick-sounding." But the poppy hooks were no accident. Nirvana had unstinting creative control over *Nevermind*. Kurt's entourage—who knew he listened to his favorite album, *Abba Gold: Greatest Hits*, almost constantly while touring—were well aware just how absurd his protestations were.

The most ironic by-product of the album's success was the acquisition of a brand-new fan base largely consisting of what Kurt

would describe as the "stump dumb rednecks that I thought we had
left behind in Aberdeen." Indeed, the crowds at the band's sold-out concerts were almost indistinguishable from the fans at a Guns n' Roses concert. So embarrassing was this turn of events that Kurt would use the liner notes of his next album to warn the homophobes, the racists and the misogynists in Nirvana's audience "to leave us the fuck alone."

As if to underscore Leland's claim that his mother didn't have any use for Kurt until he became famous, Wendy wrote a letter to the local Aberdeen newspaper shortly after *Nevermind* hit the charts, sounding like a doting mother whose son had just left the nest for the first time. "Kurt, if you happen to read this, we are so proud of you and you are truly one of the nicest sons a mother could have. Please don't forget to eat your vegetables or brush your teeth and now [that] you have your maid, make your bed." The irony wasn't lost on Kurt, who was struck by the hypocrisy of the sudden attention from Wendy and his other relatives, most of whom had wanted nothing to do with him only a few months earlier. He had left Aberdeen and his family behind for good, and no amount of sucking up would make him forget two decades of rejection.

At the height of his band's success, Kurt clearly identified with his favorite Beatle, John Lennon, who knew as well as anybody the price of fame. In an interview with *Rolling Stone*, Kurt talked about this bond with Lennon: "I don't know who wrote what parts of what Beatles songs, but Paul McCartney embarrasses me. Lennon was obviously disturbed. . . . I just felt really sorry for him . . . his life was a prison. He was imprisoned. It's not fair. That's the crux of the problem that I've had with becoming a celebrity—the way people deal with celebrities."

The next chapter in Cobain's short life was to invite new comparisons between himself and his musical idol. When George Harrison was asked how he first met Yoko Ono, he replied, "I'm not

24 | sure. All of a sudden she was just there." Kurt's bandmates, Dave Grohl and Krist Novoselic, would tell similar stories in later years about the bleached blonde who started to appear at Kurt's side shortly after *Nevermind* was released. Perhaps that's why Grohl and Novoselic both called her Yoko—at least behind her back.

2

When we set out to interview those who might offer us the best insight into the real Courtney Love, we encountered an unusual obstacle. The first two people we contacted said they were in hiding. Each gave us the same explanation: they were "afraid of her." What made this even more unusual was the fact that these two people were her father and her first husband.

Now, in the summer of 2003, we are sitting on the outdoor terrace of the Seattle Art Museum with an old friend of Kurt's who witnessed his relationship with Courtney unfold from its beginnings. After about half an hour of candid memories about her old friend Kurt, captured by our video camera for a potential documentary, the subject turns to Courtney Love. "Tell us about her," we say. She immediately turns pale. "You expect me to talk about Courtney with the camera running? Do you think I have a death wish?"

* * *

The first time Kurt Cobain spotted Courtney Love, he thought she looked like Nancy Spungen. Courtney liked that. For several years, she had been obsessed with the infamous bleached blonde whose life so closely paralleled her own. Nancy was an upper-middle-class girl turned groupie, stripper and heroin addict, whose tempestuous relationship with the notorious Sex Pistols bassist Sid Vicious—a tortured working-class youth turned punk legend—culminated in both their deaths, one mysteriously murdered, the other from an overdose. To friends, Courtney liked to claim that she had modeled her life after the so-called punk rock Juliet. A few years before she met Kurt, she had even auditioned to play the lead in Alex Cox's film biopic *Sid and Nancy* and, although failing to land the role, ended up playing the smaller part of Nancy's best friend, Gretchen.

For her part, Courtney thought Kurt looked like Dave Pirner, the front man for Soul Asylum. At their initial encounter in the Portland club where Nirvana had just opened for the Dharma Bums, she flirted with the boyish blond musician for a while and later kept tabs on the progress of Kurt and his band—even sending him a little heart-shaped box as a gift after the Nirvana buzz started to grow louder. But, like Nancy, Courtney was a self-proclaimed groupie, and Kurt was still a relatively unknown musician. By the time they met again a year later, shortly before the release of *Nevermind*, that had changed. The band had signed a major record deal and was obviously on the verge of something big. The two were attending a concert in L.A. when Courtney spotted Kurt downing a bottle of cough medicine. She chided, "You're a pussy; you shouldn't drink that syrup because it's bad for your stomach," and offered him one of her prescription painkillers. "We bonded over pharmaceuticals," she later recalled. They went home that night and had sex for the first time. "She had a completely planned way of seducing me and it worked," said Kurt, telling friends it was the best sex he had ever had.

But Courtney's boyfriend at the time was Billy Corgan, whose band Smashing Pumpkins had opened for Guns n' Roses the same week she slept with Kurt for the first time. For now, Corgan was still more famous than Kurt Cobain. Nirvana and the Pumpkins both had albums scheduled for imminent release; *Nevermind* and *Gish* shared the same producer. When the albums were released, they both exceeded expectations, making Cobain and Corgan instant rock stars. On the *Billboard* charts, however, there was no contest. By the time *Nevermind* hit number one in late December 1991, Kurt and Courtney were inseparable.

* * *

She came from a broken home and had a mother who rejected her, but that's where the similarities ended between Kurt Cobain and the woman who would soon turn his world upside down. If we were going to obtain the clues to make sense of Courtney Love's early years and discover whether she was really capable of committing the heinous act of which she had been accused, we would have to head as far afield as California, Oregon, Australia, Japan, England, and New Zealand. For economy's sake, we decided to confine our quest to the U.S. Pacific Northwest.

Courtney Love Michelle Harrison was born in San Francisco on July 9, 1965—O. J. Simpson's eighteenth birthday. A little while after she made her appearance, Courtney's father, Hank Harrison, headed over to share the good news with the members of the small San Francisco band he managed. They were still known as the Warlocks, but within a few months they would take on their more familiar name—the Grateful Dead. Harrison couldn't decide which of his friends he would ask to be the godfather. Jerry Garcia was good with kids, but Hank's roommate, bassist Phil Lesh, was the only one home, so Lesh received the honor. Instead of passing out cigars, Harrison broke out a couple of tabs of acid, and they celebrated the birth of the little rock-and-roll princess. Meanwhile, her mother's adoptive family—heirs to the Bausch & Lomb eye care fortune—marked the occasion by setting up a trust fund for the new baby. "Courtney is not the rags-to-riches rock-and-roll story," says her father when we finally persuade him to meet with us at his horse ranch in northern California. He had insisted we meet in the center of town so he could size us up and ensure we weren't working for Courtney before he would escort us to his home.

This is a man who for years has been publicly vilified by his own daughter as a grotesque, anti-Semitic, drug-crazed pathological liar. But Courtney's accusations pale beside his own oft-repeated and publicly leveled charge—that Courtney was somehow involved in the murder of her husband Kurt. What kind of father would say these things about his own child? we wanted to know the first time we met him, convinced that—no matter what the truth of his charges—we must be in the presence of an unpleasant opportunist. However, that was apparently the least of his sins.

In 1995, before a TV audience of 25 million Americans, Courtney told Barbara Walters that this man had given her LSD when she was three as part of a bizarre eugenics experiment. "He was anti-Semitic, his father was anti-Semitic," she claimed. "Three people testified that he gave me acid. He wanted to make a superior race, and by giving children acid you could do that."

So when we arrive for our first encounter with Hank Harrison, we are a little spooked, expecting to meet some kind of bizarre rock-and-roll Hitler. He hardly disabuses us of this notion as he begins burrowing into his boxes of old papers, photos and Grateful Dead memorabilia. "Check this out," he says, handing over a yellowing envelope with a letter inside. At the bottom of the letter, just under the signature, is a large hand-drawn swastika. The sender's name is unmistakable: "Charles Manson." Case closed, we think. Reading the letter itself, however, soon causes us to reevaluate. It's just a letter from Manson bad-mouthing the Dead's music.

"He sort of stalked us for a while," explains Harrison. "But that was long before the murders and stuff, so nobody paid much attention."

As he continues to forage, we take in our surroundings. On the living room wall is a framed letter on White House stationery bearing the seal of the president of the United States. Sent a few months after Kurt's death, it is a personal note from Bill Clinton commending Harrison for his work promoting suicide awareness and offering his best wishes to "you, Courtney and Frances Bean during this difficult time." On another wall hangs a Chagall oil painting that Harrison bought with the proceeds from his 1971 biography, *The Dead*—the first book ever written about the band. Although it is still considered by many as the definitive account, the book caused a permanent estrangement between Harrison and the group after he revealed that they had dealt heroin to finance their early tours. Today, thanks to Courtney's public statements, Harrison is more likely to be falsely described as a Dead "hanger-on" or "roadie" than as the band's first manager.

Eventually, Harrison apparently finds what he's looking for: hundreds of pages of transcripts from the divorce proceedings initiated by his wife, Linda Carroll, when Courtney was five years old. Nowhere in the transcripts is there a single suggestion that Harrison ever gave his baby daughter LSD, as Courtney later charged. What is revealed, however, is that Linda feared he would abduct Courtney and take her to live with him in another country after she threatened divorce. The LSD story appears to be based on the suggestion that Courtney may have been given acid while she was left with a babysitter at a hippie commune, perhaps supplying a chemical explanation for her erratic behavior later on. (In 1995, when asked about the allegation that her father had given her acid, Courtney admitted to the *San Francisco Chronicle*, "I don't know if it actually happened.") However, private detectives hired by Carroll's family had dredged up a number of other skeletons in Harrison's closet, including arrests for pot possession and petty theft while he was still in college. "They tried to portray me as a bad influence, and I just didn't have enough money to fight it, so Linda got full custody," he recalls, admitting that his father was indeed somewhat anti-Semitic but saying "that's the only true thing about her Barbara Walters story." Courtney has frequently claimed she has seen her father only a "few times" since her parents divorced. But he pulls out a trove of letters and photos of them together during various phases of her life to prove that father and daughter have at times been very close.

Clearly we can't trust anything Courtney said about her father, and we have already resolved to take most of what Harrison says with a grain of salt. But as he continues to pull scrapbooks and folders out of the boxes, including hundreds of letters and poems written by Courtney, as well as photos and documentation pinpointing the facts about various chapters of her life, we realize that we have discovered a valuable insight into her turbulent early years and a clue to the supposedly imminent train wreck that millions would later watch with voyeuristic fascination.

* * *

Courtney Love may have been too young when her parents split to blame her troubled childhood on the trauma of her parents' divorce, as Kurt's family did to explain his own downward spiral, but by the time she was seven, Courtney's mother had already divorced her second husband, Frank Rodriguez, and married husband number three, David Menely. They moved to a mansion in Oregon, where Linda and her new husband ran a free-spirited commune. Linda followed a strange assortment of gurus during those years, and, depending on the spiritual flavor of the moment, she and Menely might be chanting, meditating or screaming at the tops of their lungs while little Courtney was left to her own devices. She would later recall an assortment of "hairy, wangly ass hippies" running around doing Gestalt therapy. On the back of her album *Live Through This* is a photo of a waiflike little Courtney from this period. "We were living in a tepee and I always smelt like piss," she recalled.

When Courtney was seven, Linda and her new husband suddenly decided they were going to move to New Zealand and raise sheep. Linda told friends it was easier than raising her daughter; consequently, Courtney was left behind. In therapy for a pattern of misbehavior since she was three, Courtney was sent to live with one of her therapists, an old friend of Linda's in Eugene. "It was all done behind my back," recalls Harrison. "I would have been very glad to have her come live with me, but I was never consulted and there was nothing I could do. Courtney would always say in later years that she had never felt so abandoned."

It was during this period that Courtney became, in her own words, a "demon child." The brash young delinquent proved unmanageable for her surrogate mother, therapist or not, and she was soon shipped off to join Linda in New Zealand. She didn't last long there. Linda quickly sent Courtney off to test the compassion of another friend in the region, who in turn ended up banishing her to a Catholic boarding school in Australia. It was the first of a series of schools over the next few years that would expel her with dizzying alacrity. Courtney then headed back to Oregon, where she was shuttled from one of her mother's friends to another—each time overstaying her welcome when she was caught shoplifting, stealing money or smoking pot.

By 1977, Linda and her husband had tired of sheep ranching and returned to Oregon, where Courtney went back to live with them, mainly because Linda could no longer find anybody willing to take her in. But when she was caught shoplifting from a local Woolworth's at the age of twelve—stealing either a 49-cent lipstick or a

Kiss T-shirt, depending on Courtney's mood when she tells the story—her mother instructed the police to teach Courtney a lesson. Instead of the usual warning, she was brought before a judge and placed on probation. When Courtney ran away from home a few days later, Linda asked the authorities not to bring her home, but to a reform school called Hillcrest. In an interview with her biographer, Melissa Rossi, Courtney recalled arriving at the school in handcuffs, leg shackles and a David Bowie haircut. Years later, she would describe the dissolute period of freedom leading up to this stint in juvenile hall. "I was a runt—no tits, no period, no puberty—so I get picked on, and I realize that I can fight really well if I just pretend I'm going to murder the person. I started hanging around the mall and running with this crowd of teen whores."

She fit right in among the bad girls at Hillcrest. In a letter she sent to her father at fourteen, full of chatty references to the crush she had on Kurt Russell and the fact that *Lord of the Flies* was her favorite book, she brags that she has read her personal file and found herself described as "the most shrewd, cunning, devious person" her caseworker had ever seen. In another letter, written the same year, she writes, "I went out and knifed a girl because I didn't like her looks." It was at Hillcrest that Courtney claims she discovered punk rock for the first time after an intern working at the school returned from England and noticed her resemblance to British punk musicians. After he lent her a copy of the Sex Pistols' *Never Mind the Bollocks*, Courtney claims, she decided she wanted to be a rock star. This account is dubious because her friends would later say she always despised punk music. But there is no doubt that it was during this period that Courtney began writing poetry, some of which would form the lyrics of her later music. Harrison still has a stack of harrowing poems Courtney wrote between the ages of fourteen and sixteen. One of the most revealing is called "Future Date" and includes the lines:

I'll destroy anyone in my way
I'll kill every lousy lay—Coz I got my eye on a Future Date

By 1980, Harrison hadn't seen his daughter for several years. They corresponded frequently, however, and in each of her letters, Courtney begs him to "get me out of here." Finally, when she was fifteen, he successfully convinced the state of Oregon to release her into his custody. She moved in with her father for more than a year, the first period of relative stability that she had probably ever experienced. His second book, *The Dead, Volume 2*—chronicling the Haight-Ashbury scene from an anthropological perspective—had been released to great acclaim. (One academic reviewer described him as the "Jane Goodall of rock and roll.") Now Harrison was planning to embark on a two-year study of the monuments of ancient Ireland. For Courtney, the British music scene beckoned. She desperately wanted to go overseas with him but had settled for her father's promise to send for her once he was established in Dublin after completing a six-month research odyssey. She was to spend the interval in a Portland foster home. Harrison takes out a letter he received from Courtney while he was in Ireland in which she writes, "You're the only person who ever understood me."

As bizarre as it seems, Courtney's version of what happened next appears to be fairly close to the truth. Only sixteen, she was approached by a representative of the Japanese underworld, who promised her a lot of money to come to the Far East and strip. For more than six months, she disappeared. When she was deported back to the States, she told friends lurid stories about working in the white slave trade.

Using her newly acquired skills, she soon landed a job stripping at a Portland club until the establishment was raided by police a few weeks later, and Courtney was carted off to yet another reform school. This time she happened to mention to a school social

34 | worker she had befriended that she was an heiress. When her confidante suggested she sue for legal and financial emancipation from her mother, Courtney gleefully took action. At the age of sixteen, the child who had been passed from hand to hand so many times finally took matters into her own. Just as important, she gained access to her trust fund. She now had the freedom and the money to pursue the life she had only read about in the fanzines. Her first stop was Dublin, where she hooked up with her father. But Ireland didn't really appeal to Courtney, who saw bigger fish just a ferry ride away. She headed for Liverpool, a city undergoing a musical renaissance twenty years after the Beatles left town. In her backpack were a thousand hits of acid that she had brought with her from the States, intending to use the drugs as her entrée into the local music scene.

Before long, she was a fixture in the entourage of the neopsychedelic Liverpool band The Teardrop Explodes and was soon known as the band's most loyal groupie, latching on to the notoriously eccentric front man, Julian Cope. Later Courtney would claim that Cope took her virginity, but she has made similar claims about at least three other rock stars, so it is difficult to know if this is just another one of her wild tales. She has also claimed that, during her stay in England, she took photos for the Irish music magazine *Hot Press*, shooting the Pretenders, U2 and other big-time rock bands. But *Hot Press* editor Niall Stokes claims that, like much of Courtney's storied past, this is pure fiction. "It's fairly typical Courtney behavior to lie or exaggerate anyway," the magazine wrote in a 1995 profile. "Throughout her career, she has continually proffered colorful stories—often with several conflicting versions—about her past life to the media in order to increase her mystique and punk rock credibility."

One story that she simply chose not to address is what suddenly happened to force Courtney's abrupt return to Oregon in 1982. It was clear that she was no longer welcome in Liverpool, but the details are sketchy. "I took a lot of acid in Liverpool and basically I never recovered," she later explained cryptically. Whatever the case, Cope's band had harsh words for her in the years to come, claiming her time with them was a "destructive" one. Years later, after Courtney took up with Kurt Cobain, Julian Cope took out a large ad in the music press stating, "Free us from Nancy Spungen–fixated heroin A-holes who cling to our greatest rock groups and suck out their brains." He also told an interviewer, "She needs shooting, and I'll shoot her."

* * *

Courtney's next stop was Portland, and it was our next destination as well. This was the city she was referring to when she told *Spin* magazine, "Years ago in a certain town, my reputation had gotten so bad that every time I went to a party, I was expected to burn the place down and knock out every window." Although it's been more than a decade since she left town, there are people here who are clearly still afraid of her. Portland scenester Todd Curran remembers Courtney from the city's notorious gay dance club the Metropolis, where drag queens mixed with new-wave bohos. "She was totally outrageous," he recalls. "She was always causing a scene. The Metropolis wasn't exactly a likely setting for barroom brawls, but when Courtney was around, it was chaos." He said she popped pills like candy—barbiturates, speed, tranquilizers, painkillers.

Virtually everybody we talked to in Portland refused to be interviewed or asked that their names be changed, even though many said they actually liked her style and admired her take-no-prisoners attitude. "She was fun to watch as long as you didn't get in her way," said one former doyenne of the club scene who, although she hadn't really dissed Courtney at all, begged us not to use the video of her interview, lest it "awake the beast." But Rozz Rezabek has no such compunctions talking about Courtney for the record.

"Don't believe the hype. A kinder, gentler Charles Manson is still Charles Manson." This is the first thing he says about the woman who he claims "stole" his career. Rezabek was the front man for an up-and-coming Portland new-wave band called Theater of Sheep when Courtney swept back into town in the early '80s after her sojourn in Liverpool.

"She latched on to me right away," he recalls. "She claimed she was going to make me a star. At the time, she was always saying she thought the world was dominated by men and the only way she would make it was through a man, and I guess she chose me. She had just got back from England, where she was supposedly fucking all these rock stars. She would talk with this really phony British accent all the time. Then she started dressing me in Julian Cope's clothes and was trying to make me into some kind of British rock god." Eventually, Rezabek says, he quit music because of what he calls Courtney's incessant attempts to mold him into her image of a rock star. "If I hadn't," he says, "I would have ended up just like Kurt, with a gun down my throat. Man, I can identify with what he must have gone through." The last time he spoke to Courtney, he claims, she had just called to tell him how she had "bamboozled Barbara Walters" during her TV interview.

At some point during these Portland years, Courtney apparently decided that being a groupie would take her only so far. She would later state, "I finally said, 'I'm not on this earth to fuck a rock star, I'm here to *be* a rock star.' I would create myself." Rezabek, who ended up dating Courtney on and off for nine years, still has a box of her old poetry, journals and more than fifteen hundred letters from that period. One particularly revealing note, written by Courtney to herself when she was about nineteen, gives an early hint of an ambitious, driven woman who knows what she wants and

knows what it takes to get it. The note is titled "Here's How Courtney Will Make It":

> Gig locally tons
> Stop working at jobs
> Get financed
> Get a deal using old connections and new connections
> Movie comes out
> Tour with Furs and R.E.M.

A new breed of female rocker was just beginning to attract attention on the American punk scene, singing angry, feminist-laced,
fiercely political lyrics to driving, hard-edged musical beats. This
was music by and for Courtney's type of woman. Before long, she
had sought out and befriended two women rockers who were already attracting considerable attention on the foxcore scene—Kat
Bjelland, a brash young L.A. stripper turned punk rocker, and Jennifer Finch, the lead singer of a band called Frightwig. Within a
few years, the three women would form the genesis of what would
soon be known as the riot grrrl movement. From the outset of
their disastrous musical partnership, however, that possibility
seemed extremely unlikely.

One day, apparently at Courtney's suggestion, the three decided
to form a band, which was known as Sugar Babylon and later re-
named Sugar Baby Doll. Courtney had recently taken up the bass
but still couldn't play, so she was designated the lead singer. From
the start, it was a fiasco. According to Kat, Courtney hated punk
and wanted a more melodic new-wave sound while her bandmates
wanted to play strictly hard-core punk rock. Tantrums followed
and, within five months, the band had broken up. Soon Courtney
moved to Minneapolis to join Kat's new group, Babes in Toyland,
but it wasn't long before Courtney was thrown out of that band, reportedly for a lack of talent on the bass.

Depressed at yet another bump in her sputtering musical career, she decided she needed a change of scenery and headed off to San Francisco to live with her father once again and take some college courses. It was here that she discovered her magical elixir for the first time. In Portland, pills and acid had always been her preferred high. Now she appeared to take her drug use to a new level.

Hank Harrison's partner, Triona Watson, remembers Courtney during this period: "She would live with us for a few weeks at a time and then spend extended periods hanging out at junkie pads and never coming home. . . . She could be really sweet one moment and then turn into a monster. Once she started doing heroin, she was unbearable. I remember once she threatened to burn our house down. We just couldn't take it anymore."

For Courtney's father, the turning point came when he found syringes littering the floor of his house, remnants of a party Courtney had thrown in his absence. "When I realized my daughter was a junkie, I was stunned," says Harrison, who claims his own drug use had never progressed farther than LSD and pot. "I had done a lot of drug intervention work during the sixties, and I tried to help her, but she told me to mind my own business and kept up her habit. She was stealing from me to buy more smack, so I finally threw her out."

He takes out a letter Courtney wrote him during this period:

Dear Hank. Thank you for the stay. I know it has been terribly difficult at times due to me and the company I keep. Hope to see you fully recovered from my regressed experimentation near Xmas. Thanx esp. for school support & letting me walk on the ice of thickness of my own choosing.

Love
Courtney

Heroin is an expensive habit. Although she was still receiving about $800 a month from her trust fund, it wasn't enough, so

Courtney headed north to Alaska, where she had been offered a job stripping for the pipeline workers. Soon she was offered a more lucrative stripping gig, at L.A.'s notorious Star Strip Club. The lure of Hollywood was appealing, and for a while Courtney thought movies might offer a quicker route to stardom than rock and roll. After failing to win the coveted part of Nancy, she finally landed a major role in another Alex Cox film, *Straight to Hell*, featuring the Pogues. The movie bombed, going straight to video and landing on many critics' lists as one of the worst films of all time. However, she put part of her $20,000 acting fee to good use, getting a nose job to repair her most glaring physical flaw and transforming herself in preparation for the next chapter of her life. It was time to return to her original plan.

* * *

Starting from scratch again, Courtney placed an ad in the popular L.A. music guide *The Recycler*: "I want to start a band. My influences are Big Black, Sonic Youth, and Fleetwood Mac." Her earlier failures, she said later, had only taught her the formula for success. Within three months, her new band, Hole, was attracting a favorable buzz in indie circles. She had abandoned her old softer-edged musical style in favor of hard-core screaming and screeching beats, but underneath the noise, you could still hear the melodic influences of the catchy pop music she loved. She got rid of the David Bowie hairdo, bleached it blond and pioneered a new look that she would soon refer to as "kinderwhore"—ripped little-girl dresses and pink ribbons in her hair. With the contrived new image, fans and critics were starting to pay attention. Courtney was convinced stardom was just around the corner. But old habits are hard to break. She had forged a new sound, a new look and a new personality on her own terms, but she couldn't quite shed her groupie ways, the old notion that it might just be a little easier to ride on the coattails of a man's success. In Portland, she had tried and failed to mold Rozz Rezabek into her version of a rock star. In L.A., she was after something different—a shortcut to the top.

Courtney knew virtually nothing about punk rock. She had never liked the music nor cared about its political message. She hadn't a clue about who was in or out and, more important, who knew the directions to the musical holy grail—a record deal. By the time Courtney set eyes on James Moreland for the first time, he was already known as an L.A. punk rock survivor. Since the late '70s, he had paid his dues and then some, gaining a larger following with every year he stuck it out, grinding out his high-octane, obscenity-laced lyrics night after night. His music was not much different from the countless hard-core punk bands Courtney had scouted while doing her homework in one dingy club after another, often leaving with the front man or a backup musician. However, there was something different about Moreland the first time she saw his band perform, something that set him apart from the typical clichéd punk rocker, each sporting the same look—torn jeans, black T-shirt and a sneer. As he jumped all over the stage, screaming out the typically indecipherable lyrics, Moreland happened to be wearing a cocktail dress, fishnet stockings and ruby red lipstick with black mascara. His onstage antics, a mixture of slapstick and acrobatics, had the crowd in a frenzy. Courtney was just beginning to pioneer her soon-to-be infamous brand of showmanship with her own band, Hole. She was definitely intrigued. When she was informed by a barmaid that Moreland, known to his fans as "Falling James," was every inch a heterosexual, she knew she would have to get to know him better.

A few days later, they were married.

The way Courtney tells it, the marriage lasted only two days, but, according to her father, it was closer to two years. When we first contacted Moreland for an interview, he refused to talk about his marriage, claiming he was still "petrified" of Courtney. But Harrison, who hadn't spoken to Moreland for years, offered to arrange an interview for us after we supplied him with the phone number.

"Hi, James. This is your former father-in-law, Hank. Long time no speak." They proceeded to reminisce, trading memories of Courtney the way old soldiers swap war stories. He asked if Moreland would mind "talking to some Canadian writer friends of mine." Apparently, Falling James had recently been spooked by Courtney's reaction to the only other detailed interview he had ever given about her. In that article, he had called her "Conan the Barbarian when it comes to her career" and described her as a homophobic conservative who believed that people got into punk rock and homosexuality only to piss off their parents. "She would also say that me and other knee-jerk liberals don't know what we're talking about, because she had slept with generals at this army base in Alaska and they had a lot of secret information which proved that the wars they got us into were really for our own good," Moreland recalled. "I thought I was marrying the female Johnny Rotten. Instead I got this right-wing Phyllis Diller."

Moreland did indeed agree to talk to us, but only after Harrison assured him we could be trusted.

They were married in Las Vegas, "pretty well on the spur of the moment," he recalls, after he jokingly asked her if she wanted to tie the knot and she said yes. At first, their relationship was very intense. He had never met anybody like her, and he was enthralled by her in-your-face personality, but they always seemed to clash, mostly about politics. "We would have these huge fights and split up for weeks at a time and then get back together. She was really fucked up on drugs most of the time, and she could get uncontrollably violent."

Violent enough to have her next husband killed? "I can't really answer that because I wasn't there, but when we were married, she certainly seemed to know a lot about hit men. If somebody pissed her off a lot, she would pay this guy she knew fifty or a hundred dollars to beat them up. It was pretty scary. From my own experience, she's dangerous. She definitely has an evil side. She once tried to burn my bed when I was sleeping. A fire started and I woke up in shock. It's impossible to figure out Courtney's motives. Her disdain was powerful, and she came off as a spoiled little snot."

Moreland offered a slightly different version to *New York Press* when the conspiracy theories started to surface: "I can see [Kurt] getting into some ridiculous argument with her and getting so fed up that he ran into the house and blew his head off rather spontaneously. Most people would want to kill themselves just waking up to her. The other scenario, which is scarier and more cold-blooded, is that there was a profit motive for knocking him off. I can also see that happening, because Courtney is a violent person who, even in the midst of our anonymous, crummy, poverty-stricken little marriage, threatened to have me beaten up for two hundred dollars when I didn't do what she wanted. I was so scared of her I caved in immediately. In those days, she was just this junkie stripper and prostitute, but give somebody like that a couple million and you can't overestimate how dangerous they might be."

Moreland recalled what for him was the last straw—why their relationship finally ended. Choking down tears, he said Courtney had become pregnant with their child but refused to stop using heavy drugs, which eventually forced her to get an abortion. "It was a nightmare," he said. "I'll never forgive her for that."

Although their turbulent marriage temporarily put the brakes on Moreland's own music career, it appeared to have the opposite effect on Courtney, whose band released its first single soon after they were married. It created enough buzz to attract the attention of the respected Caroline label, which released Hole's first album, *Pretty on the Inside*, in 1991, to instant critical acclaim in alternative music circles, and earned her a reputation as the new queen of the riot grrrl movement. Madonna and Sonic Youth's Kim Gordon were among a growing legion of new fans. For those who would later claim that Kurt Cobain wrote most of her music, *Pretty on the Inside*—recorded a year before she began to date him—proved that, no matter what anybody said about her, Courtney was about more than just hype. Reviewing the album, *The New Yorker* wrote, "*Pretty on the Inside* is a cacophony—full of such grating, abrasive, and unpleasant sludges of noise that very few people are likely to get through it once, let alone give it the repeated listenings it needs for you to discover that it's probably the most compelling album to have been released in 1991."

Somewhere in the midst of the ruthless ambition, the carefully crafted image and the trail of bitter ex-lovers prepared to believe the worst of her was an undeniable talent. But like Yoko Ono, who was already among the most important figures of the '60s avant-garde arts scene before she ever met John Lennon, that talent was about to be overshadowed by a man who would be labeled the musical genius of his generation.

* * *

"Only about a quarter of what Courtney says is true," declares her on-again, off-again friend Kat Bjelland, the leader of Babes in Toyland. "But nobody usually bothers to decipher which are the lies. She's all about image. And that's interesting. Irritating, but interesting."

The way Courtney tells the story, she had only dabbled in heroin a couple of times before she met Kurt, who was already a full-fledged junkie. But Kurt's friends scoff at the suggestion—prominently repeated in a number of dubious biographies—that he turned her on to the habit. The truth appears to be somewhat more elusive.

By 1992, the stomach pain that had once caused Kurt only occasional irritation was a near constant source of agony. Most agree that his periodic heroin use became a full-fledged habit around the time *Nevermind* was released in the fall of 1991. The fact that it also coincided with the period when he and Courtney started dating may have been why there was a perception that she was responsible for his stepped-up drug use. The way Kurt publicly described it, he had "decided" to become a junkie in September 1991, to relieve the "excruciating, burning, nauseous pain" in his stomach he experienced every time he swallowed food. "The only thing I found that worked were heavy opiates," he later explained. "There were many times that I found myself literally incapacitated, in bed for weeks, vomiting and starving. So I decided, if I feel like a junkie as it is, I may as well be one." For months, however, a prescription of morphine had seemed to do the trick. Why he eventually substituted heroin, despite his needle phobia, is still a mystery.

"He had already tried heroin a few times before he met Courtney," says Kurt's old friend Alice Wheeler, the unofficial photographer of Seattle's grunge scene, who had known him since his days in Olympia. "But she definitely used it as a lure to control him. She's very sophisticated that way. It was in her best interests for Kurt to form a habit." Kurt's best friend, Dylan Carlson, tells a similar story: "She knew that the more drugs he did, the less chance that he'd be in a state to get up and leave her." However, Kurt always denied that Courtney was responsible and would later claim that he formed his habit while she was in Europe touring with Hole.

The magnitude of his drug problem was brought home to his bandmates in early January 1992, when he arrived in a virtual stupor at the NBC studios in New York for Nirvana's appearance on *Saturday Night Live*. He and Courtney had shot heroin in the hotel room earlier in the day, and, by the time Kurt arrived for the afternoon rehearsal, Dave and Krist had never seen him looking so out of it. Though Krist had a severe drinking problem and Dave had grown up a self-described "suburban stoner," neither had a lot of experience with hard drugs. Now they were decidedly worried about Kurt's near catatonic state, but neither of them had any idea as to how to approach the problem. Ever since Kurt had started spending time with Courtney a few months earlier, he had become increasingly distant from his old friends. They no longer hung out together the way they used to, lamenting and laughing at their unexpected success. After the rehearsal, Kurt returned to the dressing room, where he vomited for almost an hour. He managed to get through the show but afterward, backstage, he nearly collapsed. Dave was heard calling him a "junkie asshole."

Whether or not Courtney exercised a Rasputin-like control over Kurt, as many speculated, or whether he had simply found somebody who understood him, as he told his friends, one thing is certain: the two were very much in love, at least in the beginning. "My attitude has changed dramatically," he told *Sassy* magazine in January 1992, "and I can't believe how much happier I am and how even less career-oriented I am. At times, I even forget I'm in a band, I'm so blinded by love. I know that sounds embarrassing, but it's true." In the same interview, he revealed for the first time that he and Courtney had recently become engaged; he may or may not have known at the time that Courtney was carrying his baby, conceived two months earlier. Some of his friends, Dylan Carlson among them, say it was the pregnancy that prompted Kurt to propose and that the couple delayed the news only to avoid the stigma of a shotgun wedding. By the end of January, however, it was no longer a secret, and Kurt was ecstatic about impending fatherhood, telling everybody who would listen that he was going to be a "punk rock daddy."

By the time their baby was born on August 18, 1992, Kurt and Courtney had become the darlings of the music media, the rock-and-roll couple that everybody loved to watch. They had flown to Hawaii in February for a small wedding, attended by only a few

Nirvana crew members, Dave Grohl, and Kurt's best friend, Dylan Carlson, who served as best man. Conspicuously missing from the ceremony was Krist Novoselic, possibly because he had been getting on Kurt's case about his increasing use of heroin, more probably because neither he nor his wife, Shelli, appeared to approve of his choice of mate. Nor was a single member of either Kurt's or Courtney's family invited to attend. Before the wedding, Courtney insisted that Kurt sign a prenuptial agreement, in the apparent conviction that she would soon be more successful than her superstar husband. "I didn't want Kurt running away with all my money," she told a reporter, only half-jokingly.

Within months, their faces adorned the covers of countless magazines. In an interview with *Rolling Stone* in April 1993, Kurt finally admitted that his success wasn't the drag that he had been complaining about for months in the media and to his punk rock friends. When *Nevermind* hit number one, he revealed, he was "kind of excited, [but] I wouldn't admit that at the time." He also dismissed the media reports suggesting that he was uncomfortable with his newfound fame. "It really isn't affecting me as much as it seems like it is in interviews and the way that a lot of journalists have portrayed my attitude. I'm pretty relaxed with it." It was a heady time for Courtney as well. Her band was attracting a lot of attention after a recent UK tour, and a number of major labels had recently come calling, especially after news leaked out that Madonna's new label, Maverick, was interested in signing Hole. Years later, Madonna revealed what happened when she arrived for her first meeting with Courtney, whom she described as "miserable and self-obsessed."

"When I met her, when I was trying to sign her, she spent the whole time slagging off her husband," Madonna recalled. "She was saying, 'Hole are so much better than Nirvana.' "

After a fierce bidding war, it was Nirvana's label, Geffen, offering a million-dollar advance and unprecedented royalties, which finally signed Hole to its first major record contract, while denying 47 the lucrative deal had anything to do with keeping in Kurt's good graces. For years Courtney would brag that she had landed a better record deal than her husband.

*   *   *

Both Kurt Cobain and Courtney Love were living the dream that neither would admit to publicly for the sake of their punk rock cred. Success, money, glamour and a new baby on the way. They seemed to have it all. And then the bottom fell out.

On August 20, 1992, only two days after Frances Bean Cobain was born at L.A.'s Cedars-Sinai Medical Center, the September issue of *Vanity Fair* hit the newsstands. Three months earlier, Courtney had allowed the respected celebrity scribe Lynn Hirschberg to follow her around for a feature. One of Courtney's favorite publications, *Vanity Fair* was nothing less than the arbiter of who was hot in the entertainment business. Moreover, Hirschberg was not interested in writing the kind of rock-and-roll-couple story that had become a staple of the music press in recent months. She had said she wanted to focus on Courtney, who was now anxious to get out of her husband's shadow and jump-start her own career.

But by the time Courtney had finished reading an advance copy of Hirschberg's story faxed to her in the hospital before it hit the stands, she knew that she had gotten more than she'd bargained for. The article paints a devastating portrait of an opportunist— albeit a charismatic, talented one—married to a rock-and-roll "holy man." Weighing in about Courtney are friends and rivals who had crossed her path and come away the worse for the experience. "Courtney's delusional," her longtime friend Kat Bjelland told Hirschberg. "Last night I had a dream that I killed her. I was really happy."

Courtney, however, gives as good as she gets, slagging both Madonna and Krist Novoselic's wife, Shelli, and suggesting to Kurt that he start a new band without Dave Grohl, whom she had always despised. All in all, however, she presents herself as content with her new life. "Things are really good. It's all coming true," she says, before acknowledging prophetically that it could "all fuck up any time. You never know."

All this would be perfect, Hirschberg concludes, "except for the drugs." She proceeds to cite no fewer than twenty different music-industry sources who maintain that the Cobains have been "heavily into heroin." Though it wasn't the first time a journalist had confronted Kurt or Courtney about their rumored drug use, Kurt had usually been content just to lie. Only a few months earlier, he had told *Rolling Stone* that "all drugs are a waste of time" and that his body wouldn't allow him to take drugs even if he wanted to "because I'm so weak." Courtney's usual strategy was to admit that she had dabbled in hard drugs in the past but had now straightened herself out and might just pop the occasional valium. In the interview she granted Hirschberg, however, she apparently failed to do some basic arithmetic.

The fateful words come in a quote describing the couple's January 1992 stay in New York when Nirvana appeared on *Saturday Night Live*. "We did a lot of drugs," says Courtney. "We got pills, and then we went down to Alphabet City and Kurt wore a hat, I wore a hat, and we copped some dope. Then we got high and went to *S.N.L.* After that, I did heroin for a couple of months."

If this was true, it meant that Courtney had still been doing heroin *after* she knew she was pregnant. Hirschberg interviewed a "business associate" of the couple's who proceeded to confirm that exact scenario. "It was horrible," the source revealed. "Courtney was pregnant and she was shooting up. Kurt was throwing up on people in the cab. They were both out of it."

The wave of revulsion set off by Courtney's shocking revelation in the *Vanity Fair* piece was a devastating blow to the new parents. The *Globe* tabloid published a story headlined "Rock Star's Baby Is Born a Junkie" over a photo of a deformed newborn baby falsely purported to be Frances Bean. "I knew that my world was over. I was dead," Courtney later said. "That was it. The rest of my life . . . any happiness that I had known, I was going to have to fight for, for the rest of my life."

The day before the issue hit the stands, the couple's handlers were already in full damage-control mode, issuing a press release in the name of Kurt and Courtney saying the forthcoming article contained "many inaccuracies and distortions." At first, Courtney claimed that she had been misquoted, that she had never done heroin while she was pregnant. "I didn't do heroin during my pregnancy," she told *Melody Maker*. "And even if I shot coke every night and took coke every day, it's my own motherfucking business." But Hirschberg had fairly incontrovertible evidence that Courtney did indeed admit to taking heroin for two months after the *SNL* appearance. "I taped the interview and I wrote what I saw," the journalist insisted. *Vanity Fair* stood firmly behind the story. Then Courtney's story changed. She had indeed done heroin in the first trimester, Courtney admitted, but only before she learned she was pregnant. This story stands in glaring contradiction to both the story she told Hirschberg and the account of Kurt's best friend, Dylan Carlson, who told us he had shot up with both Kurt and Courtney before their February wedding, where he was best man.

To make matters worse, only five days after Frances Bean was born, somebody from the hospital anonymously faxed a copy of Courtney's medical records to the *Los Angeles Times* revealing that she had been receiving "daily doses of methadone, a heroin substitute used to treat narcotics addiction." Because hospital records are sealed, it is unknown whether her baby was born drug-addicted, but, as the *Times* article disclosed, such a condition would be a given if the mother was regularly using methadone at the end of her pregnancy. The article quotes the director of a nearby drug rehab center saying that babies born chemically dependent must go through methadone detox, but that "babies go through that well."

The fallout was devastating. On August 20, two days after the birth, an L.A. County child services social worker, brandishing a copy of Hirschberg's article, arrived at the hospital to interview Courtney. The new mother was scheduled to leave with the baby the next day, but, after interviewing Courtney, the social worker recommended that Frances stay in the hospital for observation. Four days later, at a state-ordered custody hearing, a judge ruled that neither Kurt nor Courtney would be allowed to see their new baby without the supervision of a court-appointed guardian.

The couple's lawyers persuaded the court to allow Courtney's half sister to act as Frances Bean's guardian. "[The half sister] barely knew Courtney," admitted Danny Goldberg, the president of Kurt's management company, "and she couldn't stand her. So we had to kind of bribe her to pretend she gave a shit."

The ordeal was taking an especially hard toll on Kurt, who had so been looking forward to fatherhood. "I felt as if I had been raped," he later revealed. For her part, Courtney was out for revenge, and all her wrath focused on Lynn Hirschberg. In 1995, Courtney admitted to *Select* magazine that she had indeed taken heroin while she was pregnant, "or else I would have sued [Hirschberg's] ass off." However, that didn't stop her from firing off repeated threats to Hirschberg, *Vanity Fair* and the magazine's publisher, Condé Nast. Hirschberg later revealed that she had received repeated death threats from Courtney, as well as a promise to cut up her dog. Hirschberg still refuses to talk to journalists about the article, claiming she is "terrified for my life."

She wasn't the only one. A few months before the article ran, Kurt had given the go-ahead to two Seattle-based British music journalists, Victoria Clarke and Britt Collins, to write a book about Nirvana and had even sat for a number of interviews with the two writers. As the longtime girlfriend of the legendary Pogues front man, Shane MacGowan—with whom she had briefly split—Clarke was well connected in the music industry and was herself no stranger to tempestuous rock relationships. MacGowan, who is considered by many as a musical genius in the same category as John Lennon and Kurt Cobain, had recently been thrown out of the band he founded because of his own self-destructive drug and alcohol use. Clarke believed she could offer a unique insight into Kurt's world.

Courtney had always revered MacGowan, with whom she had starred in the ill-fated movie *Straight to Hell*. So for months she had been all too happy to cooperate with his girlfriend. However, several weeks after the publication of the *Vanity Fair* article, she apparently heard that Clarke had attempted to meet with Hirschberg to get her side of the story and possibly obtain the tape of the original interview. That set off a chain of events that has left both Collins and Clarke terrified ever since. One day in late fall 1992, Victoria Clarke returned to her Seattle apartment to find an hysterical message on her answering machine from Courtney. The tone of the tape is chilling:

I will never fucking forgive you. . . . I will haunt you two fucking cunts for the rest of your life. . . . Going and interviewing Lynn Hirschberg is called rape. . . . Fucking bitch. . . . You're going to pay and pay and pay up your ass and that's a fact. . . . You're going to wish you've never been born!

The next day, with Courtney's voice egging him on in the background, Kurt himself left a series of messages that sounded even more threatening:

If anything comes out in this book that hurts my wife, I'll fucking hurt you. . . . I'll cut out your fucking eyes, you sluts . . . whores

... parasitic little cunts! ... I don't give a flying fuck if I have this recorded that I'm threatening you. I suppose I could throw out a few hundred thousand dollars to have you snuffed out, but maybe I'll try it the legal way first.

Quick with the damage control, Danny Goldberg denied that it was Kurt's voice on the answering-machine tape, but Kurt himself later confirmed to his biographer Michael Azerrad that he had made the threatening calls. "Obviously I have a lot to lose right now so I won't be able to do it," Kurt said. "But I have all the rest of my life.... I've tried killing people before in a fit of rage.... When people unnecessarily fuck with me, I just can't help but want to beat them to death."

Kurt's longtime friend Alice Wheeler says she isn't surprised by this aspect of his personality. "Everybody always tries to portray Kurt as some kind of saint and Courtney as this bitch," she says, "but Kurt definitely had a dark side. He could be very twisted, real mean at times. Most of the time, though, he was real sweet, a quiet gentle guy. It just didn't compute." Wheeler says that, after the incident, she and about seventy other friends of Kurt's were visited by a private detective working for Kurt and Courtney who was attempting to find out whether they had talked to the two British writers. "It was very intimidating," she recalls. "I think they were trying to send us a message that we better shut up. It seemed like a veiled threat."

Meanwhile, Clarke—who had relocated to Los Angeles within hours after she heard the messages on her answering machine—had the misfortune to run into Courtney some months later at an L.A. bar, where she claims she was attacked. "She hit me with a glass and then tried to drag me outside by my hair," recalls Clarke, who has subsequently returned to the UK, still fearful of Courtney's wrath.

Soon after, in a further attempt at damage control, Nirvana's management company Gold Mountain approached veteran *Rolling Stone* writer Michael Azerrad to write the authorized biography of the band. Mindful of his journalistic credibility, Azerrad was uncomfortable with the idea that the biography would be called "authorized" but agreed to the project as long as he retained full editorial control. Officially, the book would be written with the band's "cooperation."

"Kurt and Courtney were using Azerrad for one purpose," reveals Alice Wheeler. "They needed to convince people that their drug use had been exaggerated and that they had put all that behind them. Kurt especially was terrified of losing the baby, so he did what he had to do, even if he had to lie. We all knew what was going on. Kurt even admitted what was happening. At one point, I received a letter from their people instructing me to speak only to Michael Azerrad and not to those British writers. That's why you can't really trust a lot of the information in that book."

Indeed, *Come as You Are*, released in October 1993, is filled with passages that downplay the couple's drug use. The book takes special pains to sanitize Courtney's drug habit, implying that she had once used heroin casually but had put all that behind her. The book also appears to settle a number of the couple's personal scores, excoriating Hirschberg and other writers who had portrayed Courtney in a negative light. Azerrad details a number of relatively minor factual errors in the *Vanity Fair* piece and suggests that Hirschberg had failed to understand Courtney's sardonic sense of humor. He goes on to blame Courtney's treatment by the media on "a considerable sexist force." In 2001, long after it became obvious that his book had painted a less-than-accurate portrait, Azerrad appeared to acknowledge the fact in a statement to the Nirvana Fan Club: "It's true, I didn't realize the full extent of Kurt's drug addiction while I was writing the book. But even Krist and Dave didn't know how much Kurt was using." Despite its flaws, *Come as You Are* remains a valuable behind-the-scenes portrait of Nirvana at the peak of their career.

Because of Kurt and Courtney's almost obsessive attempts to control the information disseminated about them after the controversy involving the birth of Frances Bean, it's sometimes difficult to figure out which of their public statements over the following two years can be trusted and which should be dismissed as spin. Both checked themselves into rehab and made genuine attempts to kick their habits, and both apparently more or less failed. "I knew that when I had a child, I'd be overwhelmed and it's true," Kurt told the *Los Angeles Times* after the couple had finally won back full custody of their baby in 1993. "I can't tell you how much my attitude has changed since we've got Frances. Holding my baby is the best drug in the world."

"He adored that little girl," says Alice Wheeler. "You'd see him with the baby carrier and the diapers, the whole setup. His mood wasn't quite so morose anymore. I think he really got off on being a daddy." All of his friends echo this description, calling Kurt a changed man. "I was invited to Frances's first birthday party, and I noticed how different he was. When he was with his daughter, he just lit up," recalls Kurt's friend, Seattle rock photographer Charles Peterson. Kurt's grandfather remembers visiting the couple's Seattle house when Frances was almost a year and a half. "Courtney was going out to a club or bar or something and she wanted Kurt to come with her," recalls Leland. "But he just wanted to stay home and play with the baby. He just thought the world of Frances."

Around the fall of 1993, something else happened to lift Kurt's mood. Over the years, a succession of stomach specialists had failed to determine what was causing the unbearable agony in his lower abdomen. So mysterious was its source that some doctors even believed it was psychosomatic. Finally, one specialist decided to look a little further into Kurt's early medical history and discovered that, when he was a child, he had been diagnosed with a mild case of scoliosis, or curvature of the spine. He consulted the medical literature. Scoliosis can sometimes cause pinched abdominal nerves, and this is what had been causing Kurt's pain all these years. Once the problem was diagnosed, it took a simple prescription to erase the pain.

In more than one interview over the years, Kurt had described his stomach pain as so agonizing that it made him want to "blow his brains out," a phrase that would soon prove uncomfortably prescient. So those who knew him couldn't help but take notice when they read the first interview where he announced that the pain was gone, in the January 27, 1994, issue of *Rolling Stone*, two months before his death. "It's just that my stomach isn't bothering me anymore," he exults. "I'm eating. I ate a huge pizza last night. It was so nice to be able to do that. And it just raises my spirits."

To the average fan, these words are innocuous and would hardly register in the months to come. More than one reader, however, remembered another of Kurt's quotes near the beginning of the same interview.

The writer, David Fricke, revealed that, when he caught up with his subject in the middle of Nirvana's U.S. tour, he had expected to find what he describes as the Cobain press myth—a "pissy, complaining, freaked-out schizophrenic." Instead, he writes, he was surprised to find Kurt in a thoughtful mood, taking great pains to explain that success doesn't really suck—not as much as it used to anyway—and that his life was pretty good and getting better.

In the years since his death, the public has been fed a steady stream of assertions about the supposed despair that led to Kurt's suicide. Even many of those who have never heard a Nirvana song can practically recite the factors by rote: the pop success-induced desolation, the alienation and misery that came with his fame. All the more surprising, then, to read what he told Fricke in this interview just a few months before he allegedly killed himself: "I've never been happier in my life."

3

As the rumor spread through the ranks of the Seattle Police Department, its impact was the same on every officer, from the lowliest beat cop to the thirty-year veteran. On March 23, 1999, to the stunned disbelief of his colleagues, Sergeant Donald Cameron was suspended by the chief of police in connection with a two-year-old theft case. The stench of corruption had long hung over the SPD, which had been rocked time and again through the years by revelations of malfeasance, kickbacks, police brutality and close ties to organized crime. But Cameron, one of the department's longest-serving homicide detectives, had always appeared above reproach. Now his conduct threatened to put the department under the microscope of public scrutiny yet again.

He was affectionately known among his colleagues as "Mr. Homicide." During his thirty-eight-year career with the force, Cameron had investigated hundreds of murders and earned the respect of many, if not all, of his fellow officers for his no-nonsense approach to criminal investigation. When he pronounced a suicide verdict in the highest-profile case of his career, the investigation into the death of Kurt Cobain, Cameron's sterling reputation was repeatedly cited to back up his claim.

Now he was being accused of helping one of his detectives cover up the theft of $10,000 from a crime scene two years earlier. At first, the story went that Cameron had merely gently suggested to a subordinate officer, thirty-year veteran Sonny Davis, that he avoid a career-ending mistake and return the money he had stolen from the crime scene before it was discovered missing. But at Davis's subsequent trial, his partner, Cloyd Steiger, told the jury that he believed Cameron himself had "conspired to steal money." The accusation further rocked a department already reeling from the scandal.

After an investigation, the prosecutor publicly stated that Cameron could have been charged with a number of offenses, including rendering criminal assistance, but by then the two-year statute of limitations had expired. Cameron quietly retired from the force before he could face an SPD internal affairs investigation and disciplinary action. In the end, after two hung juries—the latter of which voted eleven to one to convict—prosecutors decided not to retry the case, and Davis was released. But the affair left a dark cloud over the department and, more important, over the reputation and career of Sergeant Donald Cameron.

The news that Cameron's integrity was being openly questioned may have come as a shock to his many friends and supporters, but it came as no real surprise to us. A few years earlier, we had a revealing encounter with Detective Cameron, and it left us with our own lingering doubts. When Cameron closed the Cobain case in 1994, he publicly declared that he would be very willing to reopen the dossier if he were presented with new evidence pointing to homicide. Three years later, we decided to take him up on his offer. We arrived at the offices of the SPD Homicide Division in 1997, followed by a BBC camera crew. Our compendium of new evidence compiled over the three years since Kurt's death included the polygraph of a man who said he was offered $50,000 to kill Cobain. After we told a receptionist we had important new information about the Cobain case for Sergeant Cameron, she went to deliver our message. We could see Cameron at a desk, seemingly unoccupied. Soon another detective came out to tell us Cameron was busy. We told him that we had come three thousand miles, from Montreal to Seattle, and that we would be willing to wait. The detective was implacable. "That case is closed," he said. "Now leave." We informed him that Cameron had promised to consider reopening the case if he was presented with credible new evidence. We said we just wanted to give him what we had. We'd even be willing to leave our file for him at the front desk. He threatened to arrest us if we didn't leave immediately. We beat a hasty retreat.

On the BBC's film footage, Cameron can be clearly seen peeking out from behind his cubicle. In the years since, he has consistently refused to comment on the case.

* * *

On August 6, 2002, three years after Cameron retired from the SPD, his old friend, Dr. Nikolas Hartshorne, climbed to the top of a steep cliff in the Lauterbrunnen Valley of central Switzerland and prepared to plummet to the ground thirteen hundred feet below. A few years before, Hartshorne had taken up BASE jumping, an extreme sport version of skydiving in which participants parachute off buildings, bridges and cliffs. Oddly enough, his interest in this dangerous sport had been sparked a few years earlier when, as deputy medical examiner for Seattle's King County, he was called to the scene of a BASE-jumping death. Fascinated, he soon tried it out himself and was immediately hooked by its walking-off-a-ledge thrill. Since then, he had recorded more than five hundred jumps and won the U.S. BASE-jumping national championship. However, Hartshorne was probably better known as the doctor who conducted the 1994 autopsy on the body of Kurt Cobain and ruled that the rock icon had committed suicide.

His fellow BASE-jumping participants referred to Hartshorne as "Dr. Death," partly because of his job, partly because of his penchant for investigating the deaths of his fellow jumpers. His motive was to learn exactly what went wrong so as to reduce the risks that had cost some forty lives in twenty years. But, as he hurtled off the menacing Swiss cliff, known locally as "The Nose," his scientific prowess proved futile. His body turned 180 degrees, facing the cliff as he fell. He struck three ledges on his descent as his chute, which had opened normally, collapsed around him. He died instantly.

We didn't yet know if the abrupt retirement of Cameron and the sudden death of Hartshorne—the two men most responsible for convincing the world that Kurt Cobain committed suicide—represented an obstacle to getting at the truth or an opportunity to find it.

* * *

The series of events that would inextricably link Detective Cameron and Dr. Hartshorne took place a few years earlier, when both men were still at the peaks of their professional careers. On Friday, April 8, 1994, each received a call at their desks shortly before 10:00 A.M. Earlier that morning, Gary Smith, an electrician, had arrived at the Lake Washington estate of Kurt Cobain and Courtney Love to install an alarm system. He and his crew had been working at the estate for several days; Smith had arrived early Friday morning to finish wiring the garage, located in a separate structure close to the main house. As he climbed to the balcony that jutted from a room above the garage, he spotted what he first thought was a mannequin through the glass of the French doors. Then he noticed there was blood in the right ear; when he saw a gun, he immediately called his supervisor at Veca Electric to report the gruesome discovery. Instead of calling the police, the company dispatcher placed a call to local radio station KXRX-FM and told DJ Marty Reimer, "You're going to owe me some pretty good Pink Floyd tickets for this one." At first, Reimer thought the call was a hoax, but, twenty minutes later, the news was flashed around the world: a body had been found at the residence of Kurt Cobain.

A week earlier, on Friday, April 1, Kurt had climbed over the wall of an L.A. drug rehab center and disappeared. Although the stomach ailment that he claimed had prompted his heroin habit no longer bothered him, he was already a severe addict. By the end of 1993, Kurt no longer needed heroin to relieve the pain—he just needed it.

During the final months of his life, one thing had become very clear to most of Kurt's family, friends and colleagues: his relationship with Courtney was in trouble. Whereas a year earlier, they were clearly very much in love, now it was obvious to just about everybody who came into contact with the couple that a vicious and largely one-sided pattern had set in. "She was always hurling abuse at him, even in public," recalls Peter Cleary, one of Kurt's Seattle drug buddies. "She would call him a dumb fuck all the time. He would just stand there and take her abuse. . . . He was like a baby."

When Nirvana headed into the studio in 1993 to record the widely anticipated follow-up to *Nevermind*, reports began to circulate that Courtney was constantly meddling in the session. She demanded that Kurt follow her advice, screamed at him constantly and nearly came to blows with both Dave Grohl and Steve Albini, the producer. Twice Albini threatened to quit, citing Courtney's continual interference. Later he went public with his complaints, telling reporters, "I don't feel like embarrassing Kurt by talking about what a psycho hosebeast his wife is, especially because he knows it already."

In January 1994, Tad Doyle, another old friend of Kurt's, also went public with complaints about Courtney, telling *Melody Maker* magazine, "She's outta control. Wherever trouble is, she'll find it or make it. . . . She's disgusting. And you can quote me on that." Soon after, Doyle's band, Tad, was abruptly dropped as the opening act for Nirvana's January 8 Seattle Center gig.

Even during their relationship's finest hour, in 1992, it would be a stretch to describe Kurt and Courtney's home life as domestic bliss. By the middle of 1993, however, the relationship had become what one observer called a "pitched battle." Cobain biographer Christopher Sandford quotes a friend of Kurt's who arrived at their home during this period to find "Courtney throwing everything that was loose against the wall and screaming at Kurt for being useless. His fault, as she saw it, was not being able to come up with a song."

Their marital troubles hit the public's radar screen for the first time in June 1993, when Seattle police responded to a 911 domestic disturbance call from the couple's Lakeside Avenue home. When police arrived, Courtney told them that Kurt had shoved her after she threw a glass of juice in his face during an argument. Kurt was arrested for assault and spent three hours in the King County Jail before being released on $950 bail. One witness to the incident told police that Kurt had been "provoked." Courtney declined to press charges, and the case was dropped.

Courtney would later claim that Kurt's drug use was the chief source of their domestic troubles, but those close to him say that Courtney was regularly shooting up herself. She had even hired a known junkie—an ex-boyfriend from California named Michael "Cali" Dewitt—as the full-time nanny for Frances Bean. Kurt's grandfather visited the house in January 1994 and was shocked by the scene. "Courtney and the male nanny were obviously high as a kite, and Frances was right there in the room," Leland recalls. "I didn't know who the fellow was at first, but when I found out he was in charge of taking care of the baby, I was very upset. There was another nanny there, too, and she was also on drugs. Later I told Wendy [Kurt's mother] that they better get rid of those nannies, or they're going to get Frances taken away again. She said, 'Why?' and I said, 'Because they're both full of dope.' She said, 'They ain't on dope,' and I said, 'The hell they ain't. You just have to take one look at them and you can see they're stoned to the eyeballs.' Then a couple of months later, I read a magazine article where Wendy was saying how nice Courtney was because she was paying for her nannies to go into drug rehab."

Dylan Carlson, one of the couple's prime drug sources, recalls the tragicomic interplay of Kurt and Courtney putting in their orders: "One of them would be on the phone asking me to bring them something," he recalls. "Then I'd get a call-waiting beep, and it would be the other one asking for drugs. Each of them would tell me not to tell the other one."

However, friends of the couple claim that money, not drugs, appeared to be the chief source of conflict. The tension between Kurt and his bandmates had reached a boiling point in mid-1993, when he insisted on renegotiating the terms of their royalty agreement. When the band signed their first major contract with Geffen Records, they had agreed all royalties should be divided equally among them. But, after *Nevermind* hit number one, Courtney was said to have been furious that Krist and Dave would be receiving an equal share of the millions of dollars in royalties, despite the fact that Kurt had written most of the songs. She demanded that he do something to alter the arrangement. "Anybody can do what they do," his friends say she nagged him repeatedly. "You're the one with all the talent." Reluctantly, he gave in and confronted his bandmates. From now on, he argued, 100 percent of the lyrics and 75 percent of the music royalties should go to him. Moreover, he demanded the changes be made retroactive to the first sales of *Nevermind*. Stunned at what they believed was a betrayal of their friendship, not to mention Kurt's punk rock ideals, Dave and Krist initially balked at the changes, arguing that the arrangement should take effect only with the next album. But Kurt stood his ground and threatened to quit the band unless they accepted his terms. Dave and Krist blamed Courtney for their old friend's decision to sell them out, and things were never the same again. They barely spoke, except about Nirvana-related issues.

With the increased income, Courtney insisted that they live in a house that befitted Kurt's superstar status. She had set her sights on the exclusive neighborhood of Denny-Blaine, where Seattle's old-money elite resided, socioeconomic light-years from the seedy university district the couple had inhabited for almost two years. Kurt was more comfortable in the kind of dives he had grown up in, and he had no real desire to see how the other half lived. But at Courtney's insistence, he shelled out more than $1 million for a 7,800-square-foot mansion up the hill from Lake Washington, next door to Starbucks chairman Howard Schultz and directly across the lake from where another Seattle icon, Bill Gates, was constructing his own palatial estate. His new neighbors were more likely to call the police when they heard loud music than to welcome the infamous grunge couple to their domain. Kurt regularly complained to friends that he was embarrassed by the opulent surroundings.

To go with the new upscale digs, Courtney wanted a nice car to replace Kurt's beat-up old Valiant. Though she didn't have a license and had never learned to drive, she convinced Kurt to buy a black luxury Lexus. Mortified by the ostentatiousness of it all, however, he kept it for only eighteen hours before returning it to the dealer.

Shortly after they moved into the new house, Kurt gave the go-ahead to his management company to proceed with a 38-date European tour scheduled to begin in early February 1994. He was exhausted from the band's recently completed American tour and considered canceling the European dates, but he was still exhilarated by the absence of his stomach problems. He told friends he enjoyed playing music again without having to endure the constant pain he had experienced since he was a teenager. As his friend Peter Cleary described it, Kurt loved to tour because it provided him with a long-craved-for independence. "The thing about touring," he explains, "is that Kurt said it's the only time he gets to call the shots. At home, he was like an emotional cripple around his wife, but on tour it was different. He was the center of attention and he was the boss." As an added bonus, Courtney would not be accompanying him on the European dates because she was in the studio mixing Hole's upcoming album.

Nirvana kicked off their tour on February 4 in Paris with an appearance on a lunchtime TV show. Afterward, Kurt—jet-lagged but cheerful—posed for publicity shots with a French photographer named Youri Lenquette, who had become a close friend during Nirvana's 1992 Australian tour. At one point, Lenquette asked Kurt to pose with a toy gun in his mouth, as he had once seen him do at Dave Grohl's house in Seattle. No one could have known how prophetic the pose would be.

On March 1, two weeks after his twenty-seventh birthday, Kurt complained he was feeling ill shortly after the band arrived in Munich to play the first of two concerts at an abandoned air terminal. He had looked exhausted for weeks and had been uncharacteristically listless onstage during recent concerts in Milan and Lisbon. At one point, he even asked a member of his entourage what would happen if he canceled the tour. The band, he was told, would be held liable for any missed shows, resulting in a bill for hundreds of thousands of dollars. Shortly before the first scheduled Munich concert, Kurt phoned Courtney, who was in London doing advance promotion for her upcoming album. True to form, the conversation ended in a screaming match. After the show, Kurt asked his agent to cancel the upcoming gig, and the following morning, he saw an Italian physician, who diagnosed a severe case of bronchitis. The doctor signed a medical slip required for insurance purposes and then recommended that Kurt take two months off to recover.

The next day, March 3, Kurt flew to Rome to meet up with Courtney and Frances. He checked in to the city's most luxurious hotel, the Excelsior, and waited for his wife and daughter, whom he hadn't seen in twenty-six days.

Details of what transpired over the next twenty-four hours are still murky. Between 6:00 and 6:30 A.M. March 4, the front desk received a frantic call from Courtney asking them to summon an ambulance. She had just found her husband unconscious on the floor of their hotel room. Kurt was rushed to the Umberto I Polyclinic hospital. Back in the United States, CNN interrupted its programming to announce that Kurt Cobain had died of a drug overdose in Rome. The report turned out to be premature: twenty hours after he arrived at the hospital, Kurt opened his eyes and asked for a strawberry milk shake.

The next day, his doctor, Osvaldo Galletta, held a press conference to announce that Kurt was recovering from a "pharmacological coma, due not to narcotics, but the combined effect of alcohol and tranquilizers which had been medically prescribed by a doctor."

Nirvana's management company, Gold Mountain, issued a statement that Kurt had suffered an accidental overdose. Not a word about suicide was ever mentioned—publicly or privately. Gold Mountain was well aware that this was not the first time Kurt had overdosed on drugs. A year earlier, on May 2, 1993, a Seattle Fire Department unit had been dispatched to Kurt and Courtney's Lakeside Avenue home, where they found Kurt "shaking, flushed, delirious and talking incoherently." He had apparently suffered an overdose after injecting $30 to $40 worth of heroin. He was taken to the hospital, where he was treated and released.

Courtney claims that, when the couple returned to Seattle a few days after the Rome overdose, the European tour abandoned, she banished drug dealers from the house and went to extreme lengths to ensure Kurt kept away from drugs. This, she said, sparked renewed tension between them. But, according to Dylan Carlson, it was again money, not drugs, that led to the conflict.

Nirvana had been offered the headlining spot at the giant alternative music festival Lollapalooza, including a generous percentage of the gate receipts, which would have brought the band millions of dollars. But when he returned from Rome, Kurt flatly declared that he wasn't going to participate in the summer tour. According to Carlson, who saw Kurt the day he returned from Rome, Courtney was furious that he was willing to turn down that kind of money.

"She went ballistic," he recalls. "She kept on screaming at him about how much money he was giving up and said if he didn't want to do it, she'd be glad to take his place."

Courtney later took great pains to paint herself as a tender but firmly antidrug maternal figure to Kurt at this time. "When he came home from Rome high, I flipped out," she told *Rolling Stone* in December 1994. She has claimed that, as a result, Kurt only did drugs behind her back because he knew she would not have tolerated any drug use. Carlson, who was still supplying them both, finds this laughable. "That's interesting," he says.

Indeed, the recollections of two Seattle car salesmen paint a very different picture. On March 22, only two weeks after they returned from Rome, Kurt and Courtney took a taxi to the American Dream used-car lot, which specialized in vintage cars. When he had returned the Lexus in January, Kurt decided he wanted a vehicle more in keeping with his image. He had spotted a classic '65 sky blue Dodge Dart at the lot, and he wanted to acquire it.

The cabdriver, Leon Hassan, remembers that the couple had "quarreled viciously" in the backseat on the way to American Dream. When they arrived, they were served by a salesman named Joe Kenney, who says they were talking about the Lexus, with Kurt trying to convince her that the Dart could do everything the luxury car could do. After a few minutes, Courtney said she had to use the bathroom. On the way, Kenney says, she dropped a handful of drugs and had to pick them up. Kenney claims he remarked to his colleague that he should get Kurt to autograph his CD soon because it didn't look like they would be around much longer, they were so strung out. "She was really tossing down the drugs," the other salesman recalled.

Meanwhile, Geffen Records was terrified about the close call in Rome. Nirvana was the company's greatest asset, worth tens of millions of dollars in profits—they could not afford to lose Kurt. Equally concerned was the president of Nirvana's management company, Danny Goldberg, who also stood to lose millions in commissions. But Goldberg, who was Frances Bean's godfather, had also become very personally close to Kurt and was genuinely concerned about his deteriorating state.

Goldberg contacted Steven Chatoff, head of a prominent drug rehab center, who recommended an "intervention," a controversial course of action that had been used with limited success on severe drug addicts. The idea was to gather friends and family members together to confront the addict about his drug use. On the morning of March 25, Kurt walked downstairs with Dylan after the two friends had shot up together, shortly after waking up. Gathered in the living room were Courtney; Michael "Cali" Dewitt, Frances Bean's nanny; Nirvana's new guitarist, Pat Smear; and several executives from Kurt's management company and record label. Led by David Burr, a drug counselor, the participants took turns confronting Kurt about his drug use and demanding he seek treatment. Unless he did, the executives threatened, they would no longer work with him and his career would be ruined. When it was Courtney's turn, she said, "This has got to end. . . . You have to be a good daddy."

Counting Dylan, who watched the intervention but did not participate, three of the people in the room, including Courtney, were junkies themselves. "Who the fuck are all of you to tell me this?"

Kurt responded indignantly, calling them "hypocrites." As biographer Charles Cross recorded, Kurt then proceeded to describe in explicit detail what he had witnessed of the heavy drug use by most of those present in the room. From the coke-filled music industry schmooze fests he had attended to the daily heroin habit of his wife, the irony was not lost on Kurt. According to Danny Goldberg, "His big thing was that Courtney was more fucked-up than he was." Kurt stormed out, declaring that nobody in the room had any right to judge him.

Courtney was terrified that Geffen and Gold Mountain would follow through on their threats to drop him; this would severely jeopardize the extravagant lifestyle to which she had become accustomed. She saved her ultimate pressure tactic for the next day. If Kurt refused to seek treatment, she would limit his access to Frances Bean. Knowing he could not risk losing his baby, he finally agreed to check into the Daniel X. Freeman Clinic—also known as the Exodus recovery center—a rehab facility in Marina Del Rey, California, long favored by rock stars and other celebrities.

In September 1992, at the height of the *Vanity Fair* controversy, Kurt had detoxed at Exodus once before, an experience he found "disgusting." He described it to his biographer Michael Azerrad: "Right away, these forty-year-old hippie long-term junkie type counselors would come in and try to talk to me on a rock and roll level, like, 'I know where you're at, man. Drugs are real prevalent in rock 'n roll and I've seen it all in the seventies. Would you mind if David Crosby came in and said hello? Or Steven Tyler?' Rattling off these rock stars' names. I was like, 'Fuck that. I don't have any respect for these people at all.' " That time, he had left a few days before the treatment ended, exasperated by unremitting group therapy sessions and twelve-step meetings. Seeking treatment back then had been all about convincing child welfare authorities that he was cleaning up his act.

On March 30, Kurt flew to Los Angeles to begin his 28-day

treatment at Exodus. He was assigned Room 206 and went through an intake session with a nurse, who attempted to determine the extent of his addiction. The next morning, he attended an individual therapy session with a counselor, Nial Stimson, who later recalled that Kurt "was totally in denial that he had a heroin problem." Stimson tried to make him understand the seriousness of the Rome incident, but Kurt told him, "I understand. I just want to get cleaned up and out of here." Meanwhile, Courtney was attempting her own withdrawal a few miles away at the five-star Peninsula Hotel in Beverly Hills, where a doctor was supervising a treatment plan called "hotel detox"—supposedly meant to shield celebrities from the media spotlight of a public rehab center.

That afternoon, Jackie Farry, one of Frances's nannies, brought the baby to the clinic to visit Kurt, who played with his daughter for about twenty minutes. Kurt complained to Farry about his battles with Courtney over Lollapalooza. The next day, Jackie brought Frances to visit again, and this time Kurt played with the nineteen-month-old baby for almost an hour, tossing her in the air and making her giggle—Frances Bean's favorite game.

After they left, Kurt went outside and smoked a cigarette with another rock star resident, his friend Gibby Haynes of the Butthole Surfers. Haynes told him about a friend who had recently escaped Exodus by jumping over the wall in the backyard. They both laughed at the story because Exodus wasn't a lockdown facility and there was therefore no reason to escape. Anybody could just walk right out the front door anytime they wanted.

Later that evening, at 7:25 P.M., Kurt told a nurse he was going outside to smoke a cigarette, this time alone. It wasn't until an hour later that the Exodus staff noticed him missing. He had scaled the same wall that he and Gibby Haynes had joked about earlier in the day.

Seven days later, his body was found in the room above his garage. Much of what happened in the interval has remained a mystery for nearly a decade, but over time, several missing pieces of the puzzle have materialized, offering the opportunity to paint a clearer picture of what happened that week.

* * *

At 8:56 on the morning of April 8, Officer Von Levandowski of the Seattle Police Department was cruising alone in his patrol car when he received a dispatch on his police radio to investigate a dead body at the Lake Washington Boulevard estate belonging to Kurt Cobain and Courtney Love. When Levandowski arrived, the electrician, Gary Smith, led him to the deck above the garage. Through the French doors, the officer saw a man with long blond hair lying on his back with a shotgun across his body. The butt of the gun was between the victim's feet, and the muzzle was at mid-chest level. Levandowski, who had recently been called to the house to investigate a domestic dispute involving Kurt and Courtney, immediately recognized the victim as Kurt Cobain. A few minutes later, a fire truck arrived at the house, dispatched by the Seattle Fire Department at the officer's request. Outside, it was raining steadily. Firefighters climbed onto the deck and broke a pane of glass on the French doors to force entry. Inside, one of them felt for a pulse and confirmed that Cobain was "dead on arrival." The firefighter asked for an I.D. from a wallet that was lying on the floor about two feet away from the body. Levandowski removed a Washington State driver's license identifying the victim as Kurt Donald Cobain, date of birth 02/20/67, and laid it out beside the body. (Many media accounts falsely reported that Kurt had removed the driver's license before shooting himself, so that whoever arrived at the scene could identify the victim even if the gunshot made his face unrecognizable.) Two more officers had arrived by now, and both proceeded to photograph the scene, one with a Polaroid, the other with a 35 mm camera. Officer Levandowski placed a call to the Homicide Division.

As he waited, Levandowski surveyed the 19-by-23-foot room, which clearly had once been used as a greenhouse but now contained no real signs of plant life, except for an overturned potted plant in the corner, and dirt-lined planting trays set up along the walls. The victim was wearing jeans, black running shoes, and an unbuttoned long-sleeved shirt over a black T-shirt with Japanese lettering. To the right of the body was a Tom Moore cigar box containing syringes, cotton, a spoon "and other items of narcotic paraphernalia." On the floor were a hat, two towels, $120 in cash, a wallet, a pack of cigarettes, a lighter and a pair of sunglasses. To the left of the body lay a brown corduroy jacket and a beige shotgun case, on top of which was one spent shotgun shell. A box of twenty-two unused shells was found inside a brown paper bag at the base of Kurt's left foot. (It had originally contained twenty-five shells.) Inches from Kurt's head, next to a large drying puddle of blood, was an opened can of Barq's root beer, three-quarters full. A paper place mat covered with red handwriting, stabbed through with a pen, lay on a stainless steel planting tray at the north wall. On reading it, Levandowski wrote in his report that it "was apparently written by Cobain to his wife and daughter, explaining why he had killed himself." (See page 283.)

Inside the pocket of the corduroy jacket was a receipt for the purchase of a Remington 20-gauge shotgun, serial #1088925. The receipt, for $308.37, was made out to Dylan Carlson and dated March 30, 1994, the day Kurt left Seattle for Los Angeles.

Before long, three SPD detectives had arrived to secure the scene, along with three members of the King County Medical Examiner's Office, including Dr. Nikolas Hartshorne, who had already been assigned to conduct the examination of the body. With difficulty, Hartshorne removed the shotgun from Kurt's left hand, which had gripped the barrel so tightly that its impression could be seen on his palm. The damage to the interior of the mouth, Hartshorne noted, revealed that Kurt had been shot there. There was one live shell in the shotgun chamber, and another in the magazine, indicating that the gun had been loaded with three shells, including the spent cartridge that had apparently fired the fatal shot. The victim was cold, in the early stages of putrefaction, suggesting that the body had been dead for some time. There were puncture marks on the insides of each elbow.

Hartshorne took photos of the body and then emptied the pockets: $63 in cash and a piece of notepaper with "Seattle Guns, 145 & Lake City" written on it. In the left front pocket, he found an address book, miscellaneous papers and another note, which read, "Remington 20 gauge, 2¼ shells or shorter, set up for light shot." In the same pocket was a used Delta plane ticket, dated April 1, seat 2F, in the name of Cobain/Kurt—the ticket he used to fly from L.A. to Seattle after he left Exodus a week earlier.

After Hartshorne had finished examining the scene, he arranged for the body to be removed to the King County Medical Examiner's Office, where he would conduct the autopsy to determine the cause of death. This was standard procedure, though his parting statement to the assembled officers—including Sergeant Cameron, who had arrived an hour earlier—was not: "This is an open-and-shut case of suicide. The victim died from a self-inflicted gunshot wound."

The media, alerted by a radio report that a body had been found at the Cobain estate, had begun to gather outside shortly after 10:00 A.M. Within minutes of Hartshorne's pronouncement, the world would learn that Kurt Cobain had committed suicide at the age of twenty-seven. His fans were shocked by the news, but, after what they learned from Courtney Love the next day, nobody was surprised.

* * *

When the *Seattle Times* published a story by award-winning investigative journalist Duff Wilson a month later detailing some curious inconsistencies about the case, it failed to cause much of a stir. The repeated assertions by Nikolas Hartshorne and Donald Cameron that the death was a "textbook case of suicide" had done their job. Most people had by then accepted the death as just another rock-and-roll tragedy—a self-destructive junkie who had crashed and burned. Besides, he had attempted suicide once before. Hours after his body was found, Courtney was telling anyone who would listen that the Rome overdose in March had in fact been a suicide attempt, not an accident as previously claimed. In Rome, she revealed, he had also left a note. The only difference this time was that he had succeeded.

But Wilson's findings were nagging him. His sources in the SPD had tipped him off to a number of facts about Cobain's death that just didn't add up. Among the most glaring was the fact that a subsequent police investigation found there were no legible fingerprints on the shotgun, the shotgun cartridge or the pen that was found stabbed through the note. But it was the note itself that raised the most questions. Despite the fact that police on the scene had immediately described it as a "suicide note," those who had seen it said that it didn't mention suicide at all. More disturbingly, the only part of the note that might have alluded to such a fate appeared to have been added at the end, in a completely different style of handwriting.

To add to the mystery, somebody had attempted to use Kurt's credit card between the time the medical examiner said Kurt died and the discovery of his body. The police never determined who was using the credit card, missing from Kurt's wallet when he was found.

But an even more troubling detail had been disclosed in another Seattle newspaper three weeks earlier. Nikolas Hartshorne had completed his autopsy the day Kurt's body was found and immediately announced that the pathological examination had confirmed his initial verdict—that Kurt Cobain had died of a self-inflicted gunshot wound. Because Washington State law classifies autopsy results as private medical records, Hartshorne's office refused to reveal the details of his findings. But on April 14, veteran reporters Mike Merritt and Scott Maier of the *Seattle Post-Intelligencer,* who had cultivated enough sources over the years to obtain the unobtainable, filed a story claiming that a source in the medical examiner's office had leaked them the results of Cobain's autopsy. A small technical detail stood out. Toxicological tests indicated that Cobain's body contained traces of diazepam (Valium) and had a blood morphine level of 1.52 milligrams per liter. Although Nikolas Hartshorne was a medical doctor, he, like most doctors, had very little background in the complex field of pharmacology and opiates, and so this measure failed to resonate. For anyone in the field, however, the statistic spoke volumes.

4

Like hundreds of thousands of teenagers around the world, Rochelle Marshall was devastated when she heard the news about Kurt Cobain's suicide. Like many of them, she and her friends started asking questions after the murder theories began to circulate. Unlike most of them, however, her mother was in a position to provide answers.

"My daughter was very disturbed at first. She was a big fan of Cobain," recalls Denise Marshall. "Then after a while, she started saying she wasn't sure he had really killed himself, and I told her, 'Well, a lot of people feel that way about a suicide because they just can't believe it, or they don't want to believe it.' But she said this was different. She wanted me to look into it."

Marshall was well suited for the task. As a deputy coroner in Colorado, she has investigated hundreds of deaths, including countless suicides and murders. During her years as a forensic medicolegal investigator, she says, she has learned one important lesson: "Things aren't always as they appear at first." After reading our first book and a myriad of other information about Cobain's death, including the police reports, Marshall has come to her own conclusion about what happened. "I'd bet a year's salary that he was murdered," she declares. "There's just not enough evidence to rule it a suicide."

Marshall explains that a number of factors have led her to this conclusion. "There are too many red flags. There's just so many questions about how the case was handled," she says. "When I read the police reports, I was amazed at how many things they did wrong. For example, the first officer on the scene handled the body when he reached into the victim's wallet to take out his driver's license. That's a big no-no. You're supposed to wait for the deputy coroner or medical examiner to arrive so that you don't contaminate the scene. You never touch the body."

She is particularly disturbed about what she believes was a rush to judgment by both the police and the deputy medical examiner, who each concluded the death was a suicide while they were still at the scene.

"That in itself is ridiculous," says Marshall. "I don't know of any case that's an open-and-shut case of suicide, and that's what they all did in this case: they immediately ruled it a suicide. You just don't do that. You wait for all the test results to come back and you investigate the circumstances before you rule. That's just how it's done."

Even in this situation, with a suicide note at the scene and the shotgun still in the victim's hand?

"That's one of the things I'm concerned about," she responds. "In the majority of suicides, there is no note. I'm always a bit suspicious when there is one, at least suspicious enough to take a closer look. And I'm particularly suspicious after reading the so-called suicide note in Cobain's case. That's hardly a typical suicide note from my experience. I have a lot of questions about the handwriting on the note. You know, nowhere in the note does he say he wants to die. He just doesn't like what he's doing, and he wants to change his life. I don't see it as a suicide note, and I think it was really unprofessional for them to judge on it so early."

None of these factors, however, convinces Marshall that Cobain was murdered. It's the heroin levels that she claims are the clincher. "When I saw the blood morphine results of the toxicology tests—1.52 milligrams per liter—I immediately said to myself, 'How could he have pulled the trigger?' That just didn't make sense. With that much heroin in his system, it would have been virtually impossible." (When heroin enters the bloodstream, she explains, it is instantly transformed into morphine—thus, the discussion of blood morphine levels rather than heroin levels.)

Marshall relates how, suspicion piqued, she began to dig through county records in an attempt to find any autopsy whose subject had blood morphine levels near Cobain's. "There were none even approaching those kinds of levels," she said. "As a matter of fact, when I started searching further through the state, I just couldn't find any cases with those levels. The amount of blood morphine in Cobain's blood was truly amazing. With levels that high, he just wouldn't have been conscious long enough to pull the trigger."

How *could* Kurt have shot himself after injecting that much heroin? While researching our first book, we put the question to the deputy medical examiner, Nikolas Hartshorne. Tolerance levels were the mitigating factor, he explained. A severe addict like Cobain has a much higher tolerance than the average user; the opiates would therefore have taken longer to render him unconscious. "He was a serious junkie," said Hartshorne. "His system could process higher amounts of heroin than [that of] the average person." Hartshorne's supervisor, Dr. Donald Reay, who was King County's chief medical examiner at the time, concurred. "It is really an issue of tolerance: how much is this person used to," said Reay. "If a person has gradually over months or years increased the dose, a person could function with that amount of drugs."

Denise Marshall is unconvinced. "Certainly, tolerance does play a factor, there's no doubt about it. I won't argue with that," she says. "But I don't care what your tolerance level is. His morphine level was so high that I really question anybody having a tolerance that high. I've seen some really amazing amounts, and I've seen them live through it, but I've never seen anybody with his levels. It's just staggering. If tolerance was that important, you wouldn't have so many heroin addicts overdosing all the time, and with levels significantly lower than what Cobain had in his blood."

The tolerance argument in Cobain's case has always relied on the premise that he was a longtime heroin user whose body had gradually over the months and years built up a tolerance to higher and higher levels of the drug. And, despite his own frequent public denials, there is no question that Cobain was at times a heavy heroin user. However, it is still an open question just how much heroin he was actually using during the final months of his life. According to the musicians who played with him during his final European tour in February and March 1994, Kurt was almost certainly heroin-free during that tour. In April 1994, Tony Barber, bassist of the Buzzcocks, who opened for Nirvana during several dates on their European tour, told *Melody Maker* magazine, "I know he was not taking drugs on that tour. He was walking around drinking Evian water and looking clean every time I saw him." In the same article, Buzzcocks guitarist Pete Shelley echoed Barber's assessment: "He seemed really clean when we were on tour. In some ways it was a bit awkward because he wasn't really joining in the very mild debauchery that went on."

Were these musicians simply unaware of Kurt's heroin use? Perhaps, but there is another more reliable source that appears to back them up. When Kurt was rushed to the hospital after his overdose in Rome on March 4, doctors said they found no traces of narcotics in his blood, only the prescription tranquilizer Rohypnol. Thus, exactly one month before his death, Kurt's blood was free of heroin, and probably had been for some time. According to Courtney's own account, Kurt started using heroin again eight days after he returned to Seattle. For the sake of argument, we can assume he continued using it during the last two weeks before he entered rehab, building up a renewed level of tolerance. However, even the Seattle medical examiner who cited tolerance as the mitigating factor said a user would have had to increase his dose "gradually over months or years" to function with the amount of drugs found in Cobain's system. But Denise Marshall cautions against reading too much into the length of his drug use. "Tolerance can build quite quickly," she explains. "Nevertheless, I still don't think anybody could be that tolerant."

According to Geoffrey Burston's medical textbook *Self-poisoning,* "The effect of heroin is of such short duration and is so intense that it inhibits any type of physical activity, either criminal or non criminal." In 1996, we asked eleven different heroin addicts whether they believed it was possible for somebody who had injected as much as Cobain had to have then shot and killed himself immediately after injecting, as the police and medical examiners claim. Each insisted it would be impossible, no matter what their tolerance level. Said an eight-year addict, "Anybody who says you can do that has never shot smack."

Coroners and medical examiners without the requisite training in opiate toxicology will often cite tolerance in cases like Cobain's, says Marshall. "My specialty is in pharmacology, specifically opiates, so I understand these issues better than a doctor who doesn't have that kind of specialized pharmacological training. They would know the basics but wouldn't have a grasp of the studies that provide the necessary data about a specific issue in our field. I run into these kinds of cases all the time where it's difficult for me to make my case because the coroner may not properly understand the science behind opiates or another type of drug. If you consult the medical and scientific literature, it just won't back up their explanation of 'tolerance' as a factor when it comes to this kind of dose. With most drugs, there is a therapeutic level, there is a toxic level and there is a lethal level. But there is no exact ceiling lethal level with opiates because the tolerance level keeps moving up. Everybody has a ceiling, of course, otherwise you wouldn't have people dying of overdoses. With opiates, as your toxic level goes up, so does your lethal level. That's why opiate users can use a lot before they die. But if you get anywhere near Cobain's levels or much lower even, you're going to be immediately incapacitated."

Blood is often described as "an honest witness." Lethal opiate levels generally vary according to factors such as tolerance and body weight, and, although there is no officially recognized ceiling, the maximum lethal heroin dose should be slightly higher than the highest known dose someone has taken and survived. Historically, toxicologists have relied upon previously published case reports of fatal intoxication to determine the concentrations of a given drug required to produce a measured blood level. In his 1986 book *Heroin Addiction*, Jerome J. Platt—former director of the Institute for Addictive Disorders at Allegheny University—concluded that the maximum known lethal dose for a 150-pound male would result in a blood morphine level of approximately 0.5 milligrams per liter. A few months before his death, Cobain weighed in at 115 pounds. According to Denise Marshall, this would have made his lethal dose even lower. "Generally, the less you weigh, the lower the lethal dose," she explains. Other studies cited in the *Journal of Forensic Sciences* also suggest the maximum known lethal dose for heroin would result in an approximate blood morphine level of 0.5 milligrams per liter. In other words, Cobain's level of 1.52 milligrams per liter was more than three times the accepted maximum lethal dose.

It would be inaccurate, however, to simply state that Cobain took a triple lethal dose of heroin. In fact, according to the medical literature, the dose he took was approximately seventy-five times the lethal dose for the average person. What's crucial is that it was triple the lethal dose for even the most *severe* addict.

Yet this statistic does not tell the entire story. While the heroin

Kurt took was undeniably enough to kill him three times over, there are many studies that demonstrate he may not have died immediately after injecting such a dose. The literature indicates he could have stayed alive for as long as several hours, even after injecting this massive amount of heroin into his system. The real question that must be asked is whether he could have remained *conscious* long enough after shooting up to have picked up the shotgun and killed himself. According to the leaked autopsy results, in fact, the cause of death was most probably the gunshot wound rather than the heroin injection, suggesting that Kurt was still alive for some time after shooting up.

In 1973, *The New England Journal of Medicine* published a comprehensive study, "Morphine Concentrations and Survival Periods in Acute Heroin Fatalities," by pharmacologists J. C. Garriott and W. Q. Sturner, who examined hundreds of heroin-related overdoses. In all the fatalities they studied to that point, the two scientists had never encountered a single case with a blood morphine level over 0.93 milligrams per liter—more than 50 percent *lower* than Cobain's level.

However, although neither Denise Marshall nor Garriott and Sturner had ever found a blood morphine level as high as Kurt's, a number of such cases do exist. A comprehensive review of blood morphine levels in 1,526 deaths involving intravenous heroin-related overdoses found twenty-six cases, or 1.7 percent, where levels were equal to or higher than Cobain's level of 1.52 milligrams per liter.

The statistics are telling. According to a study cited in the *International Journal of Legal Medicine*, approximately 85 percent of cases with levels this high will result in a so-called "golden shot," culminating in immediate death. But in the balance of the cases, the study concludes, "the death is not so rapid and a survival period in a comatose state has to be taken into consideration." Another 1996 study of survival times following opiate overdose, reported in the *Journal of Forensic Sciences*, confirms that the user experiences a state of acute shock "within seconds" after injecting the fatal dose.

In all of the twenty-six known heroin overdose cases where blood morphine levels were equal to or higher than Cobain's level, however, the tourniquets were still in place when the body was discovered, and the syringe was still affixed in the victim's arm or lying on the floor next to the body—suggesting either instant death or unconsciousness.

Yet, as Denise Marshall notes, the police reports describe no such scenario when Kurt's body was found: "Was it suicide? I don't see how physically that could have been done. I do not see how he could have injected himself with the amount of heroin to cause those levels, put the syringe and other drug paraphernalia away, folded his sleeve down, grabbed the gun, positioned it backwards in his mouth and pulled the trigger. I do not see it."

Marshall was not the only expert with doubts about the official story. In 1997, the NBC-TV show *Unsolved Mysteries* presented Cobain's autopsy results to Dr. Cyril Wecht, one of America's most prominent forensic pathologists. Harvard law professor Alan Dershowitz has described him as the "Sherlock Holmes of forensic science." Dr. Wecht was immediately dismissive of the tolerance argument cited by Nikolas Hartshorne. "For most people, *including addicts*, 1.52 milligrams per liter of morphine is a significant level," Wecht cautiously explained, "and for most of them, a great percentage, it will be a level that will induce a state of unconsciousness quite quickly. We're talking about seconds, not minutes. . . . It does raise a question, a big question, as to whether or not he shot that shotgun."

On camera, however, Dr. Wecht refused to rule out completely the possibility of suicide, declaring it "within the realm of possibility." Thus, a leading authority appeared to believe that, however remote the possibility, Cobain could indeed have shot himself, as the official version indicates. In the years since this interview took place, however, we learned that there was more to Dr. Wecht's interview than NBC broadcast that night. According to the segment's producer, Cindy Bowles, Wecht had never been fully informed of the circumstances of Cobain's death before his interview, knowing only that he had been found shot through the mouth and with a postmortem blood morphine level of 1.52 milligrams per liter. What Wecht actually said off camera *after* declaring suicide within the realm a possibility was this: "If it *was* suicide, he probably would had to have been holding the gun in his hand while he was injecting himself with the heroin, and then shot himself immediately after the injection."

Of course, we know from the police reports that this is not what happened. Before picking up the gun, Cobain took the time to roll down his sleeves, remove his drug paraphernalia and place it back into a nearby cigar box. Again, the official scenario appears to be scientifically impossible.

The new revelation regarding Dr. Wecht's verdict, however, is not the only crucial piece of information that has emerged in recent years. In 1995, after Nikolas Hartshorne and his supervisor, Dr. Donald Reay, informed us that tolerance was the mitigating factor that allowed Cobain to shoot himself—even after injecting such a massive dose of heroin—we challenged each of them to point to a single case in which somebody had taken a dose equal to Cobain's and remained conscious for more than a few seconds. Neither of them was able to cite such a case.

Two years later, in his BBC documentary *Kurt & Courtney*, filmmaker Nick Broomfield believed he had met this challenge. In the film, Broomfield featured an interview with a British physician, Dr. Colin Brewer, who insisted that somebody could indeed shoot himself after taking the amount of heroin found in Kurt's bloodstream. To prove his point, the doctor took out a photograph he had taken of one of his patients. In this photo, featured in Broomfield's film, a man could be seen balancing on one leg fifteen minutes after supposedly taking "twice the amount as Kurt." When the documentary was released in 1998, this photo alone proved a near fatal blow to the murder theory. In fact, this evidence was the single element cited by Broomfield when he changed his mind about how Cobain died. Before interviewing the doctor, the filmmaker reveals, he was leaning toward the belief that Kurt had been murdered. After the interview, Broomfield became convinced that Cobain had committed suicide.

If, in fact, a case existed where an addict remained conscious for fifteen minutes after taking such a large dose, it would indeed prove that Kurt might still have been able to shoot himself after injecting the level of heroin found in his system.

However, it has since emerged that Broomfield made a crucial error in his film—a mistake that has inflicted lasting damage to the credibility of the murder theory. The patient depicted in the photo had not actually injected heroin after all. Rather, he had swallowed *methadone*—a synthetic opiate commonly used for heroin withdrawal. The doctor later conceded that he was not even licensed to administer heroin, so he could not have duplicated the results even if he wanted to. The difference between methadone and heroin, explains Denise Marshall, is immense.

"Methadone is meant to be swallowed, not injected," she explains. "Anytime you have to swallow a drug, it has to go through your gastrointestinal tract, and that can take thirty-five to forty minutes. But when you inject a drug, the effect is instantaneous: it goes right into the bloodstream. You feel the effect within seconds."

She says the example cited in Broomfield's documentary is completely inappropriate and misleading.

"The man in the photo swallowed methadone. It's comparing apples and oranges," she says. "Yes, methadone is an opiate. I can take that much orally and go jump around, too. I don't know how I'd be in forty-five minutes, though. But methadone is also different on how it works on the body. We have opiate receptors in our brain, and that's what the drug binds to. And once the drug binds to those receptors, the receptors release another drug called dopamine, and that's what makes you feel the high. Methadone doesn't work in quite the same way as heroin.

"Clearly the filmmaker, and probably even the doctor, didn't understand the science of opiates," she says. "I can explain it like this: if you've ever had surgery or any kind of IV sedation, the moment they tell you to start counting backwards, they're putting the drug into your vein, and you're asleep before the plunger ever finishes. That's what heroin can do. And with the amount Cobain took, I'm fairly certain that's what happened to him. He was probably unconscious while the needle was still in his arm."

How, then, could Nikolas Hartshorne have got it so wrong? Renowned forensic pathologist Samuel Burgess writes in his 1992 book, *Understanding the Autopsy*, "There are many jurisdictions in this country where you would not have to be half-smart to get away with murder, quite literally . . . the fact remains that, in all too many places, the investigation of possible murder is undertaken only after pressure is brought by relatives or other interested parties, and when such investigation is instituted, it is done so incompetently that murder after murder goes unsolved and unpunished." Burgess points to faulty autopsies as one of the main culprits.

Denise Marshall agrees. "Unfortunately, that's true. A lot of autopsies are conducted very poorly, especially when the pathologist has already come to a conclusion about the cause of death beforehand. This particular case amazes me, but I see these mistakes happen every day. You know, watching all these crime shows on TV, if you went as a visitor to a crime scene, you would just think everything goes according to the book, but it's like any other job, it just doesn't. You have people that are lazy and incompetent, just like any other job. You can spend a lifetime just researching all the deaths that were ruled incorrectly by coroners and medical examiners, especially coroners that have preconceived ideas about junkies. Opiate addicts really have a bad deal. I can't imagine how many deaths are out there that were ruled accidental overdoses or suicides with junkies that were probably homicides."

One of the best examples of autopsy misdiagnosis, in fact, involves another notorious rock-and-roll suicide. In November 1997, Michael Hutchence, lead singer of the band INXS, was found dead in a Sydney, Australia, hotel room with a belt around his neck. He had apparently hanged himself from a doorjamb before the buckle of the belt broke, sending him sprawling to the floor. Finding no signs of foul play, the Sydney coroner immediately ruled the death a suicide. But within hours, Hutchence's wife, Paula Yates, declared that she was certain her husband had not committed suicide and hinted cryptically that she knew the real cause of death. Soon after, she confessed to friends that Hutchence had almost certainly hanged himself accidentally while engaging in a sex game known as autoerotic asphyxiation (AEA).

The bizarre sex act, practiced by millions, involves an intentional act of self-strangulation performed to heighten orgasm by constricting the flow of blood to the brain during masturbation. Practitioners, nearly all male, tighten belts around their necks or suspend themselves by a noose, often using a rafter or tree branch. The resulting breath deprivation, known as cerebral anoxia, results in a woozy, heightened orgasm. Yates revealed that Hutchence was a devotee of this and other dangerous sex acts such as bondage and S & M, and that he must have died when the self-asphyxiation went wrong. Said Yates at the time, "He did everything. He's a dangerous boy, dangerous, wild. He could have done anything at any time. The only thing he wouldn't have done is just left us [her and their daughter, Tiger Lily]."

When the details of Hutchence's death scene leaked out, they seemed to confirm her story. Police revealed that when his body was found, he was completely naked, sprawled out on the floor.

Nevertheless, the coroner maintained it was a suicide and refused to call an inquest to investigate whether AEA was involved. His reluctance was probably due to the fact that the fetish is virtually unknown in Australia, although in the UK, where Hutchence lived, some two hundred people die during the act every year. Two years after the case was closed, McMaster University professor Stephen Hucker, considered the world's leading authority on AEA, agreed to investigate the circumstances of the rock star's death. At the completion of his probe, Professor Hucker declared, "I have concluded that this is most likely a death due to an act of autoerotic practice that went wrong." In the Sydney coroner records, however, Hutchence's death remains a suicide to this day.

*   *   *

In 1995, a Canadian chemist named Roger Lewis became suspicious of the circumstances of Cobain's death, largely because of the remarkably high blood morphine levels involved. On his own initiative, he conducted a yearlong survey of the existing forensic and criminological literature. During the course of his review, he studied 3,226 heroin-related overdoses, more than 3,586 self-inflicted deaths, including 760 violent suicides, and a considerable number of known staged deaths. His resulting essay, "Dead Men Don't Pull Triggers," is a scientifically rigorous "reinterpretation of the officially released evidence" that argues strongly for a reopening and independent investigation of the Cobain death.

Two years after Lewis first published his essay, Bradley Speers, a twenty-one-year-old Australian pharmacology student, took issue with the findings and published his own scientifically complex rebuttal of Lewis's theory. One of his central arguments was that Kurt might not have taken the entire massive dose of heroin all at once, but that the blood morphine levels had become elevated as a result of repeated injections throughout the day. Kurt, after all, was a junkie who would have shot up every few hours during the normal course of a day. Therefore, Speers believes that there has perhaps been too much emphasis placed on Cobain's blood morphine level of 1.52 milligrams per liter.

"It may be possible," he writes, "that there was a reasonable level of morphine present in his blood before a final injection, and thus its effects are less pronounced."

But, according to Denise Marshall, this argument just doesn't stand up under scientific scrutiny. "First of all, when you are a junkie and you have a tolerance, it means your liver has become very smart," she explains. "The way you get that tolerance is from doing it a lot, and your liver says, 'I know that a big blast of heroin is coming soon because it does every four hours, so I've got to process what I have or I'm going to die when the next blast comes.' That's the same way you develop a tolerance to alcohol. That's why, when you see people who can drink you under the table, it means their liver processes the alcohol faster than yours does. And the only way that can happen is from using it on a regular basis. So no, it wouldn't build up in his body. If anything, he would process it quicker than somebody else. I would say that the 1.52 milligrams per liter would have had to represent a dose he took recently, not multiple doses throughout the day."

Apart from the evidence demonstrating the sheer scientific impossibility of the official verdict, Roger Lewis cites a number of relevant probability studies that he believes further demonstrate the unlikelihood of the suicide scenario. According to one study published in the journal *Medicine, Science and Law*, 1,862 postmortem examinations of suicides were conducted in northwest London over a twenty-year period. Twenty percent of these suicides resulted from "physical injury," including gunshot wounds. Yet not a single case involved opiates. In another study of 1,117 suicides in the British county of Avon, fifty-one victims used a shotgun. Again, not a single case involved opiates. Lewis points to these and other studies to demonstrate what he calls the "myth of the suicidal heroin addict."

In a separate study of 189 cases of fatal self-poisoning with opiates in London between 1975 and 1984, only a single case resulted in a blood morphine level exceeding 1.52 milligrams per liter—or less than 0.53 percent of the cases studied—demonstrating that even when somebody does attempt suicide with a massive dose of opiates, the chances are extremely remote of reaching the levels found in Kurt's blood.

In his study, Lewis also researched the likelihood of suicide among missing persons, since Kurt had been missing for seven days before his body was found. According to a study cited by Charles O'Hara in his criminology textbook *The Fundamentals of Criminal Investigation,* only approximately one in two thousand missing persons cases is found to be a suicide. "To the layman," O'Hara writes, "the suicide theory is one of the first to suggest itself in a disappearance case. Statistically, however, it can be shown that the odds are greatly against the suicide solution. . . . A voluntary disappearance is motivated by a desire to escape from some personal, domestic or business conflict. . . . In the disappearance of approximately 100,000 people annually in this country, it is to be expected that personal violence should play a significant part in some of these cases. Murder, the unspoken fear of the relatives and the police, must always lie in the back of the investigator's mind as a possible explanation."

O'Hara also offers investigators some crucial advice that may be particularly relevant in the Cobain case: "Certain combinations of wounds suggest a physical impossibility. To draw a conclusion of suicide, the wounds should be physically not improbable."

*   *   *

92 | The clincher for Nikolas Hartshorne was the gun in Kurt's hands. When he arrived at the scene shortly after 10:00 A.M. on April 8, the victim was still gripping the shotgun tightly. Before Hartshorne conducted the autopsy—before he even read the note—it was this detail that led him to the conclusion of suicide, he later revealed.

"With gun suicides, you always see the victim still gripping the barrel of the gun," Hartshorne told us in 1995. "That's because at the point of death, the hand freezes in place. We literally had to pry that shotgun from Cobain's hands. You could still see the markings of the gun in his palms from where he had been gripping it for days. That's a sure sign the wound was self-inflicted. That kind of evidence doesn't lie."

Denise Marshall confirms Hartshorne's explanation—but with one important reservation.

"When you see the hand gripping the gun like that," she explains, "it's called a 'cadaveric spasm.' You usually see it more when somebody uses a pistol or an automatic weapon, but it can also happen with a shotgun. Let's say you shoot yourself in the head with a .357 Magnum. When you grip that gun, and you pull the trigger and the bullet rips through your brain, it causes a cadaveric spasm, which is basically instantaneous rigor mortis. And often we find the gun still in the grip of the hand, and even when we remove the gun, the hand is still in the position like it's holding the gun. That's from the trauma, the chemicals being released. I worked on this guy recently who shot himself in a truck with a shotgun. He wedged his shotgun between his legs and the truck, and it took his head off completely, but his hands were still wrapped around it."

Wouldn't the cadaveric spasm described by Hartshorne, therefore, confirm that Kurt shot himself?

"You're overlooking the obvious," Marshall responds. "There's one other scenario that could easily explain it. From my experience, everything about this case points to a staged scene, somebody trying to make a murder look like a suicide. I think that's exactly what happened. Cadaveric spasm can still occur in a homicide."

Indeed, the forensic literature appears to contradict Hartshorne's assertion that Cobain's cadaveric spasm conclusively proved he had killed himself. According to the University of Dundee's Forensic Pathology Wounds Manual, "Occasionally suicide is accomplished with a single stroke and the weapon may be left protruding from the wound. The hand of the decedent may be gripping the weapon in cadaveric spasm; this is proof that the victim was holding the weapon at the time of death and therefore creates a presumption, *but not a proof,* of suicide."

Marshall believes somebody gave Kurt an incapacitating dose of heroin that immediately rendered him unconscious. "I think somebody had to have given him an overly pure dose, what's usually referred to as a 'hot shot.' When heroin addicts do heroin, they pretty well know exactly how much they should do. Whenever you see an accidental overdose, it's usually because they got it from someone else, and they didn't know how pure it was. With heroin, you normally dilute the purity with some kind of adulterant. Usually you trust that whoever gave you the heroin has already done this. You would never expect to get a pure dose."

Marshall is particularly suspicious of the Barq's root beer can found beside Kurt's body. "The autopsy revealed the presence of Valium in Kurt's system along with the heroin," she says. "Somebody could have easily put a large dose of valium in the can. It would have helped incapacitate him a lot quicker than without it. Valium exacerbates the effects of the heroin. It doesn't look like the police even tested the contents of the can, but they should have."

Regardless of whether or not the Valium was used to hurry the process, Marshall theorizes that if somebody who knew Cobain gave him an overly pure dose of heroin, they simply had to wait for him to lose consciousness. "Then they could have placed the shotgun in his hands, positioned it in his mouth and pulled the trigger, making the death look like a suicide. At the point of death, his hand would have gripped the shotgun barrel, and you have your cadaveric spasm.

"Unfortunately, it's not really very difficult to get away with murder," Marshall adds, "particularly when the death involves a junkie."

* * *

Vernon Geberth knows a thing or two about getting away with murder. Recently retired as the commanding officer of the Bronx Homicide Task Force, Geberth has personally investigated, supervised, assessed and consulted on more than eight thousand death investigations. Among them, he says, "I can show you a list as long as my arm of murders that were staged to look like suicides."

According to Geberth, whose criminology textbook *Practical Homicide Investigation* is considered the bible of homicide detectives, all death investigations should be handled as potential murder cases until the facts prove otherwise. "The issue is not 'Could this conceivably have been a suicide?' It is 'Could this conceivably have been a murder?' This is the only logical procedure for distinguishing staged murders from suicides. If the police were to assume without further inquiry that an apparent suicide was not murder, then other evidence and leads at the scene would never be followed up and murders would go undetected."

Like Denise Marshall, Geberth believes the laziness of investigators has made it increasingly easy to make a murder look like suicide. "The presentation of the homicide victim and the manipulation of the crime scene by a clever offender could make the death appear to be a suicide," he explains. "I have personally investigated many such cases, and the truth of the matter is that initially the cases did look like suicides."

Geberth cites a particular case he worked on, one that resembles the Cobain case in many respects. In this investigation, he was acting as a consultant for an insurance company that filed a wrongful death suit against a man they believed had actually murdered one of his relatives, whom the authorities claimed had committed suicide.

When police arrived at the scene, the victim was lying on his back in his mobile home with a rifle wedged between his legs, blood and brain matter scattered around the body. After a perfunctory investigation, the police ruled the death a suicide and closed the case.

When Geberth conducted his own investigation, however, he discovered a number of troubling inconsistencies. The deceased was known to keep at least $1,000 cash at home, but police found an empty wallet on the floor of his car and $2.50 in his pockets. What's more, the victim's bank account showed he had made a $200 withdrawal from an ATM shortly before his death, but this amount was also missing from his trailer and unaccounted for. Geberth interviewed a neighbor who had stopped by the trailer because of his suspicion "that something wasn't right." Geberth observed that the car doors were unlocked and the keys were in the ignition—unusual for the deceased. Moreover, the door to the trailer was unlocked, the stereo blasting and the thermostat inexplicably set as high as it could go, despite the fact that the deceased reportedly never kept it above 65 degrees. Family members told Geberth the victim's radar detector, always clipped to his car's sun visor, was missing, as were a pouch of tools from the rear seat and a gold calculator with the initials of the deceased. Finally, the deceased was known to have made a number of short- and long-term plans just before his death.

Convinced the evidence pointed to foul play, Geberth submitted his findings to the police and suggested they reopen the investigation. They refused to even consider it. The verdict remained suicide.

"Frankly, some cops just don't want to admit they made a mistake, no matter how compelling the evidence," Geberth says. "They're afraid it will reflect badly on their reputation. But the fact is that when you come across an apparent suicide, you have to probe deeper, find out if anybody had a motive, if anybody benefited financially from the death. Then you have to look at the forensics to see whether the medical facts fit the pattern of suicide. Often the perpetrator is counting on the authorities not to do their job. I hate to admit it, but it's relatively easy to stage a murder to look like suicide and have the crime go undetected. It doesn't take a genius."

In his 1975 book, *Fundamentals of Criminal Investigation*, Charles O'Hara cites a study of forty apparent suicides in which the victims' skulls had been destroyed by a bullet. "Naturally in such cases," he writes, "the muzzle of the barrel must be placed directly under the chin or in the mouth. It is not therefore impossible that a murder may be committed in this way, and all the more likely as it lends itself easily to the suspicion of suicide; it is a fair supposition that a person asleep, stupefied, or bound may be thus killed."

Another study comparing homicides and suicides cited by David Lester in his 1986 book, *The Murderer and His Murder*, found the typical homicide victim—a man between twenty-five and thirty-four, killed at home with a gun—fits a profile similar to Cobain's. Lester also reports on a study that found wives killing husbands constituted 41 percent of female murderers and that 85 percent of spousal murders took place in the home. But it is the presence of drugs in Cobain's system that most closely fits the findings of the study, which concludes, "Narcotics were more likely to be present in the homicides" than in the suicides.

Indeed, says Vernon Geberth, "There is one group above all where you tend to find the most staged crime scenes, and that is in the deaths of junkies. Before I was a homicide investigator, I worked in narcotics. Whenever the authorities arrive at the scene where a junkie has apparently overdosed or committed suicide, they have a tendency to write it off as just another junkie death without properly investigating the circumstances. That's why it's easier to murder a junkie and stage the death to look like suicide than it would be in the case of your average upstanding citizen."

Although statistics about this phenomenon are difficult to come by because so many staged crimes go undetected, one 1971 study is particularly revealing, looking at drug-related deaths in an area where the use of narcotics is known to be especially prevalent—the U.S. military. Two investigators, Colonel Richard Froede and Commodore Charles Stahl, examined 1.3 million surgical and autopsy cases in the files of the Armed Forces Institute of Pathology conducted between 1918 and 1970. They detected 174 examples of what they call "fatal narcotism"—cases where military personnel were known to have died from using opiates. Of these, they found a surprisingly high 3.7 percent were actually known homicides— instances where the dead soldiers received an intentional "hot shot" of heroin.

Two decades later, the U.S. military would also become the backdrop for the most important study ever conducted into the phenomenon of staged suicides—a study that provides a caution-ary tale for investigators tempted to label a death as an open-and-shut case before investigating all the facts.

* * *

In 1993, a *Philadelphia Inquirer* reporter named David Zucchino began to probe the deaths of a number of U.S. soldiers ruled sui-cides by military pathologists. After reviewing thousands of pages of investigative, forensic and autopsy reports obtained under the Freedom of Information Act, Zucchino found not only that the ba-sic facts directly contradicted suicides, but that investigators had lost or carelessly destroyed important evidence, mishandled death weapons, failed to perform routine forensic tests and pursue leads, and filed inaccurate and misleading reports.

In case after case, he found that the victims' families had challenged the suicide verdicts, only to be accused by military authorities of refusing to face up to the fact that their loved ones had killed themselves.

Among the most glaring examples Zucchino discovered pointing to staged suicides:

- In 1989, the Naval Criminal Investigative Service (NCIS) tried to convince Bill and Donna Digman that their son, Marine Captain Jeffrey Digman, had shot himself in the head, even though he would have had to contort himself upside down to produce the bullet's trajectory. The bullet, moreover, had entered Digman's head from the right side even though he was left-handed. The family hired a forensics expert, who found injuries on Digman's body consistent with a struggle and concluded that someone had probably shot Digman and arranged his body to look like suicide.

- In 1991, the NCIS informed John Sabow that his brother, Col. James Sabow, had shot himself to death in his backyard. John Sabow, a neurosurgeon, was immediately suspicious of the circumstances and hired civilian forensics experts to examine the death records. They concluded that the colonel had been murdered and his body arranged to simulate a suicide.

- The same year, the army's Criminal Investigation Command (CIC) told Sidney and Carlos Wright that their son, Army Specialist Terry Wright, shot himself in the head with a rifle. Yet a perfunctory examination showed that Wright was wearing gloves too thick to fit through the rifle's trigger housing when he died. Army investigators had discarded evidence, and no fingerprints were even taken from Wright's gun. When queried by

Zucchino, the agent who supervised the investigation admitted that he had serious doubts about the suicide ruling.

- In June 1992, the NCIS told Mary Gallagher that her son, seaman apprentice Todd Gallagher, had fallen to his death from a Philadelphia rooftop. However, two civilian doctors and two military medical technicians said they thought Gallagher's severe head injuries were caused by a beating, not a fall. Gallagher's shipmates told the NCIS that he had had a drunken argument with sailors from a rival ship hours before he died. Yet the navy still insisted he had committed suicide.

- A month later, the Air Force Office of Special Investigations (OSI) informed Royal and Linda Shults that their son, airman Allen Shults, had hanged himself with a sheet strung from a hydraulic door opener, even though Shults was taller than the level of the opener. Zucchino discovered that investigators had failed to pursue evidence that other people were in Shults's room on the night of his death. Moreover, autopsy photos of Shults's neck showed marks that a medical examiner concluded were not caused by the sheet.

In each of these cases, as well as nine others, Zucchino concluded that all the evidence pointed to murders staged to look like suicides or accidents. After his stories were published in December 1993, twenty-six more families emerged to dispute the suicide rulings made by military authorities in the deaths of their sons.

Frederick R. McDaniel, a former army criminal investigator who reviewed three of the cases for family members, found no organized conspiracy afoot to cover up the murders—only poor investigative practices. "I see utter incompetence combined with laziness and lack of experience," he told the *Inquirer.* "Nobody goes to any trouble to do a proper investigation."

Ronald F. Decker, a private investigator who spent twelve years as an air force criminal investigator, later reviewed nine of the cases on behalf of the newspaper. He concluded that each of the suicide rulings represented a quick rush to judgment based on first impressions: "These people make up their minds on suicide long before they should. Then they work like heck to prove a suicide and totally disregard any other leads pointing to accident or homicide."

The mother of one murdered soldier summed up the official attitude that she believed had resulted in the bungled suicide verdicts: "Blame the dead—they can't complain."

5

Our summons to a secret location on the coast of central California during the winter of 2003 had all the makings of a spy novel. After eight long years, and repeated requests, Tom Grant, the L.A. private investigator at the heart of the murder theory, had finally consented to play his tapes for us. Almost from the moment he was hired by Courtney Love to find Kurt Cobain in April 1994, Grant taped everything—his conversations with Courtney, with the police and medical examiner, with the lawyers, with the witnesses and with Kurt's closest friends. He had always claimed these tapes were a crucial part of his case proving that Kurt had been murdered but had refused to play them for us, saying he would turn them over to an outside law enforcement agency only when the case was reopened. To ease our doubts about them, he had played us snippets while we were writing our first book and later posted select passages on the Internet. But, to our mounting frustration, he had consistently refused to let us or anybody else hear what he called the "most damning evidence" of the Cobain case. Now we had convinced Grant that if he genuinely wanted the case to be reopened, it was time for him to be a little more forthcoming.

When we first heard Grant's murder theory in the spring of 1995, we were highly skeptical. In the febrile world of rock and roll, conspiracy theories are a dime a dozen. Every time a rock star dies prematurely, it seems, somebody comes out to claim he or she was murdered. From Brian Jones to Jimi Hendrix to Elvis Presley, theories continue to circulate—some quite convincing—that their deaths were the result of foul play. So when Grant first went public with his charges, we figured this was just one more example of a half-baked celebrity conspiracy theory. In fact, in the very first article we wrote about the case—in *Canadian Disk* magazine—we cynically speculated that Grant was in it for the money and would attempt to cash in on his charges by writing a book or by selling his story.

When we visited his Beverly Hills office for the first time in 1995, it didn't take us long to realize that Tom Grant was not your typical L.A. gumshoe. Surrounded by photos of his seven grand-children, the stocky, clean-cut P.I. looked more like a bank manager or a university professor than somebody who made his living chasing down sleaze. Nor did he look like the kind of person whose music collection contained any albums by Nirvana or Hole.

Grant had begun his career in law enforcement more than a quarter century earlier, in 1969, when, at the age of twenty-two, he joined the Los Angeles County Sheriff's Department as a deputy. Within a year, his sharp investigative skills earned him a promotion to the elite Specialized Crime Activity Team (SCAT), which worked undercover busting felony crime operations. In 1972, shortly after Grant was transferred to the Malibu County Sheriff's Department, he cracked a major arson ring and was promoted to the rank of detective, one of the youngest ever in the county. Three years later, feeling burned out by the dangerous job, he took a leave of absence to open a retail music shop near the Malibu film colony, where he sold equipment to the Beach Boys and other big-name musicians.

If there are any skeletons in his closet from his days on the force, we couldn't find them, and it wasn't for lack of trying. Each of his former colleagues whom we interviewed had nothing but praise for Grant's skills, saying he was a highly respected police officer.

After his music shop went under, Grant worked as a security consultant for a number of celebrity clients, including Sammy Davis Jr. and Sondra Locke, before becoming the lead investigator for a former FBI agent turned P.I. in 1990. Three years later, he started his own firm.

When we first met Tom Grant, we were immediately struck by his integrity—not the first quality one would necessarily expect in a private detective. Time and again, prospective clients phoned his office, only to have Grant tell them that they could do the job themselves, and then proceed to instruct them how. "I've been told I'm not much of a businessman," he confesses. "That's probably why my music store went belly-up." One caller, suspecting her husband was having an affair, asked Grant to install a hidden surveillance device in his office. Grant's refusal was immediate: "That's illegal. I don't work like that," he told her before he hung up.

Eight years later, about to reveal his tapes to us, Grant is no longer a full-time private investigator, but he has retained his license and still takes on the occasional case. In fact, in the years since our first meeting, he has been a major player in an investigation considerably more notorious than the Cobain case itself. Grant was hired by former Arkansas state clerical employee Paula Jones to find witnesses to back up her sexual harassment suit against then-President Clinton. Later, Grant was instrumental in locating the former White House intern Monica Lewinsky, who first surfaced as a result of the Jones lawsuit. Thus, Grant played a major role in the impeachment of a sitting president.

We have to ask: Does this mean that he is a member of the so-called vast right-wing conspiracy out to bring down Clinton?

"Not really," he responds. "Some of those people I worked with might be pissed at me for saying so, but I actually think Clinton was a pretty good president. As a person, he's a complete jerk, and I know that better than most. But as president, he wasn't half bad."

* * *

Grant opens the safe and takes out a huge box of cassette tapes he recorded between April 1994 and January 1995. They represent more than thirty hours of conversations relating to the Cobain case. To our disappointment, however, the tapes containing what Grant considers the most crucial evidence in support of his murder theory are still off-limits. They will be turned over to the FBI, Grant tells us, if the case is reopened.

Still, the prospect of listening to the vast bulk of what transpired immediately before and after the discovery of Kurt's body is irresistible; we are eagerly anticipating hearing whatever new clues they may reveal. On the strength of our first book, we are generally considered the foremost journalistic authorities on the death of Kurt Cobain. But as we sit listening to Grant's tapes over the next three days and well into the nights, we quickly realize just how much we didn't know about the events of April 1994—indeed, how much we had got wrong, or just plain missed.

While the tapes don't answer all the questions, they are extremely damning and provide the first objective perspective of the events surrounding Cobain's death. Together with police reports we have obtained under Washington State's Freedom of Information laws, they go a long way toward answering the still-lingering mystery of how Kurt Cobain really died.

Sunday, April 3

On April 3, 1994—Easter Sunday—Tom Grant is in his Beverly Hills office with his associate, Ben Klugman, finishing up the paperwork on an old case, when the phone rings. The caller is a woman seeking a detective to find out who is using her husband's credit card. She does not identify herself but asks Grant if he can meet her in her suite at the nearby Peninsula Hotel. "We're kind of famous," she adds.

An hour later, Grant and Klugman arrive at the Peninsula—a five-star Beverly Hills hotel favored by celebrities—and immediately recognize the woman who greets them at the door. "If you leak this to the press, I'll sue the fuck out of you," Courtney Love warns them as they enter the room.

Her husband, Courtney tells Grant and Klugman, is Kurt Cobain; he escaped from an L.A. drug rehab center two days ago and hasn't been seen since. She lied during the initial phone call, she confesses. In an attempt to limit Kurt's movements, she has had his credit card canceled by falsely claiming it was stolen. To help locate her husband, she wants Grant to call the credit card company and get a list of all the transactions made on the card before it was canceled. At this point, Grant informs her that she doesn't need a detective for that but can do the job herself. "I'd have to charge you fifty bucks just to make a phone call," he says.

"What? That's not enough money for you?" Courtney snaps back. She tells them Kurt has only one credit card and, without it, he has no access to money, since she has also had his bank cards canceled. When Grant asks whether Kurt can obtain funds from other sources such as friends, she tells him that Kurt is totally "helpless" and has no friends. "This guy can't even catch a fucking cab by himself."

Then Courtney tells the pair that she believes her husband is suicidal. He has bought a shotgun, and she fears he may be planning to use it: "Everybody thinks he's going to die."

Grant and Klugman return to the office to get a form for Courtney to sign authorizing the release of Kurt's credit card records. By the time Grant returns to the Peninsula later that afternoon,

Courtney is frantic; she has apparently taken his advice and phoned the credit card company herself.

Kurt, she discovered, had booked a plane ticket about half an hour after he left the rehab on April 1. He paid $478. This, it turned out, was the ticket he used to fly from Los Angeles to Seattle. But it appears this wasn't his only purchase. At 5:30 P.M. the same day, while he was still at Exodus, Kurt had used his Master-Card to purchase two other plane tickets on United Airlines. The credit card company could not ascertain the flight date or the destination for these two tickets, only the amount he had paid. Courtney tells Grant that Kurt may be going east to stay with his friend Michael Stipe, the leader of his favorite rock group, R.E.M. Stipe had invited Kurt to record with the band in March, before the Rome overdose, and had even sent a plane ticket, which Kurt never used.

"I don't know where the hell he is," Courtney says. "I was figuring he goes up to Seattle and picks up his guitar. And then he flies to Atlanta. . . . [R.E.M.] are recording in Knoxville. He has two tickets. I'm curious if he bought a plane ticket for somebody else."

She tries to persuade Grant to hack into the airline's computer system. She wants to know whether Kurt has taken a flight out of Seattle and, if so, with whom he's traveling. Telling him it's "done all the time," she says she would be willing to pay a hacker $5,000 to tap into the computers of Delta and United airlines. "If he's taken those plane tickets, I want to know where he's gone."

Grant demurs: "Yeah, and then the next thing you read about me is that a major P.I. in Beverly Hills has been arrested for computer hacking."

But Courtney is persistent, urging him to hire "some sleazeball" to do the job. She tells Grant she "grew up on Nancy Drew," so she knows how these things are done.

Grant tells her that, even if she wrote a check for $300,000, he still wouldn't break the law because it's not worth the risk of going to prison. "Whatever I do," he insists, "I'm going to do it legally."

From the tone of Courtney's voice, it's obvious that she is in a panic about the second plane ticket. Grant soon finds out why.

"I think Kurt wants a divorce," she says. "If he wants a divorce, that's fine. If we got into a divorce and it came down to a custody battle, I'd win in a second." She shares something else. Kurt had left her a note in Rome in which "he says he's leaving me." At this point, Grant is still unfamiliar with much of the couple's history, and he knows nothing about Kurt's recent overdose in Rome. So this revelation means little to him.

Courtney proceeds to tell Grant about the prenuptial agreement that she and Kurt had signed before their wedding in February 1992: "Despite our prenuptial, my name is on all of our homes and all of our assets. . . . I don't want a divorce out of this. The only way a divorce will happen is if I bust him for infidelity." Then she confesses that she fears exactly this scenario; she is convinced that Kurt is having an affair with a Seattle heroin dealer named Caitlin Moore, who she says has a history of "fucking rock stars."

Courtney tells Grant she's convinced that if Kurt is in Seattle, he's with Caitlin. She asks him to bug the drug dealer's house. Again, Grant refuses. Courtney then reveals that she had already sent a friend over to Caitlin's house with $100 to buy heroin as an excuse to see if Kurt was there. He wasn't. She tells Grant that Kurt has a pattern of using girls, then says, "If he's fucking her, look out . . ." Her tone softens as she tells Grant that she and Kurt "have a good marriage," but says she thinks he is upset at her because "I'm so antidrug" and that, whenever Kurt does drugs, they fight. "When he brings drugs home, I do them, too," she says. She tells him that even Kurt's mother is "terrified of him" now, claiming that Wendy "abused him a lot" when he was a child, but now Kurt appears to have forgotten about it and forgiven her.

Grant asks whether Kurt has any favorite hangouts in Seattle where he might be holed up. She tells him that he liked to check in to a seedy Aurora Avenue motel called the Marco Polo, where he would occasionally go to shoot up. Then she steers the conversation back to Caitlin, demanding Grant find a Seattle P.I. to stake out her apartment. In an undertone to herself, she says, "If you're fucking someone else, Kurt, I'm going to nail you."

She then confesses that, the day before, she planted a phony story in the press that she had suffered a drug overdose in a ploy to attract Kurt's attention and get him to contact her. A reporter from the Associated Press has now called asking about the incident. Courtney asks Grant what he thinks she could tell them:

"My record's coming out in eight weeks and all publicity's good publicity. . . . What should I tell the Associated Press? . . . If it goes in and I deny it—and I can deny it all the way to the bank—and people will believe me if I deny it and say it never happened. . . . What I can say is that [Kurt] left rehab, and I had come down to L.A. with the baby and our nanny to support him, and when he left, I got very depressed and had to be hospitalized for some sort of nervous breakdown . . . that way, there's no drugs involved and Kurt doesn't get in any trouble because it looks like he wasn't meant to be in rehab in the first place and he felt pressured and jumped over the wall. I mean, how's that for spin? It's gonna appear that I attempted suicide. Even if it says I ODed on Xanax and booze, that would be fine, but if it says heroin, I'm in deep shit. I don't use heroin anymore. I haven't since my daughter's been born, certainly. I haven't used it in almost two years except intermittently when Kurt's brought it home. . . . You know, I've been dealing with the media for a long time. Hopefully tomorrow this AP thing *will* hit that I'm in a coma."

When Grant asks her if she thinks Kurt might resent the fact that she tricked him, she shrugs off the possibility, insisting Kurt would never find out because "the people I had do this [plant the

Tom Grant has vowed to continue pursuing Cobain's killer for another ten years, "until justice is done."

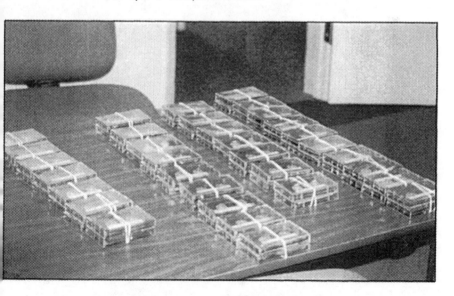

Grant's case tapes are hidden away in a secret location.

Kurt in an ambulance after his alleged suicide attempt in Rome—note Love's perfect makeup as the ambulance arrives at hospital.

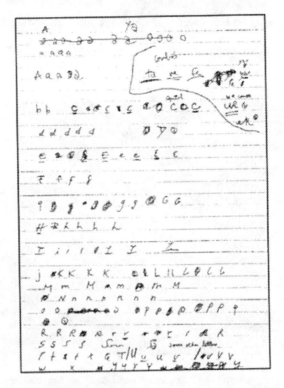

Suspicious handwriting practice sample found in Courtney's backpack the week of Kurt's death.

(above, left) Police reports prove that this stool was not barricading the door of the greenhouse shut when Cobain died, as initial media accounts claimed.

(above, right) The doorknob inside the greenhouse had a simple push-button lock, proving that a murderer could have easily locked the door shut from inside before departing.

Stan's gunshop, where Kurt's best friend bought the shotgun.

Kristen Pfaff was in the process of "leaving Courtney" when she was found dead in June 1994.

Janet Pfaff, seen holding a platinum record awarded posthumously to her daughter, has never accepted the official explanation for Kristen's death.

By all accounts, Kurt's outlook changed after Frances was born.

Better days.

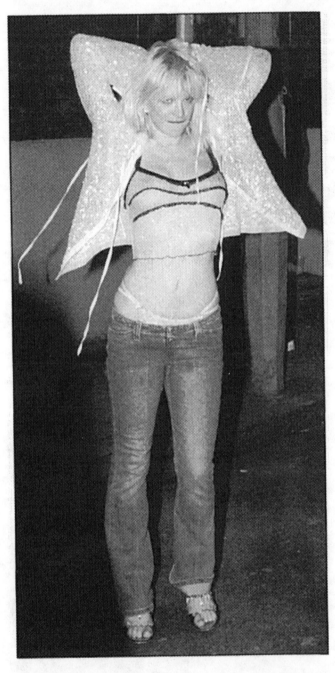

Life after Kurt. "I wish I had never married him," Courtney told an interviewer.

Leland Cobain believes his grandson was the victim of foul play.

Kurt claimed he was a happy child before his parents divorced.

Musician Allen Wrench stands on the spot where Eldon Hoke (a.k.a. "El Duce") was run over by a train, eight days after Hoke told the BBC Courtney had tried to hire him to kill Kurt Cobain. Wrench was the last person to see Hoke alive.

false story], I paid." In her world, Courtney says, people are "scared of me" so "they don't fuck with me." The fact that the press always perceives her as "completely tragic and fucked up" anyway, she continues, might work to her benefit because she has a record coming out, so "selfishly, it might even help sell records."

Although he says he didn't realize it at the time, Grant believes this conversation is highly significant.

"In retrospect," he says, "I realized that Courtney was trying to plant a trail of clues that the couple had some sort of suicide pact. You'll see later that many writers reported this pact, based on things that Courtney told the public after Kurt's death. In this discussion the first day I met her, she actually admits to me that her planted story was designed to falsely convince people that she had attempted suicide while Kurt was missing. I think it was a calculated effort to gain sympathy with Kurt's followers to help them make the seamless transition from Nirvana fan to Hole fan."

Grant's Easter Sunday conversations with Courtney are extraordinarily revealing and include the first concrete evidence of the couple's long-rumored marital breakup. But as remarkable as these April 3 disclosures appear, they may not be nearly as significant as what she failed to tell Grant that day.

* * *

Saturday, April 2

Although the Seattle Police Department never seriously considered Cobain's death as anything but a suicide, they nevertheless conducted a routine investigation into the events surrounding his demise. During this probe, they attempted to locate anybody who had come in contact with Kurt during the period he was reported missing. Though his whereabouts are sketchy during the days leading up to the discovery of his body on April 8, police were able to track some of his movements in the hours following his departure from the L.A. rehab center on the evening of April 1.

Approximately an hour after Kurt jumped over the Exodus recovery center's patio wall, he called Delta Air Lines and booked Flight 788 to Seattle, leaving from Los Angeles International Airport at 10:20 P.M. When he arrived at the airport around 9:30 P.M., he was recognized by a number of fans while checking in at the Delta ticket counter. He graciously chatted and signed autographs for almost fifteen minutes. Before boarding, he called ahead to his car service, Seattle Limousines, to inform them he'd be arriving at Seattle/Tacoma International Airport at 12:47 A.M.

During the two-hour flight, Kurt sat next to Duff McKagan, bassist for Guns n' Roses (a band, incidentally, Cobain despised). Kurt told McKagan, also a recovering heroin addict, that he had left rehab and was "going home."

When the plane landed in Seattle, Kurt's driver, Linda Walker, was waiting at the airport. She drove him directly to his Lake Washington estate and dropped him off in the driveway at approximately 1:30 A.M.

The house's only occupant while Kurt and Courtney were in L.A. was Michael "Cali" Dewitt, Courtney's old boyfriend from California who had been hired as a nanny for Frances Bean, despite his longtime cocaine and heroin habits. Cali had apparently invited a girlfriend, Jessica Hopper, to visit while she was on spring break from her Minneapolis boarding school. As a result, Jessica was present just after 6:00 A.M. the next morning when Kurt walked into Cali's room and sat on the end of their bed. On waking up and seeing Kurt, the two immediately urged him to call Courtney because "she was freaking out."

Cali later insisted that Kurt picked up the phone and called Courtney at the Peninsula but could not get through to her room. A year later, Courtney told a slightly different story in an interview with *Spin* magazine, claiming that Kurt unsuccessfully tried to call her at 8:54 A.M.:

> There was a block on the phone for everyone but him. I did not sleep. I called the operator every couple of hours to make sure, in case they changed shifts. They all knew that if Mr. Cobain called, put the fucking call through to me. At 8:54 AM, I was not asleep. He called, and for six minutes he tried to get through, and could not. For him to argue for six minutes on the phone is crazed. I cannot imagine him arguing for six minutes. He did, though. And what that told him is that I was on their side, that I had a block on the phone for him. And I did not. Kurt's whole plan was to try to wear everyone down, but he could never wear me down. I think, though, that at that very moment he thought I had given up on him.

It is a poignant story. But when the reporter from *Spin*, and later we, contacted the Peninsula Hotel, the management denied the incident had ever taken place. No attempted calls were placed to Love's room that morning, the hotel insisted, nor did Courtney leave instructions that Kurt's calls were to be put through. The hotel, in fact, logs each call received, as well as every call made from the rooms. These phone records provide a clear picture of what happened next.

Just after 7:00 A.M., Kurt called for a Graytop cab, which picked him up fifteen minutes later. Jessica and Cali claim they never saw him again. Later that day, according to Peninsula Hotel records, Courtney made eight separate long-distance calls to Cali's private number at the Lake Washington house, some of them lasting for several minutes. Yet when she hired Tom Grant the next day to find her missing husband, she inexplicably failed to tell him that Kurt had been seen at the house the day before.

"It made no sense whatsoever," recalls Grant. "When she hired me, she made it seem as if she had no idea where he had gone: she didn't even know if he was in Seattle. When I found out that Cali had actually seen Kurt at the house on April 2, I wondered what possible reason could she have had for withholding that information from me, the guy she supposedly hired to find him. What's even stranger is that she wanted us to stake out Caitlin's apartment, but she never asked us to keep a watch on the Lake Washington house, even after she finally told me a couple of days later that Kurt had been there. That's probably the first time I sensed that something wasn't right about this case."

* * *

Monday, April 4

Monday, April 4, starts with a telephone discussion between Courtney and Grant about his retainer. Money's not a problem, she tells him: "I mean, money is a problem if we get a divorce and I don't have my publishing deal, but that's not going to happen for quite some time."

She tells Grant about her recent fights with Kurt, resulting from his decision to pull out of that summer's Lollapalooza tour. Nirvana, she explains, had been offered a percentage of the gate receipts that would have netted the band an estimated $9 million. She gripes furiously about the financial repercussions of his decision, revealing that Kurt had recently told her that he didn't even want to be in Nirvana. If Kurt wants to turn up his nose at $9.5 million for Lollapalooza, she says, "We [Hole] could have fucking played Lollapalooza and gotten the cash; that's the part that pisses me off!" Now, because Kurt had pulled out, Hole won't be invited to play Lollapallooza even if they sell two million records, she fumes: "I mean, he would have got $9.5 million, and I would have

only got about $100,000, but at least I would have sold some
records, and now he's fucking that up."

When she is finished criticizing her husband, Courtney takes
aim at the other members of Nirvana, who she feels are getting too
much money for their contributions. She describes Dave and Krist
as "total losers" who made more than $3 million for songs that they
didn't write a note on. "Even his band has turned against him," she
says, revealing that neither of his bandmates had attended the recent drug intervention. She has particularly harsh words for Krist,
who she calls "the stupid one," telling Grant that, after the intervention, she asked Krist to keep an eye on Kurt. Instead, she
claims, he hotwired Kurt's car and attempted to drag him to rehab
against his will. "You just don't do that," she says.

Courtney is still obsessed with the notion that Kurt is with
Caitlin Moore. Grant has refused her request to place a bug in the
drug dealer's apartment, so she asks a friend to do it, a longtime
customer of Caitlin's. Courtney calls her friend and lets Grant listen in on the conversation. The friend tells her that he had already
been to Caitlin's apartment and there was no sign of Kurt, but that
Caitlin had been frequently leaving her place for hours at a time.
He says Caitlin claimed that Kurt hadn't been around lately.

Courtney asks whether Caitlin knew Kurt had left rehab. Her
friend says she did, leaving Courtney to wonder how she had heard
the news. "Caitlin hates Dylan, so I wonder how she'd find that
out. It wasn't on the news." Courtney offers her friend $500 to put
a bug in Caitlin's apartment, explaining, "Frances needs her dad."
She tells him she just wants to find out if Kurt is safe, insisting that
she has no intention to narc out Caitlin.

Courtney suspects that Caitlin is supplying Kurt with money to
stay at a motel because she doesn't believe that any of Kurt's other
friends are supporting him. "You know how dumb Kurt can be,"
she says. "I mean, he's brilliant but he can't even get himself a cab."

She tells her friend that she doesn't want to bust either Kurt or

Caitlin. "If he wants to be alone and he's leaving me, I'm not going to bother him," she says. She just wants "to find out where the fuck he is." If he wants a divorce, Courtney continues, she will accept that: "I just want to make him happy, and drugs are not going to make him happy."

Courtney insists that Kurt has never cheated on her, but she clearly believes that Kurt is involved with Caitlin. "If he's fucking her, look out," she tells her friend, "but you know he can be so fucked up, it's possible, right?" She reveals that Kurt cheated on two of his former girlfriends, and that he slept with another woman who used to get him drugs, although he swore he never would. Kurt's "pretty asexual," she says, and he's still wearing his wedding ring, so "I'm not really worried, but . . ."

By this point in the tapes, as she ranted repeatedly about the drug dealer, it seemed to us that Courtney's obsession with Caitlin Moore was based on little more than paranoia. Not a single friend of Kurt or Courtney that we spoke to believed that Kurt was having an affair with Caitlin. Yet it becomes clearer with each conversation we listen to that Courtney's jealousy, justified or not, played a considerable role in her actions during the week that Kurt was missing. However, it is possible that she is on firmer ground in her suspicion that Caitlin was helping Kurt hide during some of this period.

Of all the drug dealers that ever hit Seattle, Courtney tells her friend, Caitlin Moore is "the most Satanic because you know she likes the rock clientele." She believes Caitlin was the most logical person for Kurt to turn to after he left rehab because he knows she would never "narc him off to anybody."

She asks her friend whether he knows where in the apartment Caitlin keeps her phone, telling him he has two options. He can stick the bug directly on the phone or somewhere in the house.

One way or another, Courtney vows, she is going to know whether Kurt is in town by midnight that night. "If he's not in town, forget it," she says. "We're still getting a quarter million dollars for our publishing. I'm on my way. I'm not going to let Kurt stop me." She tells her friend that *Rolling Stone* magazine has just agreed to put Hole on the cover so "I can't let Kurt pull me down." She swears her friend to secrecy, saying that she knows planting a bug is a bad thing to do, but asks him whether he would rather see Kurt Cobain dead. Caitlin wouldn't care, says Courtney, "just as long as she's got his sperm in her mouth."

When Grant arrives at the Peninsula for a meeting with Courtney that afternoon, she tells him that earlier in the day, she had called the Seattle Police Department pretending to be Kurt's mother and filed a missing person's report. "They would never have taken me seriously if I filed it in my own name," she says.

The police report in question, purportedly filed April 4 by a Wendy O'Connor, reads:

Mr. Cobain ran away from California facility and flew back to Seattle. He also bought a shotgun and may be suicidal. Mr. Cobain may be at location for narcotics. Detective Terry SPD/Narcotics has further info.

Courtney's unexplained—and illegal—action in fabricating the report leaves Grant shaking his head: "Notice how she planted the idea early on in the mind of the police that he may be suicidal," he tells us later.

Tuesday, April 5

Grant spends the rest of Monday and most of Tuesday calling Seattle motels to determine if anybody has checked in under one of Kurt's aliases, which include "Simon Ritchie" (the real name of Sid Vicious). On Tuesday, at 2:50 P.M., Grant believes he has found his man. The Western Evergreen has somebody registered under the name of Bill Bailey, Kurt's favorite alias. He offers to check it out, but Courtney tells him not to bother. She says she will take care of it.

"A little while later, she told me she had called the room and it turned out it wasn't Kurt staying there," Grant recalls. "I had no reason at the time to doubt her word."

By this time, he has subcontracted a Seattle P.I. named Ernie Barth to establish surveillance on Caitlin Moore's apartment. Grant did not yet know that Kurt had been spotted at the couple's Lake Washington house by Cali on Saturday morning. But when he asks Courtney why she hadn't requested surveillance of the house, she replies, "Cali's there. He'll tell me if Kurt shows up."

And yet Cali is not there. "We later learned that Cali stopped staying at the house after Monday," Grant recalls. "After that, he stayed at the apartment of another one of his girlfriends named Jennifer Adamson. And Courtney was well aware of this because, when we obtained her Peninsula phone records, they showed that she placed several calls to Cali at Jennifer's apartment throughout the week. So she knew Kurt had been to the house, she knew Cali was no longer staying there, yet she wouldn't let us set up surveillance there. It doesn't make any sense."

Wednesday, April 6

Three days after Courtney hired him to find her husband, Grant still has not made any progress, nor has the Seattle P.I. he has subcontracted to search for Kurt. Now, back at the Peninsula, he offers to fly to Seattle to conduct his own search. Courtney gives him the OK. Three of her friends are in the room at the time, one of them a heroin dealer. Another friend, Jennifer Shank, asks why Courtney doesn't go herself. Courtney replies, "I can't. I have business I have to take care of here."

An hour later, his flight to Seattle booked, Grant bids the group farewell. As he heads out the door, Courtney shouts, "Save the American icon, Tom!"

Grant arrives in Seattle, rents a car and checks in to his hotel before heading over to the apartment of Kurt's friend Dylan Carlson at roughly 11:30 P.M. Courtney has already asked Carlson to assist Grant in the search. The two plan to drive to the Lake Washington estate, but first they stop at a café. Here, Dylan tells Grant that he and Kurt had purchased a shotgun on March 30, the day his friend left for rehab. Kurt wanted the gun registered in Dylan's name, he explains, because the police had confiscated all his guns a few weeks earlier after the couple's domestic dispute: "He was afraid of intruders, and he wanted the gun for protection for when he returned from rehab. I think there had been a burglary or something at the house recently."

Courtney's warning in mind, Grant asks Dylan if he thinks Kurt might be suicidal.

"No. Not at all," Dylan replies. "He's under a lot of pressure, but he's handling things pretty good." He admits that Kurt and Courtney have been having "troubles" lately and then says, "I don't know why Kurt married her."

They pass Caitlin Moore's apartment in Seattle's Capitol Hill district, where P.I. Ernie Barth is keeping watch in his car from across the street. Grant introduces himself and asks if Barth has any leads, but there has been no sign of Kurt in the last forty-eight hours. Grant asks Dylan whether it might be worthwhile to contact Kurt's mother in Aberdeen, but Dylan dismisses the idea: "No, Kurt wouldn't go there. He doesn't get along with his mom."

It's raining hard as the pair pull up to the Lake Washington house shortly after 2:00 A.M. The plan is for Dylan to go to the door alone so he doesn't alert Kurt to Grant's presence. Five minutes later, he returns to the car. There is no answer, but the alarm is on. Neither knows the code, so Grant asks Dylan to call Courtney and ask her how to get in. After a few minutes on a nearby pay phone, Dylan returns to the car and reports, "Courtney's calling the alarm company to get them to turn off the system. It won't be a problem." A few minutes later, they return to the house and climb in through an unlocked kitchen window. Grant's tape recorder is still running.

On the tape, there is the sound of footsteps as the two tramp through the house. Grant says, "I'm going to follow you through here because you know where everything is." Then Dylan can be heard calling, "Hello, Kurt? Kurt, are you here?" They search the house thoroughly, but there are no signs of Kurt or anybody else. Dylan says, "I've never seen the house so clean before." A television with the sound off illuminates an upstairs bedroom; Dylan says it's the nanny's room. Courtney has instructed Grant to search for any evidence that Kurt has been there, including drug paraphernalia, so he and Dylan proceed to search under the mattress. They find something, a pill package with little individual bubble packets.

DYLAN   "Here's something."

GRANT   "What's that?"

DYLAN   "It's Rohypnol."

GRANT   "That doesn't mean he's been here, huh?"

DYLAN   "No, these are what he OD'd on in Rome."

GRANT   "Would [Courtney] want us to take those?"

DYLAN   "Yeah."

GRANT   "Are those drugs illegal if we get stopped?"

DYLAN   "No, no, they're prescription from England. They're over-the-counter. They're sold there as sedatives for sleeping illness."

When Kurt's body was eventually found in the greenhouse a day and a half later, the medical examiner concluded that he had been dead for at least two days, pinpointing the probable time of death as the night of April 5 or the morning of April 6. So at the time of Grant and Dylan's search, Kurt is lying dead less than twenty-five yards away.

Later, the media were scornful of Grant's detective skills, after he failed to find Kurt's body. Why didn't the seasoned investigator check the greenhouse?

"The truth is," he says, "I didn't know it was there. It was raining very hard that night, and a floodlight was shining from the garage, and in those conditions it was impossible to see that there was a room up there."

We were somewhat skeptical of Grant's explanation the first time we heard it, convinced this was an excuse he was using to rationalize his own sloppy investigation. But in December 1995, we visited the house at night under similar weather conditions and confirmed that on a dark, rainy night, the greenhouse room was indeed invisible.

Thursday, April 7

The two men have decided to resume their search. Shortly after noon, Grant stops to pick up Dylan at his apartment. Another of Kurt's friends, Mark Lanegan, lead singer of the Seattle grunge band Screaming Trees, has agreed to help them look. Grant is anxious to establish contact with the drug dealer Caitlin Moore to determine if she has seen Kurt at any time since April 1. Grant proposes that Dylan and Mark—both regular clients of Seattle's best-known dealer—pay a visit to Caitlin's apartment under the pretext of scoring some heroin.

When they arrive at the Capitol Hill apartment building, Grant hands Dylan a microcassette player to clandestinely record the visit. About forty-five minutes later, the two emerge in what Grant describes as a "heroin haze." The tape reveals that, after scoring hits for himself and his friend, Dylan asked Caitlin whether she had seen Kurt recently, to which the dealer replied that she hasn't seen him all week.

Ernie Barth, the Seattle private investigator Grant had contracted to conduct surveillance of Caitlin's apartment, has meanwhile taken it upon himself to head over to the Lake Washington house to set up surveillance at that location. When Courtney hears about this from Grant, she is furious and immediately instructs him to call Barth off the house.

"Barth was a former Seattle cop, and he knew that it made more sense to look for Kurt at his own house rather than at the drug dealer's," Grant explains, "but, again, Courtney didn't want him there for some reason."

After dropping Lanegan back home, Grant and Dylan spend most of Thursday checking out Kurt's regular hangouts and asking around to find out if anybody has seen him. Their efforts draw a blank. Around 7:00 P.M., they drive to Carnation, a small town about thirty miles east of Seattle, where Kurt and Courtney own two small cabins and several acres of property. But it's pouring rain, night is beginning to fall and Dylan doesn't think he'll be able to locate the property under these conditions. They turn back, planning to try again the next day.

Grant drops Dylan off and returns to his hotel to get a couple hours of sleep before resuming their search later that evening. Around 8:00 P.M., the two head to Aurora Avenue, planning to visit some of the seedier hotels Kurt liked to frequent. They stop at a pay phone so Dylan can make a call. Back in the car, he tells Grant, "Courtney's had some trouble. She got arrested and she was in the hospital. Something about drugs. I need to make some more calls."

Half an hour later, Dylan manages to reach Courtney on the phone. He says she told him the arrest was all a big mistake and that she is fine. She has a request: she wants them to return to the Lake Washington house to look in a hidden compartment of the

closet for the shotgun that Dylan and Kurt had purchased a week
earlier.

"This was truly bizarre," recalls Grant. "Cali had been staying at
the house earlier in the week. I wondered why she didn't ask him to
search for the gun then, or why she didn't tell us about it when we
visited the house the night before. All of a sudden, she was instructing us to go back immediately for no apparent good reason."

Just after 9:45 P.M., the two return to the Lake Washington
house to carry out Courtney's instructions. As they enter, they immediately spot a note in plain sight on the main staircase. It had not
been there the night before. Apparently written by Cali, it reads:

> *Kurt-*
> I can't believe you managed to be in this house without me notic-
> ing. You're a fuckin asshole for not calling Courtney & at least
> letting her know that your [*sic*] o.k. She's in a lot of pain Kurt, and
> this morning she had another "accident" and now she's in the
> hospital again. She's your <u>wife</u> & she loves you & you have a child
> together. Get it together to at least tell her your [*sic*] o.k. or she is
> going to <u>Die.</u> It's not fair man. DO something <u>now.</u>

To Grant, the note didn't make any sense at all. If Cali saw evidence that Kurt had returned to the house, he would surely have
relayed the news to Courtney. Yet Courtney had not breathed a
word of this to Dylan just a few minutes earlier on the phone and
had never requested surveillance at the Lake Washington estate to
track Kurt's movements. "I became convinced the note had been
put there for my benefit for me to find that night," Grant recalls.
"That's why Courtney was suddenly so anxious for us to return to
the house, so we would find this note."

Again, they search the house, including the hidden compartment of the bedroom closet, as Courtney had requested. There is

no gun, nor any other clues that might point to Kurt's where-abouts. Again, they miss the greenhouse because of the heavy rain.

Meanwhile, a small item in the *Los Angeles Times* that morning had reported that Nirvana withdrew from their headline slot on the upcoming Lollapalooza tour, and that the band was rumored to be splitting up.

Friday, April 8

The next morning, at a gas station on their way back to the Carnation property, Dylan makes a call at a phone booth. He returns to the car a few minutes later. He has just learned that a body has been found at the Lake Washington house. Grant turns on the radio, which is broadcasting a special news report on the death of an American icon.

Kurt Cobain's journey has come to an end. Tom Grant's has just begun.

6

"**W**ait a second," says Grant after the radio reports that Kurt Cobain has just been found dead in the greenhouse. "We were just there. What's the greenhouse?"

"It's just a dirty little room above the garage," Dylan replies. "I think they keep some lumber up there or something."

They turn the car around to head back to the Lake Washington house to find out more. Grant recalls being puzzled by Dylan's attitude.

"He just found out his best friend had died, yet he hardly had any reaction. My gut instinct from the way Dylan acted was that he already knew Kurt was dead, although I didn't necessarily think he was involved."

When they arrive at the house midmorning, the place is already swarming with media. In the little park next to the house, crews from *Entertainment Tonight*, *Hard Copy*, *A Current Affair*, NBC and MTV are setting up their cameras, while reporters from *Rolling Stone*, *Spin*, *People* and *The Village Voice* arrive soon afterward. MTV's Tabitha Soren just happens to be in town and takes command for two days of nonstop live broadcasts by the network, complementing hours of coverage by CNN, Fox News and most of Seattle's TV stations. They feed on the collective grief of young America; Cobain had become the Kennedy of a new generation.

While they are parking the car across the street, Dylan points out local media personalities he recognizes and tells Grant whom to avoid and whom to trust. He refuses to get out of the car, knowing that reporters will swarm him for a comment about his friend's death the moment he emerges. "I'm not going into that zoo," he declares. By this time, a squad of detectives from the Seattle Police Department and a team from the medical examiner's office have arrived on the scene.

Grant manages to make his way through the media cordon to the small building containing the greenhouse, accessible only by a stairway on the outside of the garage. What transpires next—including whatever conversations he may have had with the police officers and medical examiners who arrived on the scene—is still a mystery because he refuses to play us the tape. "I can't go into too many details about what I learned when I arrived that morning," he explains. "Some of those details will be very important for the prosecutor who eventually tries this case, and I don't want to tip my hand too early."

In the early afternoon, Grant calls his office and speaks to Ben Klugman, who tells him that, according to the credit card company, somebody had continued trying to use Kurt's canceled credit card until early in the morning of April 8, shortly before his body was found.

But when Grant calls Detective Cameron of the Seattle Police Homicide Division to report this development, he finds Cameron strangely indifferent. Kurt was locked in the room by himself, Cameron tells Grant. Firefighters had to break the glass on the door to gain entry. Cameron's implication is clear. Locked in the way he was, Kurt would have had to be completely alone when he died.

Grant stays in Seattle for another day to interview some of

Kurt's friends before flying back to Los Angeles on Saturday, April 9. "The thing that struck me is that everybody I talked to, people who knew Kurt very well, seemed surprised," Grant recalls. "They all said the same thing, that he wasn't suicidal. Everybody from Mark Lanegan to Dylan Carlson to various Seattle friends and associates. It didn't sound like they were simply in denial or anything like that; they were all adamant. But at the time, I'm not sure I was thinking it was a murder yet. A lot of strange things had happened and I was starting to have my suspicions, but I think I rationalized a lot of it by saying, 'Well, that's Courtney's world. Bizarre things happen all the time.' She's surrounded by strangeness, so I may have rationalized all the inconsistencies at first."

* * *

By the time Courtney learned of the death from her lawyer Friday morning, the media were still unaware that she had been arrested the day before at her Peninsula suite after an anonymous 911 call was placed from the hotel about a possible drug overdose.

After paramedics transported her to L.A.'s Century City Hospital for emergency treatment, police had charged her with possession of a controlled substance (a small packet of white powder they believed to be heroin), drug paraphernalia, including a hypodermic needle, and stolen property (a doctor's blank prescription pad). She was brought to Beverly Hills Jail, leaving her baby at the hotel with one of the nannies, Jackie Farry. Courtney was released on $10,000 bail a few hours later, after promising to appear in Beverly Hills court for arraignment on May 5. That evening, she checked herself in to the Exodus recovery center, the same rehab Kurt had fled a week earlier.

It was there that her lawyer Rosemary Carroll broke the news of Kurt's death the next morning. An hour later, Courtney was on a private Learjet headed back to Seattle with Frances Bean, Rosemary Carroll, Jackie Farry and Hole guitarist Eric Erlandson.

On landing, Courtney immediately took charge. Security guards were hired to keep the media at bay, and, to thwart photographers, a tarp was placed over the greenhouse, where Kurt's body still lay, waiting for the medical examiner to remove it for autopsy. Just before the tarp was placed, *Seattle Times* photographer Tom Reese managed to snap a few photos of the greenhouse through his zoom lens. One memorable shot, beamed around the world, showed a prone, jeans-clad leg, a sneaker and an open cigar box on the floor.

Meanwhile, Kurt's mother, Wendy O'Connor, had arrived on the scene, where she told a reporter from the Associated Press, "Now he's gone and joined that stupid club. I told him not to join that stupid club," referring to the list of legendary rock stars, including Jimi Hendrix, Janis Joplin and Jim Morrison, who had died prematurely.

Outside the house, reporters descended on sixteen-year-old Kimberly Wagner, who sat on a garden wall crying. Nobody official was answering questions, so the media had resorted to interviewing one another about the impact of Kurt's death, along with any fans who happened to show up. "I just came here to find an answer," Wagner told them. "But I don't think I'm going to."

Kurt's body was removed for autopsy shortly after noon. Although police had already discreetly informed a number of reporters that he had killed himself, the King County Medical Examiner's Office issued a statement that afternoon confirming the news.

That morning, Courtney told a number of people, including executives from Geffen Records and Gold Mountain, that Kurt's Rome overdose a month earlier had actually been a suicide attempt, not an accident. It was the first time they had heard this version. The news soon leaked to the media throng, who waited outside the house, desperate for any information. Before long, the media consensus was that Kurt's suicide was tragic but inevitable. A group of distraught teenagers outside the house were attempting to come to terms with the idea. Steve Adams, fifteen, told reporters, "Sometimes I'll get depressed and get mad at my mom or my friends, and I'll go and listen to Kurt. And it puts me in a better mood. . . . I thought about killing myself a while ago, too, but then I thought about all the people that would be depressed about it." On Seattle's rock station KIRO-FM, one DJ snarled, "He died a coward and left a little girl without a father."

That night, Courtney shared a bed with Wendy and reportedly wore the corduroy coat Kurt had on when he was found. The next morning, when she agreed to talk to reporters for the first time, she began an interview with MTV's Tabitha Soren by declaring, "Everyone who feels guilty, raise your hand." She told Soren, "Something good can come out of Kurt's death. I don't know what it is yet, but something good can." At this point, Courtney took the opportunity to plug her album *Live Through This*, which was now scheduled to be released the following Tuesday. As if suddenly realizing how unseemly this might appear to viewers, she self-deprecatingly asked Soren, "How's that for sick?"

A few minutes later, she granted MTV another interview, speaking to Kurt Loder via telephone. In this conversation, she told Loder that in his suicide note, her husband had written, "It's not fun for me anymore, I can't live this life." But when the note was made public months later, it revealed that Kurt had written no such thing, nor any other direct reference to suicide. Courtney also told Loder that the physical damage to Kurt's body was so severe that he could be identified only by fingerprints. This, too, was later revealed to be a fabrication.

Later that day, she visited the funeral home where Kurt's body was waiting to be cremated. Courtney had issued these instructions soon after the body was found, despite the fact that Kurt had apparently never asked to be cremated. As she was ushered into the viewing room, Krist Novoselic was just leaving, sobbing after spending a few minutes with his old friend for the last time. Kurt was laid out in a suit, with his eyes sewn shut. Despite later media reports stating that his face had been blown off by the shotgun blast, the shell had actually inflicted surprisingly little damage. With Nirvana's production manager, Jeff Mason, looking on, Courtney reportedly stroked Kurt's face, methodically cut off a lock of his hair, then unzipped his pants and clipped a lock of his pubic hair. Then she climbed on top of his body and repeatedly cried out, "Why?"

Later Courtney spoke to *Seattle Post-Intelligencer* rock critic Gene Stout, and Caitlin Moore was still clearly on her mind. Without mentioning Caitlin by name, Courtney told Stout that she had repeatedly called the Seattle Police Department to get them to bust Kurt's dealer, complaining that she couldn't shut down her husband's drug sources. "It's like apples in an orchard," she said about heroin. "It's falling off the trees. The Seattle police won't do anything about it. I asked them, 'Don't you get embarrassed when you hear that Seattle is famous for grunge, cappuccino and heroin?' " More than a year later, Dylan Carlson introduced us to a drug dealer named "Walter," who said that he found this particular quote ironic. "At the time she said this, she was shooting up a couple of hundred dollars' worth of heroin a day," he told us. "I know because I sold it to her."

On the afternoon of April 10, about seventy guests, including dozens of members of Kurt's family, attended a private memorial service at Seattle's Unity Church of Truth. On each pew, guests found a photo of six-year-old Kurt smiling up at them. Reverend Stephen Towles told the mourners, "A suicide is no different than having our finger in a vise. The pain becomes so great that we can't bear it any longer."

Krist Novoselic delivered a eulogy in which he spoke of Kurt's punk rock ethic that dictated "no band is special and no player is royalty. . . . If you've got a guitar and a lot of soul, just bang something out and mean it—you're the superstar." He urged the assembled to "remember Kurt for what he was—caring, generous and sweet. . . . His heart was his receiver . . . and his transmitter. . . . Let's keep the music with us, and we'll have it forever."

Later in the service, a black-clad Courtney read verses from the Bible and passages from Kurt's favorite book of poetry, Arthur Rimbaud's *Illuminations.* She related a confession she said Kurt had once made to her backstage: that he never really enjoyed the roar of the crowd the way Queen's lead singer, Freddie Mercury, did.

"So why did you become a rock star, asshole?" she asked her dead husband, and then proceeded to read passages from Kurt's suicide note, which had still not been made public.

She told the guests that he had written, "I have a daughter who reminds me too much of myself," and "It's better to burn out than to fade away." The note, she said, ended with the words: "I love you, I love you."

After the service, Courtney invited the guests to a wake back at the Lake Washington house, but many chose instead to attend an alternative wake at the home of Krist and his wife, Shelli. Clearly, the acrimony between Courtney and the band had not diminished with Kurt's death. According to Alice Wheeler, who attended both wakes, "I think many people held Courtney responsible for Kurt's death to some degree. A lot of his friends wanted to know why she hadn't told anybody that Rome was a suicide attempt. If people had known, they might have done more to save him." Kurt's friend, Sonic Youth guitarist Lee Ranaldo, echoed Wheeler's words in an interview with *Rolling Stone:* "I feel like I was good enough friends with Kurt that I could have called him up and said, 'Hey, how are you? Do you want to talk?' "

Keith Richards weighed in, telling a reporter, "After the cat tried to off himself in Rome, I was surprised that the people who were supposed to be taking care of him let him buy a shotgun and mope around for days. They knew he barely escaped doing himself in already."

Meanwhile, across town, a candlelight vigil had been organized by three local radio stations at a park next to the Seattle Space Needle. Thousands gathered to pay tribute while Nirvana tunes blared from the loudspeakers. As fans burned their flannel shirts and threw themselves in the fountain, the unmistakable voice of Courtney Love was heard from the speakers—not live, but on an audiotape she had recorded earlier that day:

> I don't know what to say. I don't know what to say. I feel the same way you guys do. If you guys don't think . . . to sit in this room where he played guitar and sang, and feel so honored to be near him, you're crazy. Anyway, he left a note, it's more like a letter to the fucking editor. I don't know what happened. I mean, it was gonna happen, but it could've happened when he was forty. He always said he was gonna outlive everybody and be a hundred and twenty. I'm not gonna read you all the note 'cause it's none of the rest of your fucking business. But some of it is to you. I don't really think it takes away his dignity to read this, considering that it's addressed to most of you. He's such an asshole. I want you all to say 'asshole' really loud.

The crowd roared, "Asshole!" Then she started to read from the note:

> This note should be pretty easy to understand. All the warnings from the punk rock 101 courses over the years, since my first introduction to the, shall we say, ethics involved with independence and the embracement of your community has proven to be very true. I haven't felt the excitement of listening to as well as creating music along with really writing for too many years now. I feel guilty beyond words about these things. For example when

we're back stage and the lights go out and the manic roar of the crowd begins, it doesn't affect me the way in which it did for Freddie Mercury, who seemed to love, relish in the love and adoration of the crowd.

As before, the Freddie Mercury comparison seems to elicit Courtney's particular irritation: "Well, Kurt, so fucking what— then don't be a rock star, you asshole." She continues:

Which is something I totally admire and envy. The fact is, I can't fool you, any one of you. It simply isn't fair to you or me. The worst crime I could think of would be to rip people off by faking it and pretending as if I'm having 100% fun.

Courtney: "Well, Kurt, the worst crime I can think of is for you to just continue being a rock star when you fucking hate it, just fucking stop."

Sometimes I feel as if I should have a punch-in time clock before I walk out on stage. I've tried everything within my power to appreciate it (and I do, God, believe me I do, but it's not enough). I appreciate the fact that I and we have affected and entertained a lot of people. I must be one of those narcissists who only appreciate things when they're alone. I'm too sensitive. I need to be slightly numb in order to regain the enthusiasm I once had as a child. On our last three tours I've had a much better appreciation for all the people I know personally, and as fans of our music, but I still can't get over the frustration the guilt and empathy I have for everyone. There's good in all of us and I think I simply love people too much.

Courtney: "So why didn't you just fucking stay?"

So much that it makes me feel too fucking sad. The sad little, sensitive, unappreciative, Pisces, Jesus man.

Courtney: "Oh shut up, you bastard."

Why don't you just enjoy it? I don't know.

Courtney: "Then he goes on to say personal things to me that are none of your damn business; personal things to Frances that are none of your damn business."

. . . I had it good, very good, and I'm grateful . . .

This line suggests that Kurt decided that he no longer does. But when a copy of the note was made public months later, it turned out that Kurt had in fact written, "I *have* it good." Some people wondered whether there was any significance to the fact that Courtney misread this passage in particular.

. . . but since the age of seven, I've become hateful towards all humans in general. Only because it seems so easy for people to get along that have empathy.

Courtney: "Empathy?"

Only because I love and feel sorry for people too much, I guess. Thank you all from the pit of my burning, nauseous stomach for your letters and concern during the past years. I'm too much of an erratic, moody baby! I don't have the passion anymore. Peace love, empathy, Kurt Cobain.

Courtney: "There is some more personal things that is none of your damn business. And just remember this is all bullshit and I'm laying in our bed, and I'm really sorry. And I feel the same way you do. I'm really sorry, you guys. I don't know what I could have done. I wish I'd been here. I wish I hadn't listened to other people, but I did. Every night I've been sleeping with his mother, and I wake up in the morning and think it's him because his body's sort of the same. I have to go now."

* * *

An hour later, a twenty-eight-year-old Seattle man named Daniel Kaspar returned home from the vigil and shot himself in the head. His roommate, who had also attended, told police Kaspar had been very distraught over Kurt's death. Ever since the body was discovered two days earlier, suicide hotlines across the country had been flooded with calls from depressed teenagers. The Seattle Crisis Clinic was fielding three hundred calls a day, 50 percent more than usual. Mental health professionals feared a rash of copycat suicides. Already, reports from around the world indicated Kurt's death was having a global impact. In Australia, a teenage boy reportedly shot himself in homage to Kurt. The following day, a sixteen-year-old Turkish girl, who friends said had been severely depressed since hearing of Kurt's death, locked herself in her room, put on a Nirvana CD at full volume and shot herself in the head.

What was it about Kurt Cobain and his music that inspired this kind of emotional reaction from his fans? Seattle's local music paper *The Rocket* compared Kurt's life and death to those of two other great artists who also died at their peak, Janis Joplin, who OD'd at twenty-seven—the same age as Kurt—and Sylvia Plath, who put her head in an oven at thirty: "All three lived lives of stunning, constant pain—which arose out of both the circumstances of their tortured lives, but even more from the sensitivity that allowed them to create their beautiful, chilling reports from the bowels of hell in the first place."

Yet neither their deaths nor any of the other countless rock-and-roll tragedies over the years had touched off the tidal wave of grief and despair that now appeared to be engulfing young people around the globe.

Is it because, behind Kurt's angst-ridden lyrics, there was a message of hope in a world dominated by baby boomers? Was Kurt really "an awakening voice for a new generation," as the *Los Angeles Times* described him? Soon after the death, one fourteen-year-old boy posted his thoughts on the Internet about what Kurt had meant to him: "He was like my guru. I felt like he was leading me to something better."

Now, for millions of his followers, it was as if Kurt had abandoned them, as if he were telling them, "Why bother?" or, more appropriately, "Nevermind." Andy Rooney summed it up best during his weekly commentary on *60 Minutes:* "When the spokesman for his generation blows his head off, what is that generation supposed to think?"

*   *   *

Tom Grant was uneasy, but he was not quite sure why. When he got back to L.A. on Saturday, he knew his assignment was officially over. He had been hired by Courtney to find her husband, and now Kurt had been found. Still, he couldn't help thinking something was wrong. On Tuesday morning, he arranged a meeting for the next day with Courtney's attorney, Rosemary Carroll, whom he had talked to on a number of occasions during the previous week. He thought she might be able to clear up some of the confusion about the events surrounding Kurt's disappearance.

Wednesday, April 13

At the time of Kurt's death, Rosemary Carroll was more than just Courtney Love's lawyer. For more than two years, she had simultaneously served as the attorney for both Kurt and Courtney, as well as for Nirvana. She also happened to be married to Danny Goldberg, president of Kurt's management company, Gold Mountain, and the man often credited with "discovering" Nirvana. But the couple were much more than clients to Carroll. She and her husband had become extremely close to both Kurt and Courtney, and they had even been designated as godparents for Frances Bean. Both Kurt and Courtney said they trusted Carroll and Goldberg more than their own parents. Kurt even told friends he regarded Carroll as a surrogate mother. Rosemary knew more than a little about troubled artists. Before she met Goldberg, she had been married for many years to Jim Carroll, the notorious former junkie poet who penned the 1978 cult classic *The Basketball Diaries*. Now she was one of L.A.'s most powerful entertainment attorneys and senior partner of her own firm.

When Grant arrives at Carroll's Sunset Boulevard law offices on Wednesday morning, he immediately tells her he is "very confused" about a number of things surrounding Kurt's death.

"I was sounding her out at first. I needed to find out where she stood," he recalls. "Then, after a few minutes of talking, she lets out a sigh, puts her head in her hands and just let it all out."

Carroll tells Grant that Kurt's death just didn't make any sense, insisting that Kurt wasn't suicidal. "I knew him too well," she says.

When Grant tells her that the papers are saying Kurt had been suicidal for a long time, she responds, "No, no," and proceeds to tell him the story as she knows it.

Both Kurt and Courtney wanted a divorce, Carroll reveals. They were "hateful" toward each other, she says. Recently, Courtney had called her and asked her to find her the "meanest, most vicious divorce lawyer" she knew. Courtney said Kurt was leaving her. She also wanted to know if Carroll knew of any way the couple's 1992 prenuptial agreement could be voided.

Soon afterward, Carroll continues, Kurt called her and asked her to take Courtney out of his recently drafted will, which was still unsigned at the time of his death. It was very emotionally draining for her to be in the middle of the couple's breakup, Carroll laments to Grant. "I loved both of them."

This conversation sheds considerable light on an interview granted to BBC filmmaker Nick Broomfield in 1997 by a woman named "Jennifer," who was hired by Kurt and Courtney in March 1994 as one of Frances Bean's nannies just after they returned from Rome following Kurt's overdose. She quit at the end of March. In the interview, the former nanny tells Broomfield that Courtney was obsessed with Kurt's will during this period. Before we heard the tapes, this revelation was always puzzling because Kurt didn't leave a will when he died:

NANNY "There was just way too much will talk. A few different times. Major will talk. Just talking about his will and . . ."

BROOMFIELD "What kind of points?"

NANNY "Courtney talking about his will and— I mean, what a thing to talk about."

BROOMFIELD "And was this just sort of prior to his . . ."

NANNY "Yeah, I mean, the month that I was up there was like, I came home for what, a week, and then he died. I had quit for, like, a week."

BROOMFIELD "Why did you quit?"

NANNY "Because I couldn't stand it up there."

BROOMFIELD "And what did you think of Kurt himself?"

NANNY "Ummm . . ."

BROOMFIELD "I heard he was a very caring father."

NANNY [NODDING IN AGREEMENT] "Yeah, more caring than he was let to be."

BROOMFIELD "What do you mean?"

NANNY "She just totally controlled him—every second that she could."

BROOMFIELD "What do you think he wanted?"

NANNY "To get away from Courtney. And I think he just didn't have a way because she . . ."

BROOMFIELD "If he loved Frances so much and his family was so important, why do you think he killed himself?"

NANNY "I'm not sure he killed himself."

BROOMFIELD "Do you think someone else might have killed him?"

NANNY "I don't know. I think if he wasn't murdered, he was driven into murdering himself."

* * *

After Carroll reveals to Grant that Kurt and Courtney were in the midst of an acrimonious divorce at the time of his death, Grant tells her that Courtney had mentioned divorce at the Peninsula Hotel. He then tells her about some of Courtney's suspicious behavior he had observed the week before and wonders why she had never told him that Cali had talked to Kurt at the Lake Washington house on April 2.

Both Grant and Carroll also think it's strange that Courtney did not once go to Seattle to look for Kurt during the week he was missing.

Grant tells her that Courtney told him she had business in L.A. and therefore couldn't get away.

She had no business in L.A., Carroll replies.

But it is the suicide note that troubles Carroll the most. Courtney had refused to let her see it when they were in Seattle together. Then she adds one more twist: She tells Grant that on the night Dylan called to have the alarm switched off (Wednesday, April 6), she overheard Courtney tell him to "check the greenhouse."

"When Rosemary told me that, I knew there was something very wrong," Grant recalls. "Kurt would have already been lying there dead in the greenhouse at that time. I wondered why [Courtney] hadn't asked Cali to check the greenhouse before that."

Grant and Carroll quickly come to the conclusion that he should fly back to Seattle to find out what's going on. She asks him not to tell Courtney what they have been talking about: "Let's keep it between us."

Grant returns to his office and books a flight leaving that evening.

Thursday, April 14

On the morning of April 14, Grant arrives at the Lake Washington house where Courtney has been staying since returning to Seattle the day Kurt's body was found. A security guard posted at the door ushers him inside. Courtney is sitting at the dining room table.

"I guess I really found the right P.I. this time," she says to him warmly.

Although Grant finds her words of praise puzzling since he had actually failed to find her husband, he doesn't say so at the time. Instead, he extends his condolences and asks her how she's holding up.

"Not too good," she replies.

As Courtney gets up to get a cigarette, a woman approaches wearing a black T-shirt that says "Grunge Is Dead."

The woman asks Grant what he thinks of the whole situation.

He replies that he doesn't know what to think. What does she think? he asks.

At this point, the woman introduces herself as Kurt's mother, Wendy O'Connor, and says that something doesn't seem right to her. "Why didn't Dylan look in the greenhouse?" she asks.

Grant tells her he'd like to know the same thing. He asks Wendy if they can get together for a talk sometime in the next couple of days. She agrees and says she'd like to talk to him more about this.

At this point, Courtney goes over to Kurt's mother and whispers something in her ear.

"After that, Wendy was very evasive towards me," he recalls, "and we never did have that talk she agreed to."

Grant was anxious to read the suicide note. Knowing that Courtney hadn't let her close friend Rosemary Carroll see it, he decided he would have to trick her into letting him take a look at it.

Courtney takes him upstairs, where they can talk out of Wendy's earshot. They sit down on the bed she and Kurt once shared. Grant says, "I heard you read the note on TV the other day [referring to her taped address at the Saturday vigil]. I was confused about something. It sounded like the note said, 'I'm lying here on the bed.' If Kurt was lying on the bed when he wrote that note, why was the bed so neat when I came here the other night? It didn't look like anyone had been on this bed."

"No, Tom, I was lying on the bed," she says. "I was lying on the bed recording the message to Kurt's fans."

"Are you sure that's what you said?" he asks. "I got the impression it was Kurt saying he was lying on the bed."

"No, here. I'll show you," she says, reaching for a piece of folded paper under her pillow. "It's only a copy. The police have the original. He wrote it on an IHOP [International House of Pancakes] place mat."

Grant pretends to study the note, then says, "I can't read this without my glasses. Can I go downstairs and make a copy on your fax machine? I'll look at it later."

Note in hand, he goes downstairs and makes a copy, pocketing it so that he can examine it in detail later on.

Later that afternoon, Courtney says she wants to visit the country house in Carnation to see if Kurt had been up there during the time he was missing. Her old friend, Kat Bjelland, leader of Babes in Toyland, is visiting and decides to go along for the ride. Kat had had harsh words for Courtney in the notorious 1992 *Vanity Fair* article, telling Lynn Hirschberg, "Courtney's delusional. Last night I had a dream that I killed her. I was really happy." But, apparently, all is now forgiven as they make the hour-long drive in Grant's rental car.

Courtney is irate about a recent news story stating she had overdosed in L.A. on April 2 and vows that she would find out who the hell leaked the story "and sue that motherfucker for libel." She says she can prove that she was at the hotel at the time, because people saw her there. "It was a total lie," she says.

It dawns on Grant that Courtney is referring to the story she had leaked a week earlier, allegedly to attract the attention of her missing husband. He reminds her that she had admitted to him that it was actually she who planted the AP story.

"Huh? Oh," she says, before turning her attention back to the possibility that Kurt had been to Carnation between the time he left rehab and the time his body was found. He better not have been there with some "skank," she says to herself.

At the Carnation property, there are two cabins, one a weathered log house filled with the used furniture that came with the house, and the other a newly constructed mansion, still bare.

The three enter the old cabin, and Kat and Courtney go upstairs, only to descend a few minutes later, Courtney holding a cloth pouch. She opens the pouch to reveal a syringe inside, claiming it proves Kurt had recently been there.

They head over to the new house, where they find a sleeping bag and some cigarette butts and soda cans scattered around the room.

Courtney gathers the items to bring back, explaining she wants to have them fingerprinted to determine if Kurt had been there.

On the way back to Seattle, nationally syndicated radio commentator Paul Harvey is heard on the radio reporting rumors of a suicide pact between Kurt and Courtney. She says nothing.

"This sounded like one of Courtney's typical planted stories," Grant recalls. "Soon I started hearing a lot of rumors about this so-called suicide pact. For the first time, I wondered if the AP story she planted about her overdose on April 2, or her alleged overdose on April 7, the day before Kurt's body was found, had something to do with Courtney trying to convince people that this had all been some romantic suicide pact, and that her part of the pact had simply gone wrong."

Friday, April 15

In 1997, Seattle Police Department spokesman Sean O'Donnell told NBC's *Unsolved Mysteries* of the monthlong investigation his department had conducted into the circumstances of Kurt's death. His detectives, he said, originally began the investigation with the premise that Kurt had been murdered before officially ruling out the possibility: "That's the way they conducted this investigation, so that there was a very thorough, comprehensive investigation done from the very beginning, and everything that the detectives encountered indicated to them that this was a suicide. We actually found nothing to indicate that this was anything but a suicide."

But a long trail of evidence suggests investigators never seriously contemplated the idea that Kurt was murdered at all. Indeed, a Seattle Police Department source familiar with the investigation told us in 1996 that Sergeant Cameron made it clear at the time that the so-called homicide investigation was just a show: "We weren't supposed to take it seriously." The source, who said he didn't necessarily believe Cobain was murdered, described a "shoddy investigation" in which Cameron didn't even bother to develop the photographs taken at the scene. He said an outside law enforcement agency should reinvestigate the circumstances because "Cameron will never admit he made a mistake. He is very concerned about his reputation."

The police reports we obtained under Washington State's Freedom of Information laws appear to reinforce his charge that the homicide unit never took their investigation seriously. According to the initial incident report filed by homicide detectives, they had been summoned to the Lake Washington estate by a patrol officer at 9:50 A.M. on April 8, a little more than an hour after Cobain's body was found. The dispatcher informed detectives that uniformed officers "are on the scene of a suicide. There is a note present, and the gun is also in place." In their official incident report, filed later the same day, the SPD homicide detectives wrote "Suicide" in the box on the form indicating "Type of incident." This is a clear contradiction of the SPD spokesman's assertion that the incident was investigated as a homicide from the very beginning. It proves that from the earliest hours of April 8, each unit of the Seattle Police Department had already *officially* labeled the death a suicide.

Certainly, Grant's own attempts to share information with Cameron did not inspire confidence. Grant had already spent considerable time in the greenhouse, photographing the interior and exterior from every angle. One detail in particular stood out for him. The doors had a simple push-in-and-twist-type lock. On April 8, Cameron had informed him over the phone that Kurt was "locked inside the room," suggesting that nobody could have been inside with him. This appeared to suggest that suicide was the only possible scenario. Now, face-to-face with Cameron for the first time, Grant asks the veteran homicide detective why he had told him the door was locked from the inside. (Ever since Grant had actually seen and photographed the lock, he realized that the detective's statement was irrelevant.)

"Anyone could have pulled that door shut after locking it," Grant says.

Cameron has a ready explanation: "There was a stool wedged up against the door." This is a detail that had already been reported on both MTV and the talk show *Geraldo*, as well as numerous newspaper articles about the case. *Rolling Stone*, for example, wrote, "Sometime on or before the afternoon of April 5, Cobain barricaded himself in the room above his garage by propping a stool against its French doors." Anybody reading this would naturally assume that Kurt must have killed himself because nobody else possibly could have been in the greenhouse with him and then exited the room with a stool wedged against the door. Therefore, Kurt must have wedged the stool in front of the door himself before committing suicide.

Grant asks Sergeant Cameron if he can examine the photographs that police took at the scene. The detective refuses, offering yet more proof that he never took his murder investigation seriously. "We haven't developed the photographs and probably never will. We don't develop photographs on suicides," says Cameron.

Grant shares some of the information he and Ben Klugman have gathered, including details on the use of Kurt's credit card after he died.

Again, Cameron brushes him off: "Nothing you've said convinces me this is anything but a suicide."

At the time, Grant had no reason to doubt Cameron's word that a stool had been wedged against the door. But when, months later, he obtained the incident report filed by the first detectives who arrived on the scene, the file suggested that Cameron was either lying or had badly bungled his investigation. The report read:

> Cobain is found in the 19' x 23' greenhouse above the detached double garage. There are stairs on the westside leading to the French door entry and another set of French doors on the

eastside leading to a balcony. These doors are unlocked and closed but there is a stool with a box of gardening supplies on it in front of the door.

The report clearly demonstrates that the stool wasn't, in fact, wedged against the exit door at all. Rather, it was standing in front of the French doors on the other side of the room—doors that didn't even serve as an exit. Although the actual exit door was indeed locked, it could have been locked and pulled shut by anyone leaving the scene. Why Cameron was repeating the demonstrably false story about the wedged stool is a question he refuses to answer to this day.

Whatever the reason, the police report proves beyond any doubt that Kurt never barricaded himself in the room, and it clearly demonstrates that another person could have easily been in the greenhouse at the time of Kurt's death. Thus, one of the most convincing pieces of so-called evidence pointing to suicide is nothing more than a myth. It is a myth that has never been dispelled by a single biographer, nor by any of the media that originally reported on the barricaded door. It is a myth that many distraught teenagers would cling to in the months and years to come.

* * *

After his meeting with Cameron, Grant pays another visit to the Lake Washington house. Courtney is in the dining room discussing Hole's upcoming tour with her guitarist, Eric Erlandson. Grant asks her if she can arrange for him to meet with both Dylan Carlson and Michael "Cali" Dewitt together.

"Cali went to rehab in El Paso, or Georgia . . . no, he's in L.A. with friends," she replies. Then she shouts to Eric in the other room, "Call Cali and tell him to get back up here on the next plane."

About an hour later, while Grant is in the kitchen fixing himself a sandwich, Dylan Carlson arrives. The two haven't seen each other since April 8, when they returned together to the house after hearing Kurt's body had been found. Grant is anxious to confirm Rosemary Carroll's claim that Courtney told Dylan to "check the greenhouse." When Grant emerges from the kitchen, Eric tells him Dylan is upstairs talking to Courtney in her bedroom. The two come downstairs some twenty minutes later. It is obvious to Grant that Dylan has just shot up. Grant leads him into the kitchen to talk out of Courtney's earshot.

"When we started talking, I immediately noticed that his answers sounded rehearsed, like he'd just been prepared about what to say," Grant recalls. "He kept nodding off, I guess from the heroin, and I figured I was wasting my time trying to talk to him."

When Grant finally leaves to return to his hotel, he asks Eric to call him when Cali arrives. By evening, there is still no word, so he telephones the house. Eric tells Grant that shortly after he left that afternoon, Courtney had him call Cali and tell him he didn't have to return to Seattle after all.

"I don't know what's going on here, man!" Eric says.

* * *

When Grant pocketed the copy of Kurt's alleged suicide note from the house, he spotted a letter Courtney had just faxed somebody and quickly pocketed it as well in order to compare the handwriting later on. Then, as soon as he could, he made his exit, desperately anxious to read the note—so anxious, in fact, that he turned his car into a parking lot about a mile from the house and took the two letters out. For the next two hours, he studied the words on the suicide note:

To BoddAH   pronounced
Speaking from the tongue of an experienced simpleton who obviously would rather be an emasculated, infantile complain-ee. This note should be pretty easy to understand. All the warnings from the punk rock 101 courses over the years, since my first introduction to the, shall we say, ethics involved with independence and the embracement of your community has proven to be very true. I haven't felt the excitement of listening to as well as creating music along with reading and writing for too many years now. I feel guilty beyond words about these things. For example when we're back stage and the lights go out and the manic roar of the crowds begins., it doesn't affect me the way in which it did for Freddie Mercury, who seemed to love, relish in the love and adoration from the crowd which is something I totally admire and envy. The fact is, I can't fool you, any one of you. It simply isn't fair to you or me. The worst crime I can think of would be to rip people off by faking it and pretending as if I'm having 100% fun. Sometimes I feel as if I should have a punch-in time clock before I walk out on stage. I've tried everything within my power to appreciate it (and I do, God, believe me I do, but it's not enough). I appreciate the fact that I and we have affected and entertained a lot of people. I must be one of those narcissists who only appreciate things when they're gone. I'm too sensitive. I need to be slightly numb in order to regain the enthusiasms I once had as a child. On our last 3 tours, I've had a much better appreciation for all the people I've known personally, and as fans of our music, but I still can't get over the frustration, the guilt and empathy I have for everyone. There's good in all of us and I think I simply love people too much, so much that it makes me feel too fucking sad. The sad little, sensitive, unappreciative, Pisces, Jesus man. Why

don't you just enjoy it? I don't know! I have a goddess of a wife who sweats ambition and empathy . . . and a daughter who reminds me too much of what I used to be, full of love and joy, kissing every person she meets because everyone is good and will do her no harm. And that terrifies me to the point to where I can barely function. I can't stand the thought of Frances becoming the miserable, self-destructive, death rocker that I've become.

I have it good, very good, and I'm grateful, but since the age of seven, I've become hateful towards all humans in general. Only because it seems so easy for people to get along that have empathy. Only because I love and feel sorry for people too much I guess. Thank you all from the pit of my burning, nauseous stomach for your letters and concern during the past years. I'm too much of an erratic, moody baby! I don't have the passion anymore, and so remember, it's better to burn out than to
fade away.   peace love, <u>empathy.</u>   kurt cobain

Frances and Courtney, I'll be at your altar.
Please keep going Courtney,
for Frances
for her life, which will be so much happier
without me. I LOVE YOU, I LOVE YOU!

As Grant pores over the words on the note, something doesn't seem right. It doesn't sound like any suicide note he'd ever read. In fact, nowhere in the note did Kurt even mention suicide. And the only part that *might* be construed as such—the last four lines—appeared to have been written in a completely different style of handwriting. Grant takes out the other document he had pocketed, a handwritten letter Courtney had faxed earlier that day. Some of the handwriting seems strangely similar, but Grant is no handwriting expert. He starts the car and drives away.

"I got onto the highway and just kept going," Grant recalls.

"There were so many questions going through my mind after I read that note, and I just had to weigh them. I didn't even know where I was going. The next thing I knew, I had driven all the way to Portland, Oregon. So I just turned right around and came back. The whole time, I really didn't know what to make of it. I still had no idea what any of this stuff meant."

By the time Grant returns to Los Angeles, he is more confused than ever. He drives to Rosemary Carroll's office with a copy of the note. Carroll spends fifteen minutes poring over it and then says it's "obvious" that Kurt didn't write it. She reads the note "over and over again" and it doesn't mention suicide.

Except at the bottom, Grant points out.

Carroll, however, says the bottom section is obviously "in a different handwriting." She tells Grant that the note doesn't sound to her like anything Kurt would write. It actually sounds more like Courtney than Kurt, she says, explaining that the note contains a number of phrases that she has heard Courtney use before. Something's wrong, Carroll says, clearly troubled. She pauses, then shares her conclusion with Grant: She doesn't believe Kurt killed himself.

Grant did not know what to think. As a former police detective, he had been trained not to jump to any conclusions, but rather to follow the evidence. This evidence comes the next day when he receives a call from Carroll, who sounds somewhat flustered. She says she has something to show him—some "writings" that Courtney left at her house. She never thought to look at them until the night before. Grant asks whether they are Kurt's writings. "No, hers," Carroll replies.

Carroll is in a state of shock when Grant arrives at her house an hour later. She shows him a backpack Courtney had left behind after her visit to Carroll's house the night of April 6. Sick with doubt after reading Kurt's suicide note, Carroll had taken a look inside the backpack. What she discovered there frightened her. She takes out a sheet of paper. Written in Courtney's handwriting are two words: "Get Arrested." It is one of Courtney's typical "to do" notes to herself.

"She planned that whole thing," says Carroll, referring to Courtney's April 7 arrest.

Painstakingly, the two review what occurred after Courtney's visit to Carroll's house two weeks earlier, on the night of April 6. Hours after Courtney left Carroll's house to return to her hotel, she was indeed arrested. Responding to a 911 call reporting a "possible overdose victim," Beverly Hills police, fire department officials and paramedics arrived at Courtney's Peninsula Hotel suite the morning of April 7 to find Courtney in a state of physical distress. She was taken by ambulance to Century City Hospital, where she told doctors she was merely suffering an allergic reaction to her Xanax medication. Upon her discharge, she was immediately arrested, brought to Beverly Hills Jail and charged with possession of a controlled substance, possession of drug paraphernalia and possession/receiving stolen property.

"When she eventually went to court," says Grant, "she had a logical explanation for everything police found in her room. It turned out that the white powdery substance they thought was heroin was actually Hindu good-luck ashes; the prescription pad they thought was stolen she said had actually been mistakenly left behind by her doctor. But at the time, these things provided a perfect excuse for her to get arrested without getting into any real trouble. Rosemary's explanation that she 'planned the whole thing' makes a whole lot of sense. She needed an alibi." Grant now believes that Courtney planned to get herself arrested on April 7 so that the papers would report the fact that she was in jail in L.A. that day, the day she expected Kurt's body to be found.

"That's the day that she suddenly wanted me and Dylan to go back to the house to search for the shotgun in the closet, even though she could have asked Cali to look for it anytime that week," he explains. "I'm now convinced that she wanted us to find the body that day." Hole guitarist Eric Erlandson later revealed to Kurt's biographer Charles Cross that Courtney had already asked him to search the closet for the shotgun on Tuesday afternoon, April 5. So why did she ask Dylan and Grant to do the same thing two days later?

Carroll then tells Grant that she found another piece of paper in Courtney's backpack, one that disturbs her even more than the "Get Arrested" note. She hands the paper to Grant. On it, somebody has been practicing different handwriting styles. On each line, the person has experimented with different forms of all the letters of the alphabet, much like a schoolchild's handwriting exercise primer. But this handwriting is clearly in the style of an adult, not a child. On the top right side of the page, in a section marked "combos," the person has practiced writing two- and three-letter combinations:

ta   re   fe   ur   you   te

As he studies the sheet, Grant gets a chill. "I had no idea what it meant or who had been doing the writing," he recalls, "but Rosemary found it among Courtney's things. It sure looked to us like she had been practicing how to forge a letter."

7

By the time Rosemary Carroll understood the implications of the two notes she found in Courtney's backpack, she had already stated more than once that she didn't believe Kurt killed himself. Yet never once on Grant's tapes, before or after this conversation, does Carroll explicitly say that she believes Courtney murdered him. She is suspicious enough, however, to remove a folder from her files and slide it over to Grant. Inside are more items from the backpack: Courtney's Peninsula Hotel bill as well as an itemized list of her phone records and messages there.

It is the second message on the list that gives Grant pause. On Friday, April 1, at exactly 8:47 P.M., the Peninsula Hotel switchboard took a message for Courtney: "Husband called. Elizabeth number is (213) 850-■■■■." Courtney has always claimed she never heard from Kurt again after he fled rehab, yet here is concrete evidence that he had contacted his wife less than an hour after he left Exodus and told her where he could be reached. On the copy of the message sheet Grant shows us, he has blacked out the last part of Elizabeth's phone number, which is located within the Los Angeles area code. He says he knows who "Elizabeth" is, as well as the significance of her involvement, but can't reveal these details until the case is reopened.

On our own, however, we discovered that the Elizabeth in the message almost certainly refers to the American painter Elizabeth Peyton, who specializes in portraits of pop culture icons. Peyton, who was apparently staying in Los Angeles at the time of Kurt's disappearance, had become close friends with both Kurt and Courtney and later painted several striking portraits of Kurt after his death. For years afterward, it seemed that Peyton managed to bring up Kurt in virtually every interview she gave, as if her old friend had become a lingering obsession. From a 2000 interview with Peyton in *Index* magazine:

> . . . like John Lennon, you hear his breath. And you can have it. And if you really love that person, then you take them into your life and you make it better with them. In a different way Kurt Cobain is a good example. It was just his own fucked up life, but how many millions of people related to it? It's a beautiful thing when a collapse occurs between our own personal needs and what's in the air.

In another interview, she told *Metro* magazine that she paints portraits of "people I love," including Kurt Cobain. And, although she may be one of the keys to clearing up the mystery of Kurt's disappearance, Peyton has never discussed the events of that night nor confirmed that she is the Elizabeth referred to in the phone message.

The phone records reveal another interesting fact. On April 1, the day Kurt left Exodus, Courtney called the rehab center's patient pay phone six times, presumably speaking to Kurt on each occasion.

"That's one of the things that Rosemary was most concerned about when she gave me the phone records," recalls Grant. "She said Courtney told her she had only spoken to Kurt once that day.

She wondered why Courtney had lied to her about this. My own reaction was to wonder why Courtney never told me that Kurt had left her a message the night he left Exodus with a phone number where he could be reached. You'd think that would be something she might be expected to tell the guy she had just hired to find her missing husband. But she never said a word to me about it."

According to Charles Cross's Cobain biography *Heavier Than Heaven*—authorized by Courtney—she was "on the phone every moment trying to find someone who had seen Kurt after Saturday." Her phone records, however, testify to a more self-serving series of calls: repeated anonymous calls to the request line of L.A. radio station KROQ to play the single from her forthcoming album, *Live Through This.*

Grant and his assistant, Ben Klugman, spent the next few days tracking down the various phone calls Courtney had made and trying to match names with numbers. They discovered she had called drug dealer Caitlin Moore twice on Monday, April 4, and had been in almost continuous contact with Cali, the nanny, throughout the week, although the baby was with her in Los Angeles.

When Grant contacts Carroll to report his findings two days later, she is still fixated on Kurt's suicide note, revealing that she has a lot of "unanswered questions" that she has no idea how to go about answering.

Grant asks her how she feels about the suicide note. Carroll tells him that she feels "exactly the same way" she felt when she first saw the note: "He didn't write it."

Grant tells her that in his mind, he wouldn't be surprised to find out that Kurt did write it. But he points out that this still wouldn't necessarily mean it was a suicide note.

He asks Carroll whether she has read the article about Kurt's death in that week's *Us* magazine. She says she hasn't seen it. Grant tells her the article contains a quotation supposedly taken from the suicide note, in which Kurt is said to have written: 'I can't live my life like this any longer.' That line is not in the suicide note, he tells Carroll, who replies that "of course" it's not.

The only people who know what's in the suicide note, Grant says, are Courtney, himself and the police, so he speculates that the magazine had to have obtained the false quotation from Courtney herself. Grant says that Courtney wants the public to falsely believe that Kurt had talked about suicide in his note. Carroll agrees.

Then Grant tells her that he's "at the same place." He still feels that there is a possibility that Kurt committed suicide.

For nearly a decade, Grant has been vilified for his role in the investigation of Cobain's death. He has been called everything from a "lunatic conspiracy theorist" to a "publicity hound" to an "opportunist" who came up with the murder theory to "cash in." Yet in the decade since Kurt's death, he has refused countless financial offers from tabloid TV shows, including a significant offer from *Inside Edition*, and he has never attempted to write a book. "If I take any money or try to write a book about the investigation, my credibility will be shot," he told us. "Courtney will come out and say, 'You see, he was just after the money.' I'm never going to get myself in a position where she can say that." In late 1994, engrossed in the Cobain investigation, he turned down a major case in Hawaii, one that would have netted him between $25,000 and $100,000. After he nearly went broke in the mid-nineties because he had abandoned all his other casework, he started selling a "Cobain Case Manual"—a photocopied summary of the events—for $18 over the Internet to keep up his overhead, but these sales do not bring in any significant income, especially since he has allowed a number of websites to post the manual on the Internet for free. "I'd rather see that the information gets out there," he explains. Clearly, he isn't in it for the money. "I would have made a lot more money working in a McDonald's for minimum wage than I have made on this case," Grant says. Still, the skeptics persisted in their attacks. If he isn't doing it for the money, he must simply be a nut. After all, everybody knows Cobain killed himself.

Now, as we listen to this extraordinary taped exchange between Grant and Carroll from April 1994, a number of things become clear. The tape proves that it was not Grant who first called the suicide verdict into question, but Courtney's own close friend and attorney, a woman so close to Kurt and Courtney that the couple had designated her as their daughter's legal guardian should anything happen to them. Moreover, even after Carroll repeatedly raised the possibility that Kurt might have been murdered, Grant remained unconvinced, arguing, "I still think there's a possibility it's a suicide."

Grant recalls his feelings: "I've never really been big on conspiracy theories. . . . When I hear somebody else talk about a conspiracy, I usually scoff. . . . But by that point, I was certainly beginning to think there was a very real possibility that Kurt had been murdered. If Kurt's own close friend and lawyer believed it, I thought there had to be something to it."

* * *

On April 20, Grant calls SPD homicide detective Steve Kirkland to find out, among other things, whether the police have made any progress determining who had been using Kurt's canceled Seafirst MasterCard during the period when he was missing. Credit card records indicated that on Sunday, April 3, a charge of $1,100 was denied around mid-afternoon: this was followed by a series of rejected cash advances ranging from $2,500 to $5,000. There were two unsuccessful attempts to purchase $86.60 worth of goods on the morning of Monday, April 4, and an attempt to buy $1,517.56 worth of unnamed goods at 7:07 P.M. the following day. More mysteriously, a charge of $43.29 was attempted on Friday, April 8, at

8:37 A.M., at a time when Kurt was certainly dead—and only three minutes before the body was discovered. Who was trying to use the card, which was missing from Kurt's wallet when he was found?

When Grant spoke to Kirkland, asking whether the police had any leads, the detective was dismissive, admitting once again that the SPD never took its homicide investigation seriously. "Your investigation is into things that our investigation doesn't even apply to," Kirkland tells Grant. "You're maybe concerned with what he was doing, where he was, and all that. I'll tell you, Tom, truthfully, our homicide unit doesn't even respond to suicides. . . . We're involved with this thing because it is Kurt Cobain."

To this day, Seattle police have never determined who was using Kurt's card. Because Courtney had it canceled, the bank company could not trace the exact whereabouts of the transactions, only the date and time they were rejected. When Ben Klugman called Seafirst Bank to trace Kurt's credit card activity, he was told that the transaction records do not reflect the time of the attempted transactions, only the time they were logged in to the computer. The SPD later cited this to explain the apparent use of the card after Kurt was already dead. However, the bank official, Steve Sparks, also told Klugman that the discrepancy in the logged transaction time is "no more than about fifteen minutes." Therefore, it still does not explain the postmortem credit card use.

In addition, the bank official cleared up another puzzle resulting from the notations on the credit card records. After each declined transaction, the records read "card not present," which has led many to speculate that perhaps another member of Kurt's entourage had the card number and was attempting transactions by phone. But the Seafirst official explained to Klugman that when the merchant slides the card through the reader and the transaction is refused, the card number is then entered manually to double-check that the machine has read the correct number. When that happens, the transaction is automatically logged as "card not present."

There may be logical explanations for each of the transactions, but the police reports indicate that the SPD did not even try to investigate who was using the card. More troubling is the fact that they have never explained what happened to Kurt's credit card, which has never been found. In 1995, after Grant publicly revealed the credit card discrepancies, a reporter for *The Orange County Register* called Sergeant Cameron to ask him whether he had investigated the missing card. Cameron's response is telling: "We're not going to comment until we figure out what Grant's after."

Back on April 20, Grant proceeds to describe to Detective Kirkland examples of Courtney's puzzling behavior during the time Kurt was missing as well as some of the inconsistencies in her story. That week, Grant had met with the alarm company supervisor, Charles Pelly, who had arrived at the Lake Washington estate shortly after his employee phoned to report the discovery of Kurt's body. Pelly told Grant that, when he saw Kurt's dead body in the greenhouse, it looked like his hair "had been combed." Grant now asks Kirkland if he can see the police photos to see what Pelly was referring to. The detective refuses his request. Pelly also told Grant that Courtney had suddenly on April 7 issued instructions for the electricians to begin wiring the greenhouse with a motion detector on Friday, the day Kurt's body was found.

"When you think about it, why was she suddenly so anxious that day to put a motion detector on this tiny upstairs room that nobody even uses? I realize now that when Dylan and I failed to find Kurt's body on Thursday as she had intended, Courtney made sure the electrician had an excuse to go up there and find the body," Grant recalls.

He had not yet made this leap of logic at the time of his conversation with Kirkland, but, as he shares some of the suspicious information he has gathered to date, the detective is clearly uninterested. There is a "rock stars will be rock stars" weariness to his tone: "I've been in homicide eight years, my partner's been in homicide thirteen years and Cameron's been in homicide for twenty-five years, and I am firmly convinced Kurt Cobain killed himself. There is nothing there to indicate that he did not."

GRANT "And you think none of this other stuff has any relevance whatsoever?"

KIRKLAND "I don't know how many times you've dealt with Courtney."

GRANT "I've spent a lot of time with Courtney in the last couple of weeks."

KIRKLAND "I don't think Courtney knows what she's doing from today until tomorrow, and just because Courtney says she did something yesterday, I wouldn't necessarily believe it."

* * *

The next time Grant speaks to Rosemary Carroll, she has some news: She tells him that a reporter from the *Seattle Times* is investigating the possibility that Kurt's death might not have been a suicide, but that Dylan Carlson and Courtney had conspired to have him killed. Grant asks her whether she has the name of the reporter. She tells him that the Seattle chief of police had told this to Courtney's Seattle attorney, Allen Draher. She said the Seattle police had apparently "pooh-poohed" the possibility. Carroll then urges Grant to contact her husband, Danny Goldberg, about their mutual misgivings over the suicide verdict. She says she wants her husband to realize that she "is not completely insane" for raising doubts about Kurt's suicide.

Grant is hesitant, saying that Goldberg is known to be very supportive of Courtney and singing her praises to the media, but Carroll is insistent, telling Grant that's just what Goldberg "says publicly." A few days later, Carroll calls Grant to find out how his meeting with Goldberg went.

Grant tells her that their encounter was unproductive, explaining that he couldn't really reveal to Goldberg a lot of his strongest evidence for fear of incriminating Carroll. Citing an example, Grant says he couldn't tell Goldberg that Carroll had given him Courtney's Peninsula Hotel phone records as well as the "Get Arrested" note. Grant says he can understand Goldberg's skepticism and reveals that he is also somewhat skeptical about the whole thing. The last thing he wants to do, he tells Carroll, is to create some "conspiracy theory like they did with Kennedy, and like they try to do with everybody, if it's not there."

Carroll asks whether Grant told her husband about some of the incongruities that she had observed about the case. She is particularly skeptical about the claim that Kurt was with Dylan when he bought the shotgun. Carroll believes Dylan concocted the story.

But Grant tells her he thinks it was a waste of time talking to Goldberg because it was obvious that Goldberg doesn't want to hear anything Grant has to say.

Since he last talked to Carroll, Grant has hired two document examiners to analyze the unsigned note he and Dylan had found on the stairs of the Lake Washington house. Their conclusion was that Cali had written it. Grant shares his impressions with Carroll, explaining that when he picked up the note from the stairway of the Lake Washington house, he thought it sounded "phony." Carroll concurs, telling him that she also thought the note sounded "terribly phony."

Grant tells her it sounded like "a set-up letter," explaining that when he found the note, he had no doubt that Cali had written it, but that it still looked strange to him. The note just didn't make sense.

Carroll agrees. She believes it wasn't a sincere letter and says she believes Cali wrote it because he "knew that Kurt was dead."

They continue to talk about Cali's potential role.

Grant believes Cali might have found Kurt's dead body in the greenhouse and taken the credit card out of his wallet without reporting what he had found.

Carroll says she had thought exactly the same thing.

By the time of their next conversation, the *Seattle Times* had published the first article to appear in the media detailing unanswered questions about Cobain's death. "Kurt Cobain's death a month ago wasn't the open-and-shut suicide case Seattle police originally indicated," the article began, before detailing some of the inconsistencies. In this article, Dylan Carlson, asked why he didn't look for Kurt in the greenhouse when he went searching with Grant on April 7, tells the *Times* reporter that he didn't know there was a greenhouse above the garage.

"For all the times I'd been there, I didn't even realize there was a room above it associated with the house," Dylan is quoted as saying.

When Grant calls Carroll after this article is published, he tells her that Dylan had denied knowing the greenhouse was even there.

"That's a lie," Carroll responds.

That day, Grant calls *Times* reporter Duff Wilson to let him know what Dylan had told him about the greenhouse on April 8 after they heard Kurt's body was found, that it was just "a dirty little room above the garage" where Kurt and Courtney stored lumber. Dylan subsequently receives a call from Wilson asking about the apparent contradiction, which prompts Dylan to call Grant. He is clearly upset. He says the article implies that Dylan was concealing something because Grant said he knew about the room above the garage.

Grant reminds him of their conversation immediately after the radio reported Kurt's body had been found in the greenhouse.

When Grant asked, "What's the greenhouse?" Dylan had replied, "It's the room above the garage." To this, Grant asked Dylan why they had never looked there.

Dylan recalls the conversation and says it was because he had never "thought of it" and that he had never actually been inside the greenhouse.

Grant notes that Dylan had indeed told him that he had been up there, but that he said there was "just some stuff stored up there and that it was just a small room or something."

Dylan's memory refreshed, he says, "Well, yeah. I said it wasn't part of the house."

In fact, recalls Grant, Dylan had told him that he had once "walked around the greenhouse."

"Yeah," Dylan agrees.

When Dylan accuses Grant of implying to the *Times* reporter that he knew about Kurt lying dead in the greenhouse and didn't tell anybody, Grant explains that he was simply talking about what happened after Courtney asked him to "check the greenhouse. . . ."

Dylan denies it. Courtney didn't say anything to him about "that place."

Grant tells him that he had spoken to "other people" who said they were with Courtney when she asked Dylan to check the greenhouse.

Again, Dylan denies it, but Carroll sticks to her story.

"Wow! It's obvious that they're lying," she says to Grant later, when he reports this conversation.

Meanwhile, the media has published a number of demonstrably false accounts of the events surrounding Kurt's death, relying on anonymous sources, each of whom revealed new facts bolstering the idea that Kurt had committed suicide. On April 12, for example, the *Los Angeles Times* reported that after Kurt left rehab, "One report had him buying a shotgun and calling a friend to ask the best way to shoot yourself in the head." *Esquire* reported that, before leaving rehab, he had called Courtney at the Peninsula on April 1 and told her, "No matter what happens, I want you to know you made a really good record." In addition, a number of reports were already claiming that Kurt's death was the result of a suicide pact between him and Courtney. On April 26, the *Globe* wrote, "Incredibly, at exactly the same time Kurt blew his brains out, police say his wife, Courtney Love, shot herself up with a toxic cocktail of heroin and Xanax."

As Grant and Carroll discuss this array of false reports, they agree that Courtney must be leaking the false information to the media.

Carroll says it's "amazing" that she can do this.

*   *   *

Was Grant convinced yet? "It's difficult to say for sure when I finally came to the conclusion that this was a murder, and that Courtney was involved," he recalls. "After a while, I had uncovered enough information to remove my last few doubts. Some of them will only come out in court."

By May 8, Grant was finally ready to put Courtney on notice about his suspicions. He sent her a letter hinting for the first time at his doubts:

Dear Courtney,

I'm sure you know by now that my investigation has been somewhat more active than you might have been aware of. The purpose of this letter is to clarify my position regarding our working relationship.

You may recall our trip to Carnation on Thursday, April 14th. I mentioned during the drive that I was beginning to turn over some "rocks" that I wasn't sure you'd want turned over. I asked you if you wanted me to continue digging. Kat, who was in the backseat, said, "Oh yeah, she wants to know everything." You responded, "Yeah, Tom, do whatever it takes. I want to know everything that happened." Your instructions were clear, so in the days and weeks that followed, I proceeded to "do whatever it takes."

As the investigation continued, my attempts to get at the truth often seemed to be deliberately hindered. While reading some of the articles being written in newspapers and magazines, I discovered the information being released to the press was inaccurate and often cleverly misleading.

I consider the circumstances surrounding your husband's death to be highly suspicious. My investigation has exposed a number of inconsistencies in the facts of this case as well as many contradictions in sound logic and common sense. I'm required to report findings such as these to the police, so on Friday, April 15th, I spoke with Sgt. Cameron about some of what I've learned so far.

As I've experienced in past cases, police detectives don't often welcome the work of outside investigators. I've learned it's somewhat idealistic and naive to think the truth might be more important than professional pride.

I've decided to continue working on this case until I see it to its conclusion, without additional charge. Attached you will find an invoice which accounts for the charges billed for our services, including time and expenses. As you can see, prior to my return to Seattle on April 13th, these charges exceeded the retainer amount. However, please consider your bill paid in full. There will be no further charges.

As I pursue the truth regarding the events surrounding your husband's death, your cooperation and assistance will be appreciated, but not required.

Sincerely,
Tom Grant
THE GRANT COMPANY

"I just figured Courtney would hit the roof after she received this letter," Grant recalls.

Instead, he receives a somewhat unusual call a few days later from Courtney, who is in Ithaca, New York, at the time, staying at a Buddhist monastery. The last time he had heard from her, on April 25, she had called Grant from an Arizona "health and wellness" detox resort called Canyon Ranch, where, she told him, she was sleeping with her old boyfriend Billy Corgan, lead singer of Smashing Pumpkins. "Billy's so nice," she said. "What am I supposed to do? It feels right." This call came only about two and a half weeks after Kurt died, at a time when Courtney was being portrayed in the media as a deeply grieving widow overcome with depression about Kurt's death. The same week that she was with Corgan at Canyon Ranch, *People* magazine reported, "For now, Love is with Frances Bean in Seattle in the quiet lakefront home where Cobain died three weeks ago. 'She's grieving and trying to absorb everything that's happening to her,' says a friend. 'She's doing as well as can be expected, considering.' " Years later, after Grant's revelation had already been widely circulated, Courtney came up with a slightly revised version about Corgan's visit, telling a reporter from the *Chicago Tribune*, "After Kurt died, Billy came out to the Canyon Ranch and he like took care of me for a couple of days, but it wasn't like sex. I kept trying to make him fuck me, but he wouldn't fuck me. Everybody thinks we had something, but I was so fucking high that I would have made the maid fuck me." Yet three months after her stay at Canyon Ranch, *Entertainment Weekly* reported, "Her friends insist that she has not used drugs since entering detox just prior to Cobain's suicide, and she has been encouraging others in her entourage to clean up, even helping a few, including one of Frances Bean's former nannies, get into rehab."

Now, after she receives Grant's May 8 letter, Courtney calls him again:

COURTNEY "Tom, is this the most insane case that you've had for a long time?"

GRANT "It's pretty bizarre. It's probably even more bizarre than you realize it is."

COURTNEY "How do you mean?"

GRANT "There are so many crazy twists and so many things going on here."

COURTNEY "I mean, it's just so weird that I called you and I thought he was suicidal and now he's dead."

Instead of formally cutting off ties, as Grant expected she would do after receiving his letter, she asks whether he can do some investigative work for her on issues completely unrelated to Kurt's death.

"I realized that she was trying to buy my silence," he recalls. "She was pretty transparent about that. At first, I thought of refusing the work, but then I figured that, as long as I was working for her, I'd have inside access to her world, I'd be able to keep speaking to Rosemary and I'd be able to keep tabs on Courtney."

Among the assignments Courtney gave Grant during this period was to conduct surveillance on a well-known rock musician she was dating at the time; she wanted to know if he was cheating on her. (Grant has asked us not to name the musician out of respect for the privacy of the individual.) At one point, Courtney told Grant that a psycho fan had broken into the musician's room and splattered bloody tampons on the walls. The same fan had also left the musician a threatening note, with a reference to a nearby mental institution—suggesting that a crazy woman had been responsible. Courtney asked Grant to track down the perpetrator, explaining that her boyfriend suspected Courtney herself of having written the note and vandalizing the room.

"A couple of weeks later, Courtney finally admitted to me that it was actually her who had splattered the tampons around the room and written the note," Grant recalls. "Normally I wouldn't even mention this because it has nothing to do with the Cobain case, but I realized that the phony note could represent a pattern of behavior that may be significant."

* * *

One of the enduring mysteries of this case concerns Kurt's whereabouts between the time he was spotted at the house by Cali on April 2 and the time he died, which, according to the coroner's report, was probably two to three days later. There are only three known sightings after Kurt left the Lake Washington house on April 2. On the evening of Sunday, April 3, he was spotted having dinner with a "thin woman" at Seattle's Cactus restaurant. Earlier the same day, he had bumped into Nirvana's manager, John Silva; soon after, Kurt met a woman on the street named Sara Hoehn, who said he was in a foul mood over a report that forty thousand fans had lined up that morning in L.A. to buy tickets to an Eagles concert. Various Cobain biographies quote unnamed sources who claim to have seen or spoken to Kurt later in the week, but there is not a single confirmed sighting after April 3. A Michigan man named Brad Barnett told us that he had met Kurt in the park near his house on Monday, April 4, and that Kurt had brought him into the greenhouse, where they struck up a conversation about literature. (We have since seen evidence proving that Barnett's account was false, including wildly conflicting accounts of what he claims happened.)

Seattle police later claimed that Kurt had spent time that week at his house in Carnation because fresh tire tracks had been spotted by a neighbor. Cobain biographer Christopher Sandford reports that sleeping bags were found at the Carnation house along with an ashtray filled with recently smoked cigarettes, some Kurt's brand—Winston Lights—and some Marlboro Lights (not Courtney's brand) with traces of lipstick. Sandford reports that on the table was a black drawing of the sun above the words "Cheer up." But Tom Grant says that when he drove to Carnation with Courtney and Kat Bjelland the week after Kurt's body was found, they found no such drawing. Grant believes that Courtney planted the story as another red herring. However, it is unclear why Courtney would want people to believe that Kurt was with a woman that week if it wasn't true. Her conversations with Grant reveal that she seemed certain Kurt was having an affair with Caitlin Moore and that she was intensely jealous. A friend of the couple told us that he heard Courtney yelling at Kurt, "You're fucking her, aren't you, you bastard?" just after he returned from Rome. Yet it is possible that it wasn't Caitlin Moore who was the object of Kurt's affection during this period; Courtney may have blamed the wrong woman. Sandford writes that Kurt sent a young art student several love notes, a hand-drawn valentine and an invitation for the woman to join him in a Seattle hotel. When she declined, he allegedly phoned a dozen times a day and sent her a message stating, "I'm not obsessed with you. I just wanted to talk to you about conceptual art."

*   *   *

While he was working for Courtney on miscellaneous assignments, Grant finally managed to speak briefly to the nanny, Michael "Cali" Dewitt, who admitted to him that he had seen and talked to Kurt on April 2 when he appeared in Cali's bedroom the morning after he fled rehab. Cali also confirmed that he had informed Courtney about the sighting the same day and later wrote the note that Grant and Dylan found on the stairs.

Meanwhile, the copycat suicide phenomenon that mental health professionals had feared after Cobain's death didn't appear to be materializing. After Daniel Kaspar went home and killed himself following the Space Needle vigil, American treatment centers recorded no marked boost in teenage suicides, although youth crisis hotlines did experience a significant increase in calls from teens depressed about the death of their idol. Some professionals speculated that the American media's treatment of the death—replete with interviews quoting celebrities who harshly condemned Kurt for taking the "coward's way out"—played a role in keeping copycat suicides to a minimum. Rush Limbaugh may have contributed in an odd way, too, by calling Kurt a "worthless shred of human debris." American families were widely urged to talk to their teenagers about Kurt's death.

But, while America breathed a sigh of relief for its young, other countries were not so fortunate.

* * *

Just after midnight on July 2, 1994, an eighteen-year-old Edmonton boy named Bobby Steele puts the Nirvana song "Endless, Nameless" on the stereo and presses the REPEAT PLAY button. Minutes later, he lifts a 12-gauge shotgun from his father's collection and loads three shells. Dressed in a Nirvana "Sliver" T-shirt, he takes out his little black diary and begins to write: "July 94. I just can't live anymore. If you just think a lot, you just stop knowing that life has a purpose . . . I am not intoxicated or high. . . . I just feel bad. It's been the most painful 84 days in my life."

Eighty-four days earlier, Bobby learned that his hero, Kurt Cobain, had killed himself with a shotgun. A few weeks later, a teenage friend of the family's named Greg had locked himself in his car with the engine running and died of carbon monoxide poisoning. Bobby and his sister believed he had never gotten over Kurt's death.

Now Bobby finishes writing the words in his diary, ending with a veiled reference to the passage in Kurt's suicide note, in which he wrote, "So re-

member, it's better to burn out than fade away." Instead, Bobby writes, "It's better not to spark at all. Rob Steele."

He signs the note, then snaps a Polaroid of himself with a Kurt Cobain poster in the background. He then takes another picture of himself reclining on his bed with a copy of Nirvana's In Utero *above his head. He aligns the photos on the bed and then positions himself on the floor so that when his body is found, he will look like Kurt in the greenhouse photo. With the death-haunted words of "Endless, Nameless" playing in the background, he positions the muzzle of the shotgun in his mouth and pulls the trigger.*

* * *

In the months he remained in Courtney's employ, Grant would sometimes bring up nagging questions about Kurt's death. Although Courtney encouraged him to continue probing, he believes she was actually sabotaging his investigation.

"Whenever I started talking to people close to Courtney about Kurt's death, she'd hire me to do another job," he recalls. "It seemed that she really had very few options at this point. Getting angry would just create more suspicion."

During this period, Grant took every opportunity he could to glean information about Cali and others without arousing Courtney's suspicion. At one point, Courtney provides a candid, somewhat shocking admission about the pervasive presence of drugs in the household:

"I don't know if you know this," she tells Grant, "but I spent thirty grand putting Cali through rehab. Didn't work. Brought him over to England to be a roadie and he ran off, totally fucked me over. He ran off with this girl, a thirty-seven-year-old drug addict who was shooting $400 worth of heroin and coke a day. . . . Kurt loved [Cali], he was one of the few people that Kurt didn't have a bad thing to say about, but about two months before Kurt died,

Cali was doing drugs and taking care of my baby, and I went into complete denial about it, and I told myself he was only doing speed and that he was probably only doing speed during his night off, and I was totally deluding myself. He was totally doing heroin full blown. René [Cali's friend] was not ever allowed to watch Frances and then I found out later that René had watched Frances a number of times when Cali went to the store completely on heroin. I can tell you from personal experience that I've been on heroin and been around my daughter. I mean, the nanny was in the room, but what if she had gone through a fucking window, you know? I mean, there's a reason why people get their children taken away, and I think it's totally appropriate. That might sound hypocritical coming from somebody who uses drugs on occasion but, fuck, it's just really awful. One night, Cali turned to me and I said, 'I hear you're doing IV drugs,' and he goes, 'Well, *you* do them.' And I'm like, 'What are you now, my brother?' "

Courtney was clearly becoming uneasy about Grant's suspicions, but she never went so far as to order him off the case. During one conversation, calling from Montreal, she tells him, "I don't mind that you're attributed to the Cobain case, you're a good P.I. I've met six and they're all sleazebags, you know, and you're the first one that's come through for me, you know what I mean?"

*   *   *

As Grant proceeds with his investigation, the suicide note continues to haunt both him and Rosemary Carroll. Carroll still doesn't believe Kurt wrote it, and she wonders why Courtney has never let her see the note: "She showed the note to Seth [Lichtenstein, another of Courtney's attorneys], but she wouldn't show it to me, which, at the time, I found rather odd," she says to Grant, who, for his part, continues to be suspicious about the roles of Cali Dewitt and Dylan Carlson.

GRANT "The main thing that I'm trying to do and the only time I'll ever put a rest to this—I don't care if it goes on for the next five or ten years—is if I get a real accurate handle about what happened with Cali and Dylan. Courtney for some reason is trying to keep me from Cali."

CARROLL "Well, we know what the reason is."

GRANT "I really need to speak to him about some things."

CARROLL "Do you know where Cali is?"

GRANT "Oh, Cali moves all around. I talked to him a few weeks ago and he copped an attitude with me a bit, and I had a feeling Courtney said to him, 'Oh, you don't need to talk to Tom.' Every time I get close to Cali, it seems she ships him off to rehab or something."

CARROLL "Oh, that's why she shipped him off to rehab. I couldn't figure it out, because it was a big thing, it was costing her a fortune because she sent his girlfriend with him."

GRANT "I told Courtney, when she's in L.A., I want to meet together with her and go over some of this stuff with her, and I'm gonna tell her how bad things look for her. Because if the press get a hold of this before I can finish it up and tie up all these loose ends and figure out what went on, if the press gets a hold of all these bits and pieces, they'll write conspiracy books and magazine articles all over the place, and she's going to be the villain in this thing. And she may not be a villain."

Meanwhile, copies of *Live Through This*—hurriedly released by Geffen on the Tuesday after Kurt's body was found—were flying off the shelves and getting very positive reviews in the American music press. But Courtney's new success was temporarily overshadowed on June 16 when Hole's bass player, Kristen Pfaff, was found dead in her bathtub, apparently of a heroin overdose.

* * *

On October 16, 1994, a storage locker attendant in Langley, British Co-lumbia, makes a grisly discovery: the bodies of three teenagers slumped in a 1987 Plymouth, its engine still running. Michael Coté, Stephane Dal-laire and Stephane Langlois, each eighteen years old, had driven over three thousand miles from Quebec to B.C. to end their lives in this locker, slowly inhaling the exhaust fumes from their car. In the car's tape deck, stuck in the PLAY position, is a Nirvana tape. When the Royal Canadian Mounted Police pull the boys out of the automobile, they discover a journal in a triple-ringed binder with the words "The Last Trip" on its cover. In sixty pages of tormented text and drawings, the three teens describe their cross-country odyssey and look forward to their deaths at the end. On the last page, in Dallaire's handwriting, are the words: "When Kurt Cobain died, I died. The way I would have liked to have died is by a bullet in the head and with the same firearm that Kurt Cobain used. But it's too late now. Goodbye."

* * *

In her next conversation with Grant, Rosemary Carroll—calling from New York, where she has recently moved—says she is "freaked out" about what has been going on and tells Grant, "I think [Courtney] is pretty scared of you." Then she shares with him the theory she has developed about Kurt's death.

CARROLL "You know, I've thought a lot about this. I try not to, but I have. . . . I've thought about stuff I know in general, about

Kurt, and about Courtney, and about that whole scene up there. You want to hear my theory?"

GRANT "Yeah, sure."

CARROLL "I hate to think of all this again because I'll go crazy like I did last time, but I think all of that weirdness with Cali obviously living in the house for several days while there was Kurt's corpse in the [greenhouse]. I think it had to do with the suicide note."

GRANT "Yeah?"

CARROLL "This is my theory, and it's a lot of intuition, but that suicide note is a pastiche of things he had written before, I think, and of someone copying or tracing his handwriting. I think it was sort of cobbled together."

GRANT "You don't think Kurt wrote it?"

CARROLL "No, I think Kurt wrote each of those words at different times and different places. I think someone went through his notebooks, found passages that plausibly could be cobbled together into a suicide note and traced them."

GRANT "You think they were traced?"

CARROLL "Yeah, or forged or something like that."

At this point, she seems to hear a noise.

CARROLL "Are you taping this call?"

GRANT "I tape all my calls. Do you want me to turn it off?"

CARROLL "Oh shit, Tom, it's just my theory." (She hangs up).

Rosemary Carroll never speaks to Grant again.

Grant found Carroll's "pastiche" theory about the note intriguing, especially in light of the piece of paper she had found in Courtney's backpack on which somebody had been practicing different handwriting styles. But he subscribes to a slightly different theory about the note.

"If you read the body of that note," he explains, "it doesn't read like a suicide note at all. It reads like a note to his fans explaining why he is quitting Nirvana. I think he wrote most of the note, but that somebody possibly forged the last four lines." When Grant first aired this theory publicly, Courtney adamantly denied that Nirvana had been in the process of breaking up. In a 1998 appearance on the *Howard Stern Show*, however, Dave Grohl admitted that the band had indeed split up at the time of Kurt's death. Years later, Krist admitted the same thing to Kurt's biographer Charles Cross: "The band was broken up." This would certainly make Grant's theory—about the note being a retirement letter to his fans—plausible, even logical.

Indeed, the body of the note mentions not a word about suicide, but it does say, "Thank you all from the pit of my burning, nauseous stomach for your letters and concern during the past years." To whom else is he addressing this line if not to his fans?

The original officer on the scene, Von Levandowski—the first person to read the note—wrote in his report that the letter was "apparently written by Cobain to his wife and daughter explaining why he had killed himself." But if Kurt wrote the note to Courtney and Frances Bean, why did he sign it with his full name, "Kurt Cobain"?

For most who see the note, the most suspicious element is the incongruously large first word, "BoddAH"—suggesting Kurt had addressed the letter to his imaginary childhood friend—as well as the last four lines:

> Please keep going Courtney
> for Frances
> for her life, which will be so much happier
> without me. I LOVE YOU, I LOVE YOU!

Why are these specific words written in what appears to be a distinctly different handwriting? And if Kurt had really addressed the letter to Boddah, why does he write, "Thank you all . . . for your letters and concern during the past years"?

* * *

On November 18, in Dublin, Ireland, a sixteen-year-old girl kills herself with a shotgun. In her suicide note, she writes that she has "done it for Kurt."

* * *

A month after Kurt's death, police had told Grant that Courtney's Seattle attorney, Allen Draher, had identified the note as being in Kurt's handwriting. When Grant informed Rosemary Carroll of this development at the time, she responded, "Allen Draher didn't know Kurt at all." By this time, the SPD had already turned the note over to the Washington State Patrol crime laboratory, where it was analyzed by a forensic document examiner, Janis Parker. The police then asked Courtney for a sample of Kurt's handwriting with which to compare the writing on the note. She turned over a three-page note, written on Rome's Excelsior Hotel stationery, that she claimed Kurt had written to her in Rome before his March overdose—the so-called Rome suicide note.

"That just boggles my mind," says Grant. "Instead of asking his lawyers for a copy of a document known to be written by Kurt, they went and asked Courtney for a letter. How did they know Kurt wrote the letter she gave them? What if she wrote both letters? The thought never even seems to have occurred to them. But ever since Rosemary Carroll showed me the sheet of paper from Courtney's backpack where somebody had been practicing different handwriting styles, it certainly occurred to me."

The state forensic examiner sent back a report on April 22 stating that she was satisfied the note had been written by Kurt Cobain. She did not address the discrepancy in the handwriting of the first and last four lines. Three years later, in February 1997, NBC's *Unsolved Mysteries* hired two of the world's most prominent handwriting analysts to conduct their own analyses. This time, the producers supplied the experts with a copy of Kurt's handwriting *known* to be authentic—song lyrics he had written that were reproduced in his official biography, *Come as You Are*.

The first expert was Marcel Matley, an American forensic examiner. Matley had attained national recognition in 1995 when he sat on a commission that determined the authenticity of the suicide note written by President Clinton's former White House deputy counsel, Vince Foster, who had been found dead under suspicious circumstances in a suburban Virginia park in July 1993.

After completing his analysis of Kurt's note, Matley concluded, "The last four lines of the suicide letter, which include the words 'I love you, I love you,' were written by a different person. There are differences in the two."

The second expert consulted was Reginald Alton, a don at Oxford University, who is considered the world's foremost authenticator of literary manuscripts. He concurred with Matley: "There are more than a dozen discrepancies in the handwriting, definitely in the first line [where the word *Boddah* appears to have been added], and in the last four lines." Both experts agreed that the text in the main body of the letter was written by Kurt.

As Grant's suspicions about Courtney intensified, he asked himself what she would have stood to gain by Kurt's death. "As a police detective, I was always trained to look for the motive," he explains. "She had already told me that Kurt wanted a divorce and that they had a prenuptial agreement. But she also told me something else. During one of our earliest conversations, she basically admitted to

me that Kurt was worth more to her dead than alive." He plays a
tape of this conversation, recorded on April 3, 1994.

On the tape, Courtney tells Grant that around the time of
Kurt's coma in Rome, her ambition was to become the first female
musician to receive a million-dollar music publishing deal. She
says that she can always gauge her career by how much money she
was being offered by record companies. For example, she tells
Grant, before the *Vanity Fair* controversy, she had been receiving
$500,000 offers but, after *Vanity Fair*, she was only getting $50,000
offers. So, after Kurt's coma, Courtney called her entertainment
lawyer and said, "I bet the offers fell off after the coma." On the
contrary, her lawyer replied. In fact, the offers had doubled. When
Courtney asked why, the lawyer told her it's because everybody
thinks "you're going to outlive him." At first, Courtney says, she
thought this idea was "morbid and sexist," but then she realized
that she didn't care. "Go for it," she told the lawyer. "Try to get two
million dollars."

* * *

On November 20, in Niagara Falls, Ontario, an unnamed seventeen-
year-old male hangs himself in his basement bedroom. The day after his
funeral, his nineteen-year-old best friend hangs himself from a tree in the
park. The suicides are described in the media as Cobain-related. Both boys
were devotees of Nirvana; the mother of one blames "death music" for the
suicides.

Two weeks later, a twenty-year-old Californian named Lyle Senac,
jokingly emulating Kurt's suicide, accidentally kills himself in front of his
friends by propping a 12-gauge shotgun on the floor, then kneeling with
his mouth over the barrel. Eventually, there would be sixty-eight docu-
mented cases of Cobain copycat suicides worldwide. The real figure is likely

in the hundreds, since most suicides don't leave a note. Because it's not an intended suicide, Senac's death doesn't count in those statistics.

* * *

By December 1994, eight months after Kurt's death, Grant is finally ready to go public with his suspicions and chooses a national forum to do so. Appearing on the *Gil Gross Show*, broadcast over the CBS radio network throughout the United States, he states his belief that Kurt Cobain was murdered. The Seattle police, he says, are not guilty of a cover-up, only a rush to judgment. He refuses to disclose the name of the person he believes committed the crime.

"I felt I had to go public," Grant recalls. "All the copycat suicides were starting to haunt me, all these kids killing themselves because they thought that's what Kurt did. At first, I thought the best strategy would be to avoid naming names. I assumed the media would be less nervous." Nevertheless, within days, he receives a letter from Rosemary Carroll's firm accusing him of airing his "baseless" allegations for the sake of "personal profit and notoriety," and warning him to cease and desist with his charges or the firm would refer the "matter to the authorities for possible criminal prosecution."

"That made me mad," Grant recalls. "Rosemary knows that she was the one who first said Kurt was murdered and who encouraged me to pursue the investigation. Now here she was threatening me with legal action if I went public. I thought that was very cowardly of her." His response, dated December 29, 1994, is blistering:

Dear Rosemary:
Having received the letter from your firm threatening me with lawsuit and possible criminal prosecution, I have to wonder what

must be going on in your head! My loyalty to you and the confidentiality of our conversations ends abruptly when I am threatened for doing a job I was encouraged by you to do.

From the beginning, you played a major role in directing this investigation and exposing some facts and details that implicated Courtney as part of the conspiracy that eventually led to Kurt's murder. I'm convinced you know in your heart the truth about what happened. It's time for you to come forward and speak to the authorities about what you know.

I'm aware there's lots at stake here for you. Your career, your marriage, possible financial losses and who knows what else? You may not realize it yet, but these things are in jeopardy whether you come forward or not.

You impressed me as the type of person who has their priorities in order. What good are we as human beings if we're so afraid that we allow people to get away with murder?

The world of secrecy is a dangerous place to live, especially when your mind holds information that could help convict a killer. I've placed my life in danger here in order to bring about justice and put an end to what may turn out to be more than just one killing. In addition, kids are continuing to commit suicides themselves, thinking Kurt did it so it must be the way to go! The last of these incidents occurred just a couple of weeks ago.

Although I'm still in some danger, I feel my silence would have created an even greater threat to my life. Getting rid of someone *after* they talked is just plain stupid and can only bring more attention to the case. The real danger exists *before* the person talks.

I think I've given you something to think about. Call me if I can help. If you choose to oppose me in this, all I can say is good luck. You'll need it.

Sincerely,
Tom Grant

Carroll never responded.

A week later, on January 5, 1995, Grant takes to the radio airwaves again, this time on the nationally syndicated *Tom Leykis Show*, where he outlines his case in detail for more than an hour. It is during this appearance that Grant publicly airs the heart of his theory for the first time, charging Courtney Love and Michael "Cali" Dewitt were involved in a criminal conspiracy that resulted in the murder of Kurt Cobain.

After Grant drops this bombshell, Leykis opens the phone lines to listeners. One of the first callers happens to be Gary Dewitt, Cali's father, who is understandably outraged:

GARY DEWITT "I can't believe that this guy's going to make a huge score for absolutely no reason at all. Kurt Cobain killed himself. Period."

LEYKIS "So, you believe our guest is out only to make a buck?"

DEWITT "Of course. . . . He's out for the big score. There's a lot of money in it."

LEYKIS "Have you seen any of the evidence to prove that what the police said, that this is a suicide, is true? Have you seen the evidence?"

DEWITT "No, but I've known Courtney about five years and Mike is my son, and believe me, neither one of them is capable of something like that . . . and when I heard this on the radio, I couldn't believe it, so I called Sergeant Cameron at the Seattle police, and they're treating this guy like a nut."

LEYKIS "Let me ask you a question. Is it possible that cops don't like P.I.s messing in their business? Is that possible?"

DEWITT "Naw. That's movie stuff."

After the show, Courtney leaves a message on Grant's answering machine at 4:00 A.M.: "Hi, Tom. This is Courtney. . . . I just heard the radio thing. . . . I haven't heard you tell an out, ya know, I lis-

tened to the thing and didn't hear you tell, tell like outright lies. . . .
I wish you were doing it for the money, and the realization that you're doing it because you think it's right hurts me a lot."

Two weeks later, Grant receives another call from Courtney, who has just begun a tour of Australia and New Zealand. Her tone is more pained than angry:

COURTNEY "If this is in your fucking head, I'll do anything to get it out of your head. . . . I don't think you're crazy, just a little bit paranoid. . . . People would kill me if they knew I was calling you."

GRANT "I'm after the truth."

COURTNEY "That's why I fucking called you. I'll do anything I can do to get you not to think this. This is nutty and not true. I'd like for you to have every piece of evidence to prove that I had nothing to do with it."

Grant asks her for a copy of the autopsy report, explaining that only the postmortem records can prove that Kurt committed suicide. Courtney's response is unexpected: "I spoke to Nikolas [the deputy medical examiner] the other night. . . . He said he'd come over to my house when I get back. He's angry at you. He won't give you the records. . . . As long as Nikolas is the coroner, I'm not afraid."

The Nikolas in question was Dr. Nikolas Hartshorne, the deputy medical examiner who conducted the autopsy in April and ruled Kurt's death a suicide. In late 1995, when we were researching our first book, a source close to Hartshorne told us that, while he was still in college, he had befriended Courtney Love and her first husband, James Moreland. He met Moreland while he was still in medical school when, as a punk rock promoter, Hartshorne organized Nirvana's third-ever Seattle show, at the Central Tavern in 1988. This means the bill that night featured not just one but both of

Courtney's future husbands, since the headliner just happened to be Moreland's band, the Leaving Trains.

We decided to pursue this lead and, posing as Canadian university students who were doing a paper on the Kurt Cobain copycat suicide phenomenon, contacted Hartshorne for an interview. He agreed to meet with us at his office in December 1995.

During our interview, Hartshorne confirmed that he had been friends with both James Moreland and Courtney Love, whom he described as a "great girl." When we asked him if his friendship with Courtney might have constituted a conflict of interest in the investigation of her husband's death, Hartshorne replied, "Absolutely not."

He then confirmed that he had determined Kurt's death was a "textbook case of suicide" when he first arrived on the scene and admitted that the police never seriously contemplated the possibility of murder at all. He described Tom Grant's theory as "ludicrous."

"They [the homicide unit] came to the scene because of the popularity of the individual," he told us. "I mean, Elvis is still walking around out there, and when you have somebody this prominent, you like to get the best people in there to make sure all your *i*'s are dotted and *t*'s are crossed. Look at all the people who think it's a conspiracy. If they hadn't done all this work, you would have many more people mucking about saying it's murder." Hartshorne paused for a moment, and we couldn't help noticing the huge Kurt Cobain poster looming over us from its spot on the wall. We were in the very room where Hartshorne had conducted Kurt's autopsy a year earlier.

"The suicide was [Kurt's] decision," he continues, "and you have to respect him for whatever his decision was. He had that right."

Now, in the New Zealand phone call, Courtney continues telling Grant about her recent conversation with Hartshorne: "I asked Nikolas if there was doubt in his mind whether this is a suicide, and he said, 'I've seen people fake suicides before, and this isn't one of them.' "

She then tells Grant that she is "having dinner at Nikolas's house" when she returns to Seattle on February 16 and she will ask for the autopsy records then.

A month before this conversation took place, Courtney had given an interview to *Rolling Stone* magazine in which she claimed that Kurt had left her another, hitherto unmentioned letter before he died:

> It's kind of long. I put it in a safe-deposit box. I might show it to Frances—maybe. It's very fucked-up writing. 'You know I love you, I love Frances, I'm so sorry. Please don't follow me.' It's long because he repeats himself. 'I'm sorry, I'm sorry, I'm sorry. I'll be there, I'll protect you. I don't know where I'm going. I just can't be here anymore.'

Grant was intrigued, not least because the note appeared to confirm that Kurt was not planning to kill himself at all, but rather was leaving Courtney. Her cooperation on the autopsy report promised, Grant takes the opportunity to ask her about the second note.

GRANT "What about the other note? You mentioned in *Rolling Stone* about another note that he wrote to you."

COURTNEY "It's like a letter and it's not really, like, a suicide note. It's like, it seems more like, it was, like, in a sealed envelope, and it was just, like, to me, and it seems like he wrote it in rehab."

GRANT "Where'd you find it?"

COURTNEY "It was in my bedroom, under my pillows."

GRANT "Under your pillows?"

COURTNEY "Yeah, and I didn't tell anybody about it but Rosemary, and I told Sergeant Cameron about it; I let him see it."

GRANT "There's only one problem with that, Courtney."

COURTNEY "What's that?"

GRANT "I looked under your pillows."

COURTNEY "Well, uh . . ."

GRANT "Just like we looked under your mattress."

COURTNEY "It was there."

GRANT "That's how I found the Rohypnol, between your mattresses. That note wasn't under the pillows on the bed."

COURTNEY "Tom, it was, and I showed it to Sergeant Cameron, and he can prove it. I own it. I'll show it to you. Whatever you— if you want to see it."

GRANT "Yeah, I'd like to see it. I'd like to see it. But what I'm telling you is, it was not there the night before the body was found, or the night before that. Because we, you know, you can ask Dylan about this, we picked the pillows up. We were looking for drugs. We looked under the mattresses. That's where the Rohypnol was. There was no note in an envelope."

In the same December 15 *Rolling Stone* interview, Courtney claimed that in his so-called Rome suicide note, Kurt had written, "You don't love me anymore. I'd rather die than go through a divorce." Grant asks her about this note.

COURTNEY "It's not very nice. It's mean to me."

GRANT "Did it say anything suicidal?"

COURTNEY "It says something definitely suicidal on the first page. It said—it's mean to me—it says, like, 'Dr. Baker says I have to choose between life and death. I'm choosing death.' That's a quote on the note."

Grant is clearly shaken by this revelation. Courtney has repeatedly told friends and journalists that Kurt left a suicide note in Rome. This is how most people have come to the conclusion that his suicide in Seattle was merely a successful second attempt after the first failed attempt in Rome. But this passage about Dr. Baker, a psychiatrist who treated him at Canyon Ranch, clearly refers to Kurt's decision to continue using drugs rather than revealing an intention to kill himself. Dr. Baker had told Kurt that he had to stop using heroin or it would eventually kill him. In the note, Kurt appears to be saying he has chosen to continue his drug use rather than stating an intention to kill himself. Is this all there was to the so-called Rome suicide note?

Grant asks her if this is the only thing Kurt wrote about suicide in his Rome note, remembering that Courtney already told him on April 3 that in the note, "Kurt says he's leaving me."

COURTNEY "It talked about wanting to die rather than going through a divorce."

GRANT "Do you still have the note?"

COURTNEY "No, I burned it."

GRANT "You burned it?"

COURTNEY "When he gave it back to me the day after Kristen died, Sergeant Cameron advised me, 'This will never do you any good, or your family,' so I burned it."

GRANT "Why would somebody tell you to get rid of that?"

COURTNEY "Because it wasn't really nice. It talked about getting a divorce."

At this point in the conversation, Courtney goes off on a tangent about the blood at the scene when Kurt's body was found.

COURTNEY "One thing that bothered me when I went up there— because I don't think [Kurt died] on the third for two reasons, because when I went in the room . . . I laid in that blood, there was only one clump of it. You know that photograph they ran on the cover of the [*Seattle*] *Times?* Well, the way Kurt's laying, where the feet is, that's where the blood was."

GRANT "That doesn't make any sense either. How could there be blood at his feet and not at his head?"

COURTNEY "Somebody wrote something on the Internet about 'arcing blood.' . . . The only thing that bugs me is why is his blood where his feet are?"

GRANT "That's not the only thing that bugs me."

COURTNEY "Why is his blood where his feet are? Why is that the only place where there's blood?"

GRANT "I've never heard that before from anybody."

COURTNEY "That's where it was, Tom. You saw it. You were with me, I think. It's all a fucking hallucination. Weren't you there?"

In retrospect, Grant believes she was trying to plant a red herring to lead him down the wrong path: "I think Courtney wanted me to start talking publicly about the blood, about all kinds of garbage that can be easily disproved, so that I would ruin my credibility the way this guy on public access has done." He is referring to a Seattle man named Richard Lee, who has hosted a weekly cable public access TV show called *Kurt Cobain Was Murdered* since April 1994. Lee has been widely derided as a "crackpot" for his own bizarre theory, which suggests that Courtney murdered her husband, and the crime was then covered up by Geffen Records and the city of Seattle. One of Lee's central arguments is the lack of blood at the scene when Kurt's body was found.

Grant ignores Courtney's questions about the blood and tells her that if she really wants to allay his concerns, she can take a polygraph exam and ask Michael "Cali" Dewitt to take one as well:

COURTNEY "[Cali's] fucked me over. I know that in your job, paranoia is reality, but in my world, paranoia is also reality. . . . I believe you when you tell me that [Cali] knows something. I truly believe that in my heart. I know he does, you know he does, and

I don't know what the hell it is, but I think he might have heard the gunshot is what I think . . . that's what my gut instinct tells me . . . I think he heard the gunshot."

GRANT "Would Mike be willing to come down and take a polygraph?"

COURTNEY "For you?"

GRANT "Courtney, here's the bottom line. The truth is really easy to get to. I'm just after the truth. If Cali can get down here and take a polygraph, we can clear this up before it goes any further. Let's get him down here and get a polygraph done, and then he's off the hook."

COURTNEY "You think [Kurt] was forced down or something. He only had about sixty or eighty dollars' worth of heroin in his body [when he was found dead]."

GRANT "Well, here's what can bring this to a real quick end and solve all your problems. If I have a copy of the coroner's report and if Cali comes down for a polygraph, this thing will be brought to a real quick end. It's as simple as that."

COURTNEY "I'll do a bloody polygraph for you, if you keep it secret. I don't know why—I love him so much."

GRANT "You love who?"

COURTNEY "My husband. I love Cali, too, by the way."

GRANT "That's why we can help Cali. If we can get Cali cleared through a polygraph, then he's out of it, and believe me, then I'm going to start looking like a fool and nobody's going to pay any attention to me anymore."

COURTNEY "He's with my daughter right now. I want him to be able to stay up there and not deal with this right now. I'm not going to turn around and call him at home and say 'go to Tom Grant's office.' . . . I don't think Cali is lying, because he's my friend. I hired him and I also pay him a lot of money, and he's one of my best friends, so I don't think he would lie to me, but he *might* be lying to me."

Grant believes her next statement indicates that she is getting ready to let Cali take the fall for her if things start to sour, if the police start to close in on the truth:

COURTNEY "Mike was bad. I found [heroin] spoons in his room. He watched my child sometimes when he was on drugs, and Kurt was furious; he was firing Mike because he kept doing drugs. Kurt liked to have notes when he talked to someone, and I have a note he wrote, it's pretty lengthy, it's all the reasons why Cali can't be our nanny anymore because he's continuing to do drugs, and yada yada. . . ."

Grant pinpoints this conversation as especially significant: "I think she was trying to get it into my mind that maybe Cali killed Kurt because Kurt was about to fire him," he explains. "She was planting Cali's motive in my mind."

* * *

In January 1995, an eleven-year-old boy from Ile d'Orléans, Quebec, is found hanged in the basement of his family home. At the boy's feet, his father finds a note reading, "I'm killing myself for Kurt." In the obituary, his mother pleads for other children not to listen to the "negative music" of Nirvana.

* * *

Nearly nine years have passed since Grant first publicly accused Michael "Cali" Dewitt of engaging in a conspiracy with Courtney Love to kill her husband. In 1995, we challenged Grant to show us any evidence at all pointing to Cali's involvement. Why was he accusing Cali rather than Dylan Carlson of playing a part in the conspiracy? we demanded. After all, it was Dylan who bought the shotgun and who apparently lied about the greenhouse.

"No, I ruled out Dylan as an accomplice early on," explains Grant. "When I was going around Seattle with him looking for Kurt, he kept saying how he didn't understand why Kurt married Courtney: he was bad-mouthing her. And after Kurt died, he repeatedly said his friend wasn't suicidal. It wouldn't make any sense if he was involved. I reached a conclusion that Dylan was being used by Courtney, but that he wasn't part of the planning."

Is Grant now ready to be more forthcoming about his reasons for citing Cali's involvement?

"The only thing I'm willing to say at this point is that there was a conspiracy between Courtney and Michael Dewitt, and there may be others involved," he responds. "Remember, I never said I can solve this whole case all by myself or single-handedly prove that Courtney or Cali killed Kurt. There's still some questions that need to be asked. That's where the police need to go around with a badge asking the questions. It's too easy to blow off a P.I. People can't get away with lying to the police so easily."

Neither Courtney nor Cali has ever responded to Grant's allegations, but Charles Cross's Courtney-authorized biography offers some dubious details about Cali's activities the week Kurt disappeared—details that appear at first glance to deflect suspicion from both Cali and Courtney. In this account, Cali is said to have wakened on the morning of Saturday, April 2, to find Kurt sitting on his bed. He claims he told Kurt to call Courtney and then drifted back to sleep, exhausted from a cocaine binge the night before. What follows is an account that stretches credulity: a description of Courtney's repeated calls to the house later that morning as she tries to locate Kurt.

Back at the Cobain house, the main phone rang every ten minutes but Cali was afraid to answer it, thinking it was Courtney.

When he finally answered, he told her he hadn't seen Kurt. Still fried from drugs, Cali thought Kurt's bedside visit was simply a dream.

Cross writes that two days later, Cali finally remembered that he had seen Kurt, and only then did he relay the news to Courtney. By the time Cross's book was published, Tom Grant had already publicly disclosed the fact that when she hired him, Courtney had inexplicably failed to tell him that Kurt had been spotted at the house on Saturday morning. This new account provides a convenient explanation as to why not.

The problem is that it is demonstrably false. Grant interviewed Cali in May 1994, and in this conversation, the nanny confirms that he informed Courtney about seeing Kurt on the very same day he saw him, Saturday, April 2. Grant also interviewed Eric Erlandson the same month, and in this conversation, Courtney's guitarist revealed that Cali told him he had seen Kurt on April 2 and informed Courtney about it that day. Moreover, Dylan Carlson told the *Seattle Times* on May 11 that he had received a call from Cali on April 2 saying he had seen Kurt and that Kurt was "acting weird." The account in Cross's book, therefore, has to be false. But where did it come from? Cross supplies no source. If it came from either Courtney or Cali, the implications are troubling.

Equally perplexing is another account in Cross's book about Cali's activities on April 7, the day before Kurt's body was discovered. According to this account, Cali had been staying at the apartment of his girlfriend Jennifer Adamson, because he was "afraid to be in the Cobain house." When Courtney found out about this on Thursday, Cross writes, she was "incensed," and she demanded Cali return to look for Kurt immediately. So that evening, Cali and Jennifer drove to the Lake Washington house with a friend, arriving at "dusk." They searched through the house, finding no sign of Kurt. This is when Cali jotted the note in which he accused Kurt of "being in the house without me noticing" and placed it on the stairs. Various media accounts, including Cross's book, have reported that the TV was on in the master bedroom, tuned to MTV with the sound off, suggesting that Kurt had been in the house watching TV. (This is apparently what Cali is referring to in his note.) However, when Grant and Dylan Carlson searched the house the night before and again on Thursday evening, they found the TV turned on in *Cali's* bedroom, not Kurt's.

Cross writes that after Cali, Jennifer and their friend, Bonnie Dillard, finished searching the house "with night falling," the trio, "with a great sigh of relief," got in the car and began to head down the driveway. As they were pulling away, Bonnie told Cali and Jennifer that she thought she had seen "something above the garage. . . . I just saw a shadow up there." But Jennifer reportedly believed her friend was simply being "superstitious," and so they didn't turn the car around to check the greenhouse.

It is an eerie story and makes for fascinating reading. Unfortunately, it could not have happened. According to the SPD reports we obtained, a Graytop taxi was dispatched to the Lake Washington house on April 7, arriving at approximately 4:00 P.M. The driver picked up a "white male in his 20s, 5'8–9", medium to thin build, some facial hair, and dark hair," and drove him to the airport. This description is clearly Cali's, as the SPD confirmed when they interviewed him a week later. Cali told police that he had indeed taken a taxi to the airport on the afternoon of Thursday, April 7, to catch a plane to Los Angeles because "Courtney accused him of hiding Kurt after he fled the hospital, so he flew to L.A. [on April 7] to tell her face-to-face that he wasn't." As a result, Cali—like Courtney—was in Los Angeles the day Kurt's body was discovered.

So if Cali left the house by taxi at 4:00 P.M. Thursday afternoon to go to the airport, it would have been impossible for him to have searched the house with Jennifer Adamson and her friend at dusk, "with night falling," that evening, written the note and placed it on the stairs, and then left the house in Adamson's car, as Cross describes in his account. According to the U.S. National Weather Service, the sun set that day at 7:47 P.M., almost four hours after Cali's departure for the airport.

Moreover, Cross writes that Courtney only learned on Thursday, April 7, that Cali wasn't staying at the house and that she was "incensed" when she learned that he had been staying at the apartment of his girlfriend Jennifer Adamson. This is why she allegedly sent him back to the house to search for Kurt on Thursday. Yet her Peninsula Hotel phone records prove that she had repeatedly called Cali at Jennifer Adamson's apartment many times that week, starting as early as Tuesday, April 5, suggesting that Courtney was already well aware Cali was no longer staying at the Lake Washington house. Another obvious fiction, but what does it mean?

Who is responsible for planting these falsehoods in Cross's biography? Clearly, somebody who wants the world to believe that Kurt was still alive, but preparing to die alone in the greenhouse, after Cali left the house for the last time.

Three years later, Courtney would award the construction company owned by Cali's father a very lucrative contract worth hundreds of thousands of dollars to renovate her Lake Washington house just before she put it up for sale. She had already secured a high-paying A & R job for Cali at Geffen Records.

Still, we have never seen a shred of convincing evidence proving that Michael Dewitt was involved in Kurt's death. When we confront him about this, Grant is evasive: "The only thing I'll say at this point is that this was a murder staged to look like a suicide. If I play my hand too early and reveal everything that I have before the police get involved, I suspect that evidence will suddenly disappear, stories will change and those involved will tidy up their trail."

8

Vernon Geberth believes there is a formula for getting away with murder.

"If you want to stage a murder to look like suicide, it helps to leave a suicide trail," explains the former commanding officer of the Bronx Homicide Task Force, who is considered America's leading expert on staged crime scenes. "That is, it helps to plant the idea in people's minds that the victim was already suicidal. That way, investigators will be predisposed to rule the death a suicide."

Geberth's words may or may not explain the unusual series of events that took place on March 18, 1994—roughly two weeks before Kurt died. On that day, police received a 911 call from Courtney stating that her husband had locked himself in a room with a gun and was threatening to kill himself.

When police arrived at the Lake Washington estate, they did indeed find Kurt locked in a room. However, according to the police report, when he opened the door, Kurt immediately told the officers that he had actually locked himself in "to keep away from Courtney." He insisted that he wasn't suicidal and he didn't want to hurt himself. And, contrary to what his wife had reported in her 911 call, he had no gun.

When the officers questioned Courtney about her phone call,

she was forced to admit that she "did not see him with a gun, and he did not say he was going to kill himself." When he had locked himself in the room and refused to open the door, she said, "knowing that he had access to guns, she contacted 911 for his safety and well-being." Just to be safe, the officers confiscated four guns from the house, a box of ammunition and a bottle of Kurt's stomach medication pills.

Two weeks later, of course, Courtney would file another false police report, the missing person's report in which she claimed to be Kurt's mother, Wendy O'Connor. Here, too, she mentioned guns and suicide, reporting that Kurt "bought a shotgun and may be suicidal."

Could these two false police reports have been an attempt to lay a "suicide trail"? If so, it was remarkably effective. In the SPD incident report, filed the day Kurt's body was found, the first officer on the scene described the death as a "suicide" and told homicide detectives that he was aware Cobain's "family had filed a missing person's report with SPD. The family's fear was that the victim was suicidal, and he had recently bought a shotgun."

Grant has absolutely no doubt about Courtney's intentions. "Of course she was trying to plant an official trail showing Kurt was suicidal before his death," Grant says. "Just look at her actions. She filed not one, but two false police reports less than two weeks before his death. Each mentioned suicide, each mentioned a gun. Why else would she do that? Why did she lie to the police? She did the same with me when she hired me. She kept telling me that he was suicidal, he had bought a shotgun and that 'everyone expects him to die.' The problem is that when I spoke to those who knew him best, they all told me the same thing: that he wasn't suicidal, and that he loved guns, so the fact that he bought a shotgun wasn't at all evidence that he planned to kill himself."

We found exactly the same thing when we spent a month in Seattle in December 1995. For more than a year, the media had been painting Kurt as a depressed, self-loathing, suicidal junkie who had finally succumbed to the demons that had been haunting him for years.

For weeks, we interviewed Seattle musicians, drug dealers and others who had inhabited the outer fringes of Kurt's world. Although some described him as "moody," "morose" or "antisocial," no one believed he was suicidal. Most agreed he was a changed man after Frances Bean was born. But how well did any of these people really know Kurt? Most were nodding acquaintances at best; some probably exaggerated their friendship. Nobody seemed particularly qualified to talk about Kurt's state of mind at the time of his death. As a result, we were determined to land an interview with the person who is said to have known Kurt best, his closest friend, Dylan Carlson. At the time, Ian Halperin was a professional musician. A former member of his band, Casio, a Bulgarian who had moved to Seattle a year earlier, told us he was friends with Dylan and could probably arrange a meeting.

They were getting together to jam over the weekend, and Casio promised that if we dropped by, he would introduce us. At the time, the twenty-six-year-old Dylan was the leader of Earth, a struggling Seattle "ambient metal" band, which had been signed to the Sub Pop label a few years earlier.

At the appointed time, we arrived at an address in Seattle's university district where the jam session was scheduled to take place. If Stephen King had ever written a novel about the grunge scene, he would have set it in this house—a three-story Gothic Victorian, which, from the outside, looked as if it had seen its share of ghosts. Inside, it didn't take us long to figure out that the house was a "shooting gallery"—a location where junkies come to buy heroin and shoot up. All over the house, strung-out addicts were plopped on couches and threadbare mattresses. We found Ian's musician friend Casio in the basement, banging away on a set of old Tama drums, while Dylan Carlson jammed along on a beat-up Fender guitar. A few minutes later, they took a break, and Casio introduced us as his friends from Montreal. To explain the video camera, we told Dylan that we were shooting a documentary on the decline of the Seattle scene. (At the time, we were indeed planning to produce a documentary.) We didn't mention Kurt Cobain or that we knew Dylan was his best friend. It was Dylan who eventually raised the subject. Once he did, he was all too willing to discuss his old friend and the circumstances behind Kurt's death. He talked to us at length that day and at a subsequent meeting.

They had met in Olympia a few years earlier, Dylan explained, and soon became the best of friends, even though they were very different in many ways. We asked him to give us an example.

"Well, for one thing, I'm a Republican. I was a big fan of [the elder] George Bush; I liked what he stood for. Kurt couldn't stand him. He really liked Clinton." Indeed, Kurt was widely credited with helping Clinton win the presidency in 1992 by convincing a generation of young Americans to vote for the sax-playing Democrat. Later, Chelsea Clinton was said to be a huge Nirvana fan.

After touching on Kurt's drug habit ("He didn't do as many drugs as people think"), Courtney Love ("I only met her the day before their wedding in Hawaii when I was the best man. . . . I always got along pretty well with Courtney. . . . She pays my rent sometimes. . . . She bailed me out of jail when I got arrested for drugs"), and his love for guns ("I can't stand that whole gun control crowd"), Dylan finally came around to the subject of Kurt's final days.

"You know, I'm the one who bought him the gun," he told us casually. When we ask why, he explains, "He had a robbery or something, and he said he needed it for protection. He wanted me to buy it because the cops had recently confiscated all his guns, and he was afraid they would take it away again if it was in his name. I think he was also kind of afraid of stalkers. His hero was John

Lennon, you know, and Mia [Seattle punk rocker Mia Zapata] was murdered the year before, so I guess he had his reasons."

Wasn't Kurt known to be suicidal? Hadn't he already attempted to kill himself in Rome the month before?

"At the time, Kurt definitely wasn't suicidal or I would never have bought the gun," he insists. "He was my best friend, so I would have known if Rome was a suicide. No way. A year earlier, I would have believed it because of the pain, but he wasn't talking like that anymore. He was making all kinds of plans for when he got back from rehab."

The comments echoed what Dylan had told a reporter from the *Seattle Post-Intelligencer* a week after Kurt's death: "Kurt was facing lots of pretty heavy things, but he was actually pretty upbeat. He was prepared to deal with things facing him. . . . Kurt just wanted to make music, and he didn't want to do the grind."

Dylan also told us that he and Kurt "used to go shooting together all the time, just targets and stuff. Kurt didn't like to hunt. We'd go into the woods and shoot at tin cans."

Kurt had told *Rolling Stone*'s David Fricke roughly the same thing a few months before his death: "I like guns. I just enjoy shooting them . . . when we go out into the woods, at a shooting range. It's not an official shooting range . . . there's a really big cliff so there's no chance of shooting over the cliff and hurting someone."

Kurt told Fricke that he didn't think it was dangerous to have guns in the house: "It's protection. I don't have bodyguards. There are people way less famous than I am, or Courtney, who have been stalked and murdered. Look, I'm not a very physical person. I wouldn't be able to stop an intruder who had a gun or a knife. . . . It's for protection reasons. And sometimes, it's fun to go out and shoot. . . . It's the only sport I have ever liked."

Yet despite Kurt's professed penchant for guns and his obsession with protecting his family, Courtney continuously cited his purchase of the shotgun as evidence that he was planning to kill himself during the week he was missing.

When Fricke interviewed Courtney for *Rolling Stone* in December 1994, he reminded her of his interview with Kurt a year earlier: "When I pointedly asked him about guns in our interview, he started talking about target practice."

Courtney responded: "He totally fucking lied to you. He never went shooting in his life. One time he said, 'I'm going shooting.' Yeah. Shooting what? He never even made it to the range."

Why Kurt had Dylan buy a gun for him on March 30, the day he left for rehab, is one of the enduring mysteries in the case. The shotgun Dylan purchased was a Remington Model 11 20-gauge, "set up for light load." Kurt had told Dylan that he was afraid of intruders and that there had recently been a number of trespassers on the grounds of his Lake Washington home. His choice of gun would seem to confirm this. Setting up a shotgun for light load is what gun dealers often recommend to their clients for home protection because a bullet shot in one room won't penetrate walls and endanger those on the other side. Moreover, it is clear that both Kurt and Courtney were indeed concerned about protecting their home from intruders during this period because they had just contracted Veca Electric to install a complete home security system. (It was an electrician from this company who discovered Kurt's body on April 8.)

But the best indication that Kurt had purchased the shotgun for protection rather than to kill himself is the fact that, when police found the gun, it had been loaded with three cartridges, including the one that killed him. Why would Kurt load three cartridges in the gun if he intended to shoot himself in the mouth? Surely one would do.

Yet by the time the police reports were made available, these and other arcane details of the case were deemed insignificant. After all, Kurt was said to have barricaded himself inside his room. What's more, as Courtney said, Kurt had already tried to kill himself in Rome a month earlier. He had even left a note, she said. Nobody had any reason to doubt her word.

* * *

To establish what really happened in Rome, it is crucial to distinguish between contemporary accounts and Courtney Love's more widely reported version of the events, published after Kurt's death.

We know for certain that the day after Nirvana's March 1 Munich concert, Kurt saw a doctor, who diagnosed him with bronchitis and recommended he take two months off from touring. The next day, March 3, Kurt flew to Rome, where he was meeting Courtney and Frances Bean, who were flying in from London. Kurt checked in to Suite 541 of Rome's five-star Excelsior Hotel to await their arrival. Around late afternoon, Courtney arrived at the hotel with Frances Bean and Cali Dewitt. Little is known about what happened during the interval, but sometime between 6:00 and 6:30 A.M. the next day the Excelsior front desk received a call from Courtney requesting an ambulance. When paramedics arrived, they found Kurt unconscious and rushed him to Rome's Umberto I Polyclinic hospital, where his stomach was pumped.

Twenty hours later, Kurt awoke at Rome's American Hospital, where he had been transferred at Courtney's request. The next day, his doctor, Osvaldo Galletta, held a press conference to announce that Kurt was recovering from a "pharmacological coma, due not to narcotics, but the combined effect of alcohol and tranquilizers that had been medically prescribed by a doctor." It wasn't until ANSA, Italy's national press agency, named the tranquilizers that people began to ask questions.

Kurt was reported to have mixed champagne with a prescription tranquilizer called Rohypnol. In Rome, this drug is most commonly known as a sedative or sleeping pill, so the disclosure didn't attract much attention. But in the United States, Rohypnol was already better known by its sinister nickname: "The Date Rape Drug." On university campuses in particular, the tranquilizer had become notorious for its use as an illicit means of sexual conquest. Dropped in someone's drink, the odorless pill dissolves quickly and can rapidly induce a blackout or decrease in resistance. On awakening, the victim is often unable to remember what happened. Police departments all over the United States were reporting women waking up naked in frat houses or unfamiliar surroundings, the victims of sexual assault while under the influence of the drug. In 1996 alone, the U.S. Drug Enforcement Agency reported more than a thousand such cases nationwide. According to the National Institute on Drug Abuse, Rohypnol, particularly when mixed with alcohol or other drugs, may lead to respiratory depression, aspiration and even death.

Could somebody have dropped an incapacitating dose of Rohypnol into Kurt's drink without his knowledge? That's exactly what Tom Grant speculates: "I think that Courtney mixed Rohypnol into Kurt's drink to induce an overdose. I firmly believe this was her first attempt to kill him."

Boosting Grant's theory, it was later reported that the Rohypnol was in fact Courtney's prescription, not Kurt's. After his death, the British music magazine *Select* reported that one of its journalists interviewed Courtney in her London hotel room on March 3, hours before she flew to Rome to join Kurt. One passage in the article seems eerily significant:

There is a box of Rohypnol on the big mahogany table in the middle of Courtney Love's London hotel room, among the scat-

tered papers and cigarette boxes. "Look, I know this is a controlled substance," she smiles as she empties one of those fizzy
stomach upset powders into a tumbler of water and washes back
a Rohypnol. "I got it from my doctor. It's like Valium."

After Kurt's death, when Courtney claimed for the first time that
Rome had been a failed suicide attempt, the tranquilizers figured
prominently in stories she told about the incident. According to
her version, she had "retrieved two empty blister packs of Rohypnol next to Kurt—he had taken sixty of the aspirin-size pills, indi-
vidually removing each from a plastic-and-foil container." She
later told *Rolling Stone,* "I can see how it happened. He took fifty
fucking pills."

Of course, if Kurt had really taken fifty or sixty Rohypnol pills, it
would prove that Rome was indeed a suicide attempt. However,
there is not a single witness who actually saw the empty Rohypnol
packets—not the paramedics, nor any hotel official. The media
and biographers have simply accepted Courtney's version of the
incident as the truth.

When we interviewed Dr. Osvaldo Galletta, the doctor who
treated Kurt after his overdose, he vehemently denied that Kurt
had taken the massive quantity of Rohypnol described by Courtney. Neither did he believe that Kurt's overdose was deliberate.
"We can usually tell a suicide attempt," he told us. "This didn't
look like one to me. He mixed tranquilizers and alcohol and when
you do that, you're playing with fire." After Kurt's death, Dr. Galletta told reporters, "The last image I have of him, which in the
light of the tragedy now seems pathetic, is of a young man playing
with the little girl [Frances]. He did not seem like a young man
who wanted to end it all."

Galletta's doubts and the absence of witnesses would all be irrelevant if Kurt really left a suicide note in Rome. And it appears to

have been Courtney's revelation about the note that convinced the press and public that Rome had been a suicide attempt. But, as we heard Courtney tell Grant, the letter Kurt left her doesn't appear to have been a suicide note at all, but a husband's declaration of independence from a wife he detests. In it, as Courtney confessed to Grant, Kurt wrote that he was leaving her: "It's not very nice. It's mean to me. . . . It wasn't really nice. It talked about getting a divorce." The one part of the note that might be reasonably construed as referring to suicide—where Kurt declares he is "choosing death"—is lifted entirely out of context.

Even members of the Seattle Police Department who saw the Rome letter didn't believe it was a suicide note. According to one SPD source who is critical of his department's investigation, "Love gave us another note which she said Kurt had written in Rome. She said it was a suicide note, but it wasn't. It was a rambling letter which was very unflattering to her. There are some veiled references which you'd have to stretch to conclude referred to suicide."

At the time of Kurt's Rome overdose, Geffen Records itself issued a statement declaring that Kurt's mixing of alcohol and tranquilizers "was definitely not a suicide attempt—it was strictly accidental." But perhaps the most significant public statement about the Rome incident may be that of Janet Billig, the spokesperson for Nirvana's management company, Gold Mountain. Billig told *Rolling Stone*—*after* Kurt's death—that she had talked to Kurt about the note in Rome and "Kurt insisted it was not a suicide note. He just took all of his and Courtney's money and was going to run away and disappear." This would appear to confirm what Courtney told Tom Grant on April 3, that in the note, Kurt "says he's leaving me." In light of this revelation, it is especially interesting to read what Courtney told *Select* magazine while Kurt was still in the Rome hospital recovering from his coma: "If he thinks he can get away from me that easily, he can forget it. I'll follow him through hell."

In Charles Cross's *Heavier Than Heaven*, Rosemary Carroll reveals a crucial piece of the chronological puzzle for the first time. She had already made it clear to Tom Grant that Kurt wanted a divorce from Courtney but had never told him precisely when Kurt first made his intentions known. Cross supplies the missing data: on March 1 in Munich shortly before going on stage for his last concert, and two days before he met up with Courtney in Rome.

Backstage, he phoned Courtney and their conversation ended in a fight, as had all their talks over the past week. Kurt then called Rosemary Carroll and told her he wanted a divorce.

Within sixty hours of this telephone call, we know that Kurt flew to Rome, wrote a three-page letter to Courtney declaring he was leaving her and fell into a coma after ingesting the date rape drug, Rohypnol. Yet when Courtney described their encounter to *Rolling Stone*, she painted a romantic scenario:

Kurt had gone all out for me when I got there [Rome]. He'd gotten me roses. He'd gotten a piece of the Colosseum, because he knows I love Roman history. I had some champagne, took a Valium, we made out, I fell asleep.

The story teems with contradictions, yet one thing in particular has always troubled us. If, as Grant claims, Courtney intended to kill Kurt in Rome, why did she call an ambulance after she found him unconscious, thereby saving his life? Why didn't she simply leave him to die? In fact, we have always cited her actions in Rome as one of the primary flaws in Grant's murder theory. And, while it doesn't disprove the fact that Kurt was murdered, it appeared to exonerate Courtney herself in the crime.

We are certain that Grant has no hard evidence to back up his serious allegation that Rome was an attempt by Courtney to murder her husband, and we criticized him in our first book for making this unsubstantiated allegation. In response, he offered a number of questionable theories. Maybe she realized too late that Kurt hadn't ingested enough Rohypnol to kill him, Grant speculated, and she wanted to make herself look good by appearing to save his life. But in the years since we first aired our doubts, some additional information has surfaced, causing us to rethink our initial skepticism.

The first and most serious disclosure comes from Courtney herself. Umberto I Polyclinic hospital has confirmed that Kurt arrived by ambulance at approximately 7:00 A.M., at which point doctors immediately pumped out his stomach. This timeline would seem to correspond with the Excelsior Hotel's statement that the front desk received a call from Courtney's room shortly before 6:30 A.M. requesting an ambulance. Yet eight months later, Courtney told David Fricke of *Rolling Stone* how she had found Kurt unconscious some *two to three hours* before she called for an ambulance:

> I turned over about 3 or 4 in the morning to make love, and he was gone. He was at the end of the bed with a thousand dollars in his pocket and a note saying, "You don't love me anymore. I'd rather die than go through a divorce". . . . I can see how it happened. He took 50 fucking pills.

Why did she wait for more than two hours before calling for an ambulance at 6:30 A.M.? Was she waiting to first make sure he was dead? Or was she simply misquoted by *Rolling Stone?* Here is the version she told *Spin* magazine:

> And so we ordered champagne, 'cause Pat [Smear] was with us for a little while, and Kurt doesn't drink, and then we put Frances to bed. And we started making out, and we fell asleep. He must

have woken up and started writing me a letter about how he felt rejected. But I'm not sure I believe that because he wasn't rejected. We both fell asleep. Anyway, I woke up at, like, four in the morning to reach for him, basically to go fuck him, 'cause I hadn't seen him in so long. And he wasn't there. And I always get alarmed when Kurt's not there, 'cause I figure he's in the corner somewhere, doing something bad. And he's on the floor, and he's dead. There's blood coming out of his nostril. And he's fully dressed. He's in a corduroy coat, and he's got 1,000 American dollars clutched in one hand, which was gray, and a note in the other.

Here she confirms that she not only discovered him at 4:00 in the morning, but also thought he was "dead."

When the ambulance transported Kurt to the hospital some two to three hours later, Courtney rode in the back with her husband. When they arrived at the hospital just before 7:00 A.M., the famed Italian paparazzo Massimo Sestini, tipped off about their arrival, was waiting to snap photos when the ambulance doors swung open. His widely published photo shows Courtney in full makeup. Many who have seen this photo are struck by the fact that, although her husband was dying, she had the presence of mind to apply her makeup before the ambulance arrived.

Various media accounts have described Kurt's first request upon awaking from his coma: a strawberry milk shake. Only Charles Cross records Kurt's first actions. His mouth still full of tubes, he took a pencil and a notepad and scribbled a note to Courtney, who was waiting by his bedside. The first words he wrote were "Fuck You." Then he demanded the tubes be removed from his mouth and asked for the milk shake. Presumably, only Courtney knows the significance of Kurt's angry gesture.

Cross's *Heavier Than Heaven* provides another intriguing detail

206 about the incident in Rome. Sometime that morning, "a female identifying herself as Courtney had left a message with the [head of Geffen Records] saying Kurt was dead." This call was apparently why some American media outlets, including CNN, wrongly reported that Kurt had died. After an hour of panic and grief at Geffen, Cross reports, "it was discovered the caller was an impersonator." Who discovered this? And more disturbingly, how did they know it wasn't really Courtney who called? Did she simply deny it later on? Or by that time, had they learned Kurt was still alive and, thus, assumed the call was a hoax? Geffen won't say, and Cross provides no source for this revelation.

If the caller was Courtney, it shows she initially believed Kurt was dead, and therefore may have called the ambulance under the false impression that she had already succeeded in killing her husband. After all, Courtney herself later told a reporter that she thought Kurt was dead. However, this is pure conjecture and is far from convincing evidence that she attempted to murder Kurt in Rome.

Unless a more convincing explanation surfaces, her call for the ambulance may be the most compelling indication that Courtney is innocent of the terrible accusation that has been publicly leveled against her for nearly a decade.

* * *

For years, the murder theorists have argued that Kurt was never suicidal but was only pinned with the label by Courtney after his death. However, Kurt's own statements suggest he had at least toyed with the idea at certain times in his life. Indeed, it was Kurt, not Courtney, who in 1993 gave *Rolling Stone* reporter Michael Azerrad the following explanation as to why he started using heroin:

I was determined to get a habit. I *wanted* to. I said, "This is the only thing that's saving me from blowing my head off right now."

In another interview with *Rolling Stone* a year later, he provides an equally prescient quote:

For five years during the time I had my stomach problem, yeah, I wanted to kill myself every day. I came close many times. I'm sorry to be so blunt about it. It was to the point where I was on tour, lying on the floor, vomiting air because I couldn't hold down water.

However, it was in this very interview, published less than three months before his death, that Kurt declares, "I have never been happier in my life" because "my stomach isn't bothering me anymore."

The oft-cited fact that Kurt had originally titled Nirvana's last album *I Hate Myself and I Want to Die* would also seem to suggest that suicide wasn't far from Kurt's mind during this period. Only after pressure from his label did Kurt consent to change the title to *In Utero*. When we asked Dylan Carlson how he could say Kurt wasn't suicidal, given the sheer volume of such references over the years, he shrugged. "That was all just a joke," he said. "Kurt said so himself. And when he talked about blowing his brains out, anybody who knew him knew that was just how he talked when he described the pain. I don't think he meant it literally. It was an expression he used."

A few months before Kurt died, *Rolling Stone* reporter David Fricke asked him how literally he meant the title *I Hate Myself and I Want to Die*:

As literal as a joke can be. Nothing more than a joke. And that had a bit to do with why we decided to take it off. We knew people wouldn't get it; they'd take it too seriously. It was totally satirical, making fun of ourselves. I'm thought of as this pissy, complaining, freaked-out schizophrenic who wants to kill himself all the time. . . . And I thought it was a funny title. . . . But I knew the majority of the people wouldn't understand it.

Does this explain why so many of Kurt's close friends and associates insisted *after* his death that Kurt wasn't suicidal, even though he had frequently made statements that could reasonably be interpreted otherwise?

"The thing you have to remember about all the talk of Kurt being suicidal," explains his Seattle drug buddy Peter Cleary, "is that all the talk only started when Courtney came out after the death and said Rome was a suicide attempt and the media picked up on all her examples of Kurt being suicidal. That's when all these people started saying, 'Of course he was suicidal, just listen to his music.' But that's a bunch of crap. Sure he was a moody guy and got depressed quite often. That applies to a hell of a lot of people, including me. But nobody ever talked about Kurt being suicidal before he died. Nobody. Why do you think everybody who knew him was so surprised when Courtney said that Rome was a suicide attempt? I've read all this ignorant bullshit in the media pointing to the fact that Kurt wanted to call *In Utero* '*I Hate Myself and I Want to Die.*' It was a joke, for chrissake. That was his warped sense of humor. He was the most sarcastic guy you'll ever meet. He was not suicidal, at least not when I knew him, and I knew him for the last year of his life."

Yet who is to say? Perhaps it is naive to dismiss Kurt's frequent references to suicide as gallows humor or the kind of banter rockers, and youth in general, have always indulged in to shake things up. Whether his death resulted from murder or suicide, it's hard to deny that Kurt was a troubled soul, and it's not outside the realm of possibility that, like many young Americans, he may have contemplated suicide at various times in his life.

One of Kurt's longtime friends, Seattle photographer Alice Wheeler, says she never knew Kurt to be suicidal. Unlike Peter Cleary, however, Wheeler firmly believes that Kurt killed himself. In fact, she says most of Kurt's circle concluded he was suicidal "in retrospect."

"I went to the wake at Krist's house after Kurt's memorial service," she recalls, "and there were all these people there trying to make sense of the whole suicide thing. Krist came up to me and asked, 'How could we have missed the signs, Alice?' And then he started analyzing Kurt's lyrics and replaying everything that he had ever said, and saying that it should have been obvious. He really felt guilty, I think."

Yet did the "signs" really point to suicide, or did they signify another momentous life decision? We know that Kurt had already told his lawyer on March 1 that he had decided to divorce his wife. Janet Billig, spokesperson for his management company, confirmed that he wrote a note to Courtney the same week announcing his intention to "run away and disappear." Krist later described this period to Kurt's biographer Charles Cross, explaining, "There was something going on with him in his personal life that was really troubling him. There was some kind of situation." Thus even his oldest friend was unable to pinpoint Kurt's emotional state as suicidal during his final weeks, sensing instead that something else was wrong.

After the Rome overdose, Dylan Carlson was the first of Kurt's friends to see him when he returned to Seattle. He later described Kurt's mood to the *Seattle Post-Intelligencer:* "Kurt was facing lots of pretty heavy things, but he was actually pretty upbeat. He was prepared to deal with things facing him."

After Kurt's death, his friend Mark Lanegan, leader of the

Screaming Trees, told *Rolling Stone*, "I never knew [Kurt] to be sui-cidal, I just knew that he was going through a really tough time."

Another of Kurt's friends, Seattle music photographer Charles Peterson, ran into him on the street "a week or a week and a half" before he died. Kurt's mood, Peterson recalls, was decidedly cheer-ful: "He seemed really happy to me, happier than I had seen him in a long time: not that he was usually unhappy, but he was often pretty sickly, and he looked like he was doing a lot better. My first book had just come out and he was really nice about it: I think he was sincerely pleased for me. He was wearing this heavy overcoat and sunglasses to appear incognito, but ironically, they just made him stand out even more. We went to the Linda Tavern and had a few beers, and he gave me his new phone number. There didn't seem to be anything wrong as far as I could tell."

Kurt's late grandmother, Iris Cobain, talked to him shortly be-fore he entered rehab at the end of March and told the *Seattle Times* that "everything seemed fine" and that "he seemed to be happy." The only thing Kurt told her about the Rome incident, she said, was that it was an accident. In this call, he made plans to go on a fishing trip with his grandfather in April.

A number of suicide studies have found that some people seem very happy and upbeat just before they commit suicide because they have made a decision and feel relief about it. Yet studies also show that these people rarely make long-term plans. Moreover, Kurt's mood does not appear to have suddenly shifted from de-pressed to upbeat only in the final days and weeks of his life. Rather, his friends insist the change in his personality happened months before his death, when his unbearable stomach ailment was finally diagnosed and treated. It was in fall 1993 that he told *Rolling Stone*, "I've never been happier in my life."

Did something happen between this interview and his departure from the Exodus rehab facility on April 1 to change his mood? Did his stomach ailment suddenly return? Could the intervention on

March 25 have triggered something dark in Kurt's personality? Was he especially depressed when he entered Exodus on March 30? In the two days Kurt spent at Exodus, he talked to several staff psychologists at the facility, none of whom considered him suicidal. Moreover, the last person to visit Kurt at Exodus on April 1, an old artist friend named Joe "Mama" Nitzburg, told *Rolling Stone:* "I was ready to see him looking like shit and depressed. He looked so fucking great."

In the weeks leading up to his death, then, it is clear that most of his friends, associates and even the mental health professionals who treated him did not believe Kurt was suicidal.

Now Tom Grant produces an astonishing taped conversation he recorded with Courtney in late April 1994, proving that she, too, believed Kurt wasn't suicidal after he returned from Rome.

COURTNEY "People with Ph.D.s saw him the day he left [rehab] and nobody, nobody expected that he would leave, let alone that he would be suicidal," she told Grant. "And I don't think that he was really suicidal when he came home. But whoever he was with drove him to it."

This remarkable admission stands in stark contrast to what Courtney publicly told the media for months after Kurt's death about her husband's suicidal tendencies as well as what she told Seattle police on April 4 when she filed the missing person's report. It also directly contradicts what she told Tom Grant on April 3, when she first hired him to find her husband: "He's suicidal. . . . Everybody expects him to die."

* * *

By the time Courtney approached Charles Cross in 1999, it was clear that Tom Grant's murder theory wasn't going to go away. Although he was once mocked as a conspiracy theorist, Grant's website was now receiving more than a million hits a year. Nick Broomfield's BBC film about the case, moreover, had become one of the highest grossing documentaries of all time. Grant was beginning to attract the attention of mainstream media, and many credible journalists appeared to believe for the first time that there might be something to his charges. Gene Siskel himself gave Broomfield's film a "thumbs down" because, he complained, the film hadn't explored the possibility of murder as deeply as it should have and had left many leads unpursued. Worse still, the murder theory was beginning to take a toll on Courtney's bottom line. Hole's 1998 album, *Celebrity Skin,* had been widely expected to be one of the year's top sellers. Instead, it was a massive sales disappointment. Many attributed its relative failure to the thousands of Cobain fans who vowed in Internet chat rooms to boycott the album. Something had to be done.

Charles Cross was the longtime editor of the respected Seattle music weekly *The Rocket,* one of the first publications to cover Nirvana in its pages. Cross was not necessarily a friend of Courtney's, but they had known each other for years and got along well. By the time Courtney approached him, he had already decided to write a Cobain biography, but he wasn't having much luck finding a publisher. That changed when Courtney made him an offer he couldn't refuse. Kurt had kept a journal for years, and she was now offering Cross the exclusive right to read the journal and quote from it in his book. The terms of their agreement, if any, have never been disclosed, and the book is not officially described as an "authorized biography." But when it was released in the fall of 2001, many readers were immediately struck by how carefully the book conformed to Courtney's version of events. One reviewer at Amazon.com even wrote that the publisher "should have put Courtney as the author."

Indeed, the book contains scores of facts about Kurt's death that

Cross could have obtained only from Courtney herself. Although he doesn't once mention Grant's murder theory, it is almost as if the book is addressing and refuting each of Grant's allegations in turn. This would be a welcome contribution to the debate if Cross acknowledged this as his intention, but he doesn't. Instead, his book is a neat compendium of unsourced anecdotes that just happen to contradict Grant's version of events. Unfortunately, many of these anecdotes are demonstrably false. The most glaring example concerns the events of April 7, when Cali is said to be searching the house for Kurt at dusk, even though police reports prove he took a taxi to the airport at 4:00 P.M. that day to join Courtney in Los Angeles. Similarly, Courtney is exonerated for her failure to tell Grant that Kurt had been seen at the house on April 2 because the man who saw him there first thought it was a "dream."

Although Courtney's version of events is tirelessly replayed throughout the book, the most egregious example of slavishness has to be in the final chapter, when Cross describes Kurt's death. Here Cross takes Courtney's suicide-obsessed portrayal of her husband and runs with it, creating for Kurt a near–Norma Desmond moment:

> He lit a Camel Light and fell back on the bed with a legal-sized notepad propped on his chest and a fine-point red pen. The blank piece of paper briefly entranced him, but not because of writer's block: He had imagined these words for weeks, months, years, decades. He paused because even a legal-sized sheet seemed so small, so finite. . . . As he wrote, the illumination from MTV provided most of the light, since the sun was still rising. . . . He quietly walked down the nineteen steps and the wide staircase. He was within a few feet of Cali's room and he didn't want anyone catching sight of him. . . . Like a great movie director, he had planned this moment to the smallest detail, rehearsing this scene as both director and actor. . . .

More than one reviewer has asked how Cross could have possibly known what Kurt was thinking and doing in his final moments. Cross defended his narrative leap, insisting, "It's clear to anyone who's read the book to that point that I've done an incredible amount of research and that I'm not making things up out of thin air. I'm not creating evidence; I'm just taking evidence that I have discovered . . . and piecing it together to try to tell the story of those last few minutes."

Since Cross cites no evidence backing this account, it is a dubious explanation at best, and there is in fact evidence to contradict his description of Kurt's last moments. Cross, for example, describes Kurt picking up a "legal-sized notepad" on which to write his suicide note. In reality, however, the so-called suicide note was written on the back of an IHOP place mat, as Courtney confides to Tom Grant in one taped conversation. Police later photocopied the note on legal-sized paper, which probably accounts for Cross's error.

Still, Cross is a respected music journalist known for his integrity, and his book—a warts-and-all account filled with valuable insights into Kurt's childhood, life and career—is in many respects the best and most thorough biography ever written about the rock icon. Cross even discovered some important new evidence about Kurt's final weeks, revealing for the first time that Kurt announced his intention to divorce Courtney two days before the Rome overdose. According to Alice Wheeler, who was one of Cross's research assistants, it was Cross who first suggested to Courtney that she publish Kurt's journals as a book. Wheeler described Cross's relationship with Courtney as "tight." But there is no evidence that Cross simply did Courtney's bidding or wrote what she told him to. Instead, he appears to have accepted much of what she told him at face value, and allowed himself to be manipulated into writing an account that served Courtney's interests very well.

In 1995, Nine Inch Nails musician Trent Reznor, with whom

Courtney had a brief affair the year before, told *Details* magazine that she was a master at manipulating the press: "She was obsessed with the media and how she's perceived. What I didn't realize was that 95% of it was her directly calling editors. She's got a full media network going on."

This could in part explain why most media have refused to take an objective look at the facts, choosing instead to accept a one-sided version of events that simply does not stand up under scrutiny.

9

___

Leland Cobain had just dropped his bombshell. As hardened as we were by the clamor of evidence and opinion about this case, we were, quite simply, stunned. For years, the Cobain family had refused to talk publicly about Kurt's death, and there was never an intimation that any of his relatives had questioned the suicide verdict. Sheltering themselves from a prying press, they had remained silent for nearly a decade. Courtney's father, Hank Harrison, had long ago declared that Kurt was murdered, but his credibility was thought to be suspect and, more important, he had never actually met his son-in-law. Now here was the man said to have been closer to Kurt than his own parents, telling us he believed his grandson was the victim of foul play. We asked Leland how long he had harbored this suspicion.

"I knew it almost right from the start," he declared. "Something just didn't sit right with me about the description of that shotgun."

The news had come on the morning of Friday, April 8, with a call from Kurt's mother, Wendy. "She said she didn't want us turning on the TV and finding out about it," Leland recalled. "It nearly killed Iris, my wife. She couldn't even go to the memorial. I did, but she wouldn't go. Her and Kurt were very close."

A few days later, Leland saw a news report describing the scene where Kurt's body was found. When he heard the description of the body, he said, he knew immediately that his grandson had not killed himself: "They said that shotgun was laying on his chest. They'll never make me believe that you can take a shotgun and put it on your chest that way and then put it in your mouth and then pull the trigger, because once you do that, you can't hold that gun to pull the trigger. Once your arms are stretched out as far as they'll go to get the trigger, and [the gun] goes off, especially with it in his mouth, that thing will jump clear off his body. I've got a shotgun in there that if you don't hold it tight to your shoulder, it will knock you right on your butt."

He points to his gun collection, which includes a 12-gauge shotgun he uses for duck hunting. "The shotgun was still laying on his chest. I couldn't understand that; it didn't make sense. Anyone else I talked to who knows about guns said they couldn't understand that either. You know, there's a lot of *poof* that comes out of that shotgun, and especially when it's in his mouth, it's going to blow the shotgun back out of his mouth and off his chest."

A seasoned hunter, Leland considers himself something of an authority on the subject. His argument centers on the "kick" of Kurt's gun, yet Leland admits that he has never actually shot a 20-gauge Remington, the type of gun that killed Kurt. To test his theory, we decided to go to a range and test-fire a similar shotgun ourselves. The results were inconclusive. The 20-gauge is in fact considerably less powerful than the 12-gauge owned by Leland. Although it packs a definite kick when fired, it doesn't seem capable of knocking someone over the way a lower-gauge shotgun can. This is why the 20-gauge is popular with female hunters as well as with beginners. If Kurt had indeed committed suicide, would this gun have simply popped out of his mouth and come to rest vertically on his chest after he fired it, as the official scenario suggests?

It's possible, but not likely, says Denise Marshall, the Colorado deputy coroner: "I won't say it can't happen like that. I've seen many suicides with shotguns, and they usually brace it between their legs really well, and you won't really see it laying on the chest, but you'll see it wedged between their legs, and it will fall to one side or the other. I haven't seen the photos in this case, but from what I read in the police reports, it does sound like a staged scene."

In 1998, while we were promoting our first book, we appeared on a nationally syndicated radio show hosted by '70s rocker Ted Nugent. As a board member of the National Rifle Association since 1995, Nugent has become better known in recent years as a gun advocate than as a musician. He, too, was suspicious about the description of Kurt's gun.

"I'm one of the leading gun experts in this country, and I've read the police reports describing the gun evidence," Nugent told his audience. "I'm telling you right now that Kurt Cobain did not commit suicide. He was murdered." He did not elaborate on what led him to this conclusion.

If Kurt didn't commit suicide, what does Leland think happened?

"I think somebody murdered him. You know, he had just turned down a $9 million offer for the Lollapalooza deal. I honestly think Courtney had something to do with it. I might get myself in a lot of trouble for saying that. She must have had [something to do with it], because they had a prenuptial agreement where what she had was hers and what he had was his, and if they divorced, that's what they got. They didn't get anything of the other's. But if one of them died before, they got the other's stuff. So that's how Courtney got everything. I haven't heard how they figured it out for Frances, whether they put something in escrow for Frances, or what. They should have."

We ask Leland if he thinks Courtney herself committed the crime.

"No, no, I don't think she actually did it, but I think she *had* it done."

What makes him think Courtney is capable of such an act?

"Well, she's a manipulator, that's for sure. She wants things her way. She got Kurt hooked on drugs; he may have already done them before he met her, but she made sure he got hooked. She's capable of anything. . . . Why did she cremate his body so goddamned quick? By the time we went to that memorial service, he was already cremated. Kurt never asked to be cremated. I think they were getting rid of the evidence, that's what I think."

Leland reflects back to the weeks before Kurt's death and says that his grandson seemed very happy when they last spoke: "He was making all kinds of plans for the future. He said he wanted to come up and go fishing with me. We had never gone fishing before, but I had a boat back then, and we made plans to go fishing. I had been up to the house in Seattle before his last tour, when Iris was in the hospital up there. Kurt brought her that vase full of orchids when he went to visit her in the hospital." He points to a vase in the cupboard. "Then we went out to dinner, just me and him, and I had just bought myself a brand-new Ford pickup truck, a four-by-four. When we headed back to the house, it was dark and I let him drive. He really liked that truck. Then when I talked to him before he died, he said to me he wanted to come up and go fishing with me, and he was going to buy himself one of those Ford trucks that I had; he really liked it. He wanted to take me with him to buy a truck."

In the years since, Leland has thoroughly familiarized himself with the facts of the case, examining the police reports and other evidence. He says he's now more convinced than ever that Kurt was murdered.

"The toxicology tests said he was so loaded with heroin that he couldn't have even picked that shotgun up," he says. "There's a lot of other things that don't sit right. Kurt didn't do himself in."

We ask him whether Kurt's father shares his suspicion.

"Naw, he doesn't even talk about it. He gets pissed if I do," Leland replies. "Donny gets mad at me whenever I talk to him about Kurt."

* * *

Courtney's father, Hank Harrison, has also followed the case closely over the years, and he, too, is more convinced than ever that Kurt was murdered and that his daughter was involved. But unlike Leland Cobain, he now claims to have evidence to back up his theory.

In 1996, before the release of our first book, we appeared with Harrison on a Canada-wide multimedia lecture tour. The bill was split into two segments: we talked about the case during the first half of the presentation, and then Harrison discussed life with Courtney as well as his own colorful career. On stage, he never actually accused his daughter of complicity in Kurt's murder. "I have never said that Courtney killed him. I don't know whether she killed him or not," he said more than once. Yet behind the scenes, he repeatedly leveled this accusation. "I certainly wouldn't put it past her to have Kurt killed," he told us. "Face it, she's a psychopath." When we asked him how a father could say these kinds of things about his own daughter, he defended his position, explaining, "I love my daughter very much, believe it or not. That's why this is so difficult for me."

That same year, he went public with his accusations for the first time, telling *High Times* magazine, "I know for a fact that [Kurt] was trying to divorce [Courtney] and she didn't want the divorce, so she had him killed or knew it was going to happen. . . . I don't want to put my daughter in jail. I've been caught up in a bizarre web of events which has affected my life. It would be very much like if your child came home with plans for a nuclear weapon in their briefcase and you wanted to know where the hell he got them. Well, my daughter came home with a dead husband and I damn well want to know what happened."

Two years later, not entirely convinced of his sincerity, we appeared with Harrison on Maury Povich's television talk show, where we had a heated exchange with Harrison on the air:

HANK "When Kurt first died, I had a gut feeling that something went wrong, so did my mother, her mother and other people in Kurt and Courtney's family. She once stabbed a girl in Oregon in the schoolyard, kind of a precursor to the real news."

IAN HALPERIN "What's your motive, Hank? Any father who openly accuses their daughter of murder must have a hidden agenda."

HANK "No hidden agenda whatsoever. I'm right in the front about everything. I have a heavy conflict going. There's 100,000 people out there taking drugs because of Courtney."

IAN "But you haven't answered the question. Why are you doing this?"

HANK "Well, why don't you ask the Unabomber's brother?"

MAURY POVICH "Whoa, are you trying to tell me you see yourself the way you see Ted Kaczynski's brother in this?"

HANK "He was a hero for turning Kaczynski in, and I'm here looking like a jerk. I just want to get to the bottom of this. There isn't anybody in our family who has got the guts to come forward."

At times, Harrison can come off as a bit of a buffoon, as when he turned to the camera in Nick Broomfield's documentary and said, "I've got her number. . . . I've got her nailed. It's still tough love and I'm still the father. Pop off to me and maybe we can work something out, but keep on bad-rapping me, I'll keep kicking your ass. Courtney, don't take me on, I'll kick your ass. I don't care how big a show it is, I don't care if she's got $177 million."

At other times, however, he comes across as a caring father and grandfather who regrets the seemingly permanent estrangement from his daughter and is deeply concerned about the welfare of Frances Bean. He fears the girl, who turns twelve in 2004, is growing up in an environment of drugs and general excess. More than once, we saw him burst into tears as he described how Courtney has never let him see his granddaughter. He also frequently claims to love his daughter.

Harrison, who is writing a biography of Kurt Cobain, claims to have had a "mystical connection" with the son-in-law he never met. When Kurt died, he says, it was as if "my heart had been ripped out of my chest." At the time of his death, Harrison hadn't seen or spoken to Courtney since November 1993, five months before Kurt died, when she invited him to a concert at Slim's, a San Francisco music club where Hole was opening for the Lemonheads. An early computer buff who helped develop the first version of the Acrobat PDF format when he worked for Adobe Systems, Harrison describes how he taught his daughter how to use the Internet on his Apple Powerbook while he and Courtney had coffee at Cafe Trieste before the show that evening.

Backstage, Courtney introduced him to Evan Dando of the Lemonheads, who asked him for an autographed copy of his book about the Grateful Dead. Harrison claims that he saw Dando kissing her backstage and saw him again naked in his daughter's hotel room bed the next day. (Two months after Kurt's death, an undated photo circulated in several tabloids of a wasted-looking Courtney in bed with Dando. They were kissing. Courtney later claimed it was a staged "publicity shot.")

The night of the San Francisco show, Courtney promised her father that she and Kurt would try to come up to the ranch soon with the baby. "I was always telling her that I wanted to take [Kurt] bungee jumping, which is a proven treatment for heroin addiction," he recalls, explaining that he started America's first LSD telephone intervention program in 1965, talking people through bad acid trips. "I'm convinced that I could have got Kurt off drugs. She thought I was crazy." Courtney later confirmed to the *San Francisco Chronicle* that she had indeed invited her father backstage that night but that "he was only interested in talking to people who were more famous than me."

For months after Kurt's death, Harrison logged on to the Internet to conduct more than two hundred online "interventions" with teenagers who were expressing suicidal feelings about Kurt's death. A year later, sometime after he first heard Tom Grant's murder theory and became suspicious that Courtney was involved in her husband's death, word was leaked of his upcoming biography. Courtney's lawyers quickly sent him a letter threatening a lawsuit if he went ahead with plans to write the book. He ignored the threats and fired off a letter of his own:

Dearest Courtney:

Since you refuse to call or answer my letters, I must assume you are hiding something. What gives with rumors about Kurt's death? As you know, I began to write a book about Kurt two years ago, but now you insist I cease development on this project. Why? You give me no good reason and yet you slander and libel me every chance you get. I won't sue you, but I will answer the allegations in the book. Furthermore, I can't help but wonder why you want to stop me from writing a book about this wonderful man. I will donate all my royalties to suicide prevention. If you insist, I will stop work immediately and get on with the *Stones of Ancient Ireland* and my novel *The Beekeeper*, but I need to know the truth. What's going on? Why don't you just come out and volunteer to take a polygraph test to silence the critics once and for all? Please meet me halfway. I have arranged a lie detector examination for you at my own expense. The results, no matter what the outcome, will never be made public. If you pass, I will cease writing the book or collaborate with you as you see fit. If I do not hear from you, I will continue writing. Taking the test and passing it will assuage your grandmother's fears. I would like her to see the baby, but barring that at least she will know you had nothing to do with Kurt's horrible death. In the final analysis, we have a dead poet and a lot of suspicions which will never go away without a public hearing. If Kurt wasn't murdered, what is being covered up? Why the big silence? Why not throw open the case and get to the bottom of it once and for all?

> *Love always,*
> *Hank*

An early version of the book, entitled *Kurt Cobain: Beyond Nirvana*, was made available on Harrison's now defunct website several years ago, but, because his investigation into Kurt's death is ongoing, it has yet to be published in book form. He claims now that his investigation is nearly complete and that the book will probably be published in 2005. All royalties, he insists, will be donated to suicide prevention. Grant is dismissive of Harrison, believing that he serves only to discredit the case. For his part, Harrison is impressed by Grant's research but thinks it is flawed because "he can't get the credentials to hang with the junkies and dopers like I can."

Although he declines to elaborate on the new evidence he has gathered, a hint may be found in an interview Harrison granted to a Nirvana Internet fan site in 2000. Asked whether he thinks Cali might have murdered Kurt because he was the only person known to have been at the house at the time of Kurt's death, Harrison responds,

That's just bullshit. Who told you that? Grant? Did you know that the alarm was turned on and off seven times between Easter Sunday and the time the body was found? Also remember that the body was located by the alarm system employee, Gary Smith, who was dispatched to the house because Courtney put a rush order in for lights on Tuesday night after she got out of jail the 6th. Kurt was dead by that time and about five people knew where he was. Tom Grant and Dylan Carlson only account for 2 code entries and neither Tom nor Carlson had the code unless you think maybe Tom Grant did it. I have the alarm service records. Cali left town by car on Monday and did not stay at the house after Sunday. He crashed at his father's house in Seattle because his father is a contractor. In fact, Cali's father was the same contractor who did the tear down and refurbish job two years later. So Cali may have slipped him the GHB or Rohypnol but probably did not do the shotgun part. Whoever did the shotgun part knew all about guns, but what you must remember about the alarm code is that whoever did it had the code. Several people had the code. . . . Kurt died in the house, probably in the living room and was dragged out. They took him up to the greenhouse and shot him, but the thing is that by the time they got him up there hours and hours went by.

Though Harrison's comments cry out for elaboration, he declines to say anything further about what he has found, claiming he is saving the evidence for his as-yet-unpublished book. But he does disclose that he recently found a letter that Courtney sent him when she was a teenager—a letter that convinces him more than ever that she had something to do with Kurt's death. In it, she writes, "I'm going to marry myself a rock star, and kill him." As revealing as this letter might be about Courtney's teenage personality, it hardly constitutes proof of her guilt. But for those who find meaning in such writings, it may be instructive to look at the lyrics of a 1990 song Courtney wrote called "Turpentine"—the first song Hole ever recorded: "Now you're mad and you're snubbing me / Stinks of metal in the junkie tree. . . . / Rip it in turpentine / Put your leg up over your head / I better walk you to your suicide."

One of Harrison's arguments is particularly compelling: Why were there no legible fingerprints found on the shotgun? As Harrison says, "Dead men don't wipe fingerprints off their own guns."

Indeed, the lack of fingerprints has always been one of the anomalies of the case. When the police dusted for fingerprints, they actually found four latent prints. But, according to the deputy medical examiner, Nikolas Hartshorne, "We know those prints belonged to Kurt because we had to pry the gun out of his hand when we found him." Yet nowhere else on the shotgun was there a single print found, legible or otherwise.

SPD spokesman Sean O'Donnell had a ready explanation for the lack of fingerprints: "I think it's clear that anyone who is familiar with firearms and their use would know that as they hold a weapon, that frequently that weapon will move in their hand. Additionally, when that weapon is discharged, that causes a jerking motion, which causes the hands to move over the surface of the weapon. And all of those factors could cause any fingerprints that may have been left on the weapon to be unusable."

We consulted a retired FBI fingerprint specialist named Max Jarrell to ask him whether O'Donnell's explanation made sense. He was not convinced. "You're more likely to have trouble lifting prints off a handgun than a shotgun," Jarrell explained. "With a shotgun, there's a much larger printable surface. You're much more likely to find some usable latent prints. I find it unlikely that his hand would have wiped off all the fingerprints after he fired it."

Moreover, Hartshorne himself had declared that, because of the cadaveric spasm, Kurt's hand immediately gripped the barrel of the gun after firing it. Therefore, it couldn't have slid over the surface of the weapon as O'Donnell described. Also unexplained is the fact that the police found no prints on the pen thrust through the so-called suicide note.

But, according to Jarrell, the absence of prints alone does not prove that a murder took place. "Whether a person leaves fingerprints or not depends on a number of factors. A lot depends on how much oils are on your hands. If someone has just washed their hands, for example, they might not leave prints. I've certainly seen cases where somebody left no fingerprints on a surface that we know they touched."

However, we know that the shotgun was handled by at least three separate people: the salesman who sold Dylan Carlson the gun on March 30, Dylan himself, and, finally, Kurt. Yet none of the three men's prints were found on the gun. Is it possible that each of these people had washed their hands just before handling the gun?

In the end, argues Colorado deputy coroner Denise Marshall, there is a lot of very convincing evidence to call the suicide verdict into question, including the lack of fingerprints, the triple lethal dose of heroin and the postmortem credit card use: "There is certainly enough evidence in this case to have the medical examiner's verdict changed from 'suicide' to 'undetermined,' and I think that's exactly what should be done," she explains. "I've worked on a number of cases where we've had the verdict changed to 'undetermined,' and with less compelling evidence than I've seen here. This would serve to reopen the case and ensure a proper investigation is finally undertaken."

But Marshall adds a big disqualification: although there is enough evidence to change the verdict from "suicide" to "undetermined," none of this evidence will conclusively prove that Kurt was murdered. Only the crime scene photos will do that, she explains. Marshall has consulted a number of experts about this case, including one of America's most respected forensic pathologists, who insisted that, before anyone can say for certain that Kurt's death was a staged suicide, a pathologist would have to examine the photos taken at the scene. "The photos should tell the story," she says. "He'd be looking at the blood splatter. You see, if somebody actually held Kurt's hand around the gun and pulled the trigger, some of the blood would probably have splattered on their hand, leaving a void on Kurt's. You can analyze that void in the photos and determine whether or not it was a staged suicide."

This echoes what the former Bronx Homicide Task Force commander Vernon Geberth told us: "I'd have to see the photos. The photos tell you everything."

Could the importance of these photos possibly explain a letter we obtained from the Seattle Police Department under a recent Freedom of Information request? On February 13, 1995, less than a month after Tom Grant first went public with his murder theory, Sergeant Don Cameron sent the following internal memo to his superior, Lieutenant Al Gerdes, commander of the SPD Homicide Division:

> As you are aware, the suicide of Kurt Cobain has once again become a media issue. Allegations by a California private investigator Tom Grant have rekindled the concerns of Courtney Love over the preservation/security of the crime scene photos. Grant is alleging Courtney was responsible for her husband's death and we covered up the murder. Because of the rekindled media interest in her husband's suicide, Courtney Love has gone to her attorney with concerns over the release of any crime scene photos. Courtney's attorney, Seth Lichtenstein, called and asked if the photos could be destroyed to prevent any mistaken release. I have advised Mr. Lichtenstein the 35 mm film had not been developed, nor would it unless it became necessary. . . . I am not sure Mr. Lichtenstein is satisfied with this but I explained, with Grant still running amuck, we would look foolish and certainly unprofessional if we destroyed the only photographs of the crime scene. Mr. Lichtenstein may go higher on the chain of command so I thought I had better let you know.

The Seattle Police Department refuses to confirm or deny whether the photos remain in their files today.

10

Five months after the death of her daughter in June 1994, Janet Pfaff received a call from the producers of *The Oprah Winfrey Show* with an invitation to appear. They were planning a segment about the parents of drug addicts and wanted Janet to come on and talk about Kristen, who had died of an apparent heroin overdose.

Janet politely declined. She told the producers that she just wasn't emotionally ready to talk about her daughter so soon after the tragedy. Only now is she prepared to admit the real reason she refused to appear: "I am not convinced my daughter's overdose was accidental, so how could I go on the biggest show in the world and talk about it?"

* * *

Kristen Marie Pfaff was born in the Buffalo suburb of Williamsville, New York, on May 26, 1967. Her parents divorced when she was young, and her mother remarried shortly afterward. When Kristen was nine, her half brother, Jason, was born.

Kristen was educated in Buffalo's Catholic school system, where she became proficient in classical cello and piano at an early age.

Her mother recalls that, while other girls her age were playing with dolls, Kristen was recording Girl Scout songs that she adapted to her own lyrics.

She graduated from Sacred Heart Academy in 1985 and then briefly attended Boston College before receiving a scholarship to study in Holland. Two years later, she enrolled at the University of Minnesota, where she majored in women's studies, became a committed activist and worked as a crisis counselor for rape victims. After earning 150 credits, Kristen decided to leave college to pursue her lifelong dream of a music career. "I graduated myself," she told a Minnesota newspaper. "I just decided to start a band and forget about school."

Kristen soon immersed herself in Minnesota's underground music scene, where she decided that she preferred playing hard rock to the staid classical music she had performed since the age of five. She taught herself to play bass guitar, which she mastered quickly. Her first project, Drool, featured members of the notorious Minneapolis garage bands, the Cows and God's Bullies; shortly afterward, Kristen teamed up with two local musicians, Joachim Breuer and Matt Entsminger, to form a new trio called Janitor Joe, with Kristen on bass and keyboards. "Kristen was an incredibly driven person," recalled Breuer. "Whatever she set her mind to, she could accomplish."

Within a year, Janitor Joe was the talk of the Minnesota music scene. In 1993, the respected indie label Amphetamine Reptile Records released the band's debut album, *Big Metal Birds*, to great acclaim.

Kristen's musicianship was beginning to attract attention beyond the Minnesota indie scene, but her fame had not changed her gentle personality. "She was the most peaceful, friendly person you could meet," recalls former Janitor Joe music producer Pat Dwyer. "Kristen had a beautiful presence. And she was one damn talented musician and artist."

One night in 1993, after Janitor Joe finished a gig at a small L.A. club, Eric Erlandson and Courtney Love came backstage and introduced themselves to Kristen. Hole had just signed with Geffen Records, and they were about to head into the studio to record a new album. Their bassist, Leslie Hardy, had recently left the band, and they needed a replacement. Saying they were "blown away" by Kristen's assertive style, they told her she would be a perfect addition to the group.

Kristen had a good thing going with her own band, which was beginning to attract widespread attention. "She agonized over that decision for a long time," says her father, Norm Pfaff. "Janitor Joe was just getting rolling, but she recognized the opportunity of being in a successful band on a big label." After some convincing, and a generous financial offer, she agreed to join Hole on a temporary basis.

"I wish to God she would have never made that move," says her mother, Janet. "I was totally against it. I never trusted Courtney and Eric. They were deeply into drugs. I thought that Kristen was better off in Minnesota. I tried to convince her not to go, but she didn't want to let such a big opportunity slip by."

Kristen rented an apartment in Seattle, where the band rehearsed before heading to a studio in Atlanta to record their new album, *Live Through This*. Before long, Kristen had hooked up with the band's guitarist, Eric Erlandson, Courtney's ex-boyfriend, who told friends he was taken with Kristen's stunning long jet-black hair and striking figure. Within weeks she became hooked on heroin.

Janet tried to persuade her daughter to quit the band and enter a detox center, but there was little she could do with Kristen so far away. Jason, however, saw the depth of his sister's addiction firsthand: "I think she might have already tried heroin before she met Courtney, but in Seattle, Courtney got her addicted. She would always make sure that Kristen was supplied with as much heroin as she needed. I was there at the time. Kristen had asked me to move to Seattle to be with her for support, so I witnessed a lot of the crazy things that went on. One time, Kristen showed me a purse Courtney gave her. It had needles inside that Courtney had put in it. Courtney and the rest of the band pushed Kristen into drugs beyond control. Of course, Kristen had a mind of her own, so she has to take some of the responsibility."

According to Kristen's close friend Kathy Hewitt, Kristen and Courtney got along well at first, but the relationship went rapidly downhill after the band flew to Atlanta to record *Live Through This*. Kristen was a formally trained musician with strong opinions about the song arrangements. Courtney could barely play an instrument. Hysterically defensive about her musical abilities, she did not take well to Kristen's suggestions and threatened to fire her more than once.

Hewitt believes Courtney set out to break Kristen emotionally, an experience that left her friend traumatized: "Courtney yelled at Kristen all the time. She wanted to make sure Kristen knew who was boss. I think Kristen was afraid of Courtney. She thought she was out of control. She said Courtney was the most egomaniacal, insecure and power-hungry person she had ever met. Kristen was interested in making good music. Courtney was more interested in making headlines for all the crazy stuff she did every day."

To make matters worse, Kristen had established a deep bond with Kurt. They spent hours talking together. As Jason recalls, "Kurt was extremely fond of Kristen. It made Courtney very jealous. Courtney kept a close eye on them. I don't think that they were involved—in fact, I'm pretty sure they weren't—but Courtney was jealous because Kristen was so beautiful and smart. And she had a lot in common with Kurt. They used to talk a lot about books, art and music. I don't think it made Courtney very happy."

Courtney once complained to Jason that Kurt and Kristen were "connecting too much." Two weeks later, when Kurt gave Kristen a copy of the novel *Perfume*, Jason says, "Courtney hit the ceiling."

Around Christmas 1993, Kristen broke up with Eric, a relationship Kathy Hewitt describes as "nightmarish": "It's hard to say whether Kristen was ever in love with Eric. I think it was more a relationship of convenience. Kristen had just arrived in Seattle, and Eric was right there to greet her with open arms. I think the relationship eventually dissolved because Kristen wanted a change from the seedy life of drugs and booze." Soon after the breakup, Erlandson began to date Hollywood actress Drew Barrymore.

The album completed, Kristen moved back to Minneapolis in February to await the start of Hole's summer tour. It was there that she received the news of Kurt's death. "She was devastated," Janet recalls. "It was a big loss for her. She lost someone she really respected. They had a lot in common. It was a big wake-up call for her. Kristen stopped doing drugs the day Kurt died."

Reeling, Kristen entered a Minneapolis detox center and began the job of straightening out her life. In May, she told the local alternative paper the Minnesota *Nightly* how happy she was to be home: "I'm really having a great time doing the things I'm doing now here, getting back to friends, playing music together, which I really missed. I couldn't get going in Seattle because the local scene was so stagnant. There's a lot more going on in Minneapolis." Kurt Cobain, she told the interviewer, "broke my heart." She failed to elaborate.

Meanwhile, she had made the decision to rejoin her old band, Janitor Joe. Revitalized, the Minneapolis band flew to Europe in May for a brief tour. Kristen was adamant she would never go back to Hole.

"I met Courtney for the first time at the Phoenix Festival in England in 1993," says Janet Pfaff. "She was never able to look me in the eye, and I could never figure out why. I thought she was very rude. I never trusted her, and I could see how she treated Kristen.

When Kristen told me she was quitting Hole, she told me that she would never rejoin them, no matter how successful the album was. She wasn't really quitting Hole, she was quitting Courtney. She just couldn't stand to be around Courtney anymore, especially after Kurt's death. I think she was scared of her. She wanted to make a new start."

As Kristen told her Janitor Joe bandmate Matt Entsminger, "These people are all crazy. Let them find another idiot to play the bass. I'm history."

Courtney was livid when she heard the news. *Live Through This* had just been released to great acclaim, and many critics were crediting Kristen's bass playing for the band's unique new sound. She was being hailed as one of the top female rock bassists in the country. "The day Kristen joined Hole is when we took off," Erlandson told *Spin* magazine. "All of a sudden, we became a real band." To quit just as Hole's long-anticipated tour was set to begin was to plunge Courtney's carefully ordered plans into disarray.

Before settling in Minneapolis for good, however, Kristen made arrangements to visit Seattle one last time—just long enough to clear the things out of her apartment. For reasons she can't rationally explain now, Janet begged Kristen not to go: "I felt something bad might happen. I just did not want her to go back. I had this strange inner feeling that told me not to let her go. But she wasn't a kid anymore. There was just so much I could tell her. It was her decision."

When Janet's pleas fell on deaf ears, she asked her cousin Michael, a security guard, to accompany Kristen to Seattle to help her gather her belongings, and even purchased Michael an Amtrak ticket to travel there. But when Janitor Joe's European tour was extended, and Kristen's Seattle trip was postponed a week, her cousin couldn't make it. Kristen asked her friend Paul Erickson, leader of the Minneapolis band Hammerhead, to come with her and help her move.

They arrived in Seattle on June 14. The next day, Paul and Kristen packed her furniture and other belongings in a U-Haul for the return trip to Minneapolis. They planned to set out the next morning.

After Paul finished helping Kristen pack up the U-Haul, he volunteered to spend the night in the truck to guard her belongings from thieves. There were said to be more heroin addicts per square foot in Kristen's Capitol Hill neighborhood that year than in any other district in the United States; theft by junkies was rampant. Sometime that evening, Kristen called her Janitor Joe bandmate Joachim Breuer, who later said that Kristen sounded "as chipper and happy as she'd ever been. She couldn't wait to get back to Minneapolis."

Around 8:00 P.M., Paul left Kristen alone in the apartment so she could take a bath. As he was sitting in the truck a few minutes later, he saw Eric Erlandson enter the apartment and then leave again roughly half an hour later. Paul returned to the apartment around 9:30 and knocked on the locked bathroom door. He heard Kristen snoring inside. He knew she often fell asleep in the bath, so he returned to the truck to sleep for the night.

When Paul awakened the next morning, he returned to the apartment to see if Kristen was ready to hit the road. He discovered the bathroom door still locked. When he knocked and got no response, he kicked down the door. Kristen was kneeling in an inch or two of water in the tub, unconscious. The phone had already been disconnected for the move, so he rushed to a phone booth around the corner to call 911. She was dead by the time police and paramedics arrived. In a cosmetics bag on the bathroom floor, police found what they described as "syringes and narcotic paraphernalia."

On June 17, a spokesman for the King County Medical Examiner's Office declared Kristen's death accidental; he did not name the person who conducted the autopsy. When we obtained a copy of Kristen's death certificate, it revealed that the task had been performed by none other than Nikolas Hartshorne, who listed the cause of death as "Acute Opiate Intoxication" caused by an accidental "[injectable] use of drug."

"It seemed clear that the frequently self-destructive grunge music demimonde had claimed another victim," concluded *People* magazine, a little out of its depth. The media were quick to blame the city's notorious drug culture, but also its take-no-prisoners music scene. Rock stars died, they concluded, and curiously, they all seemed to die at the same age. More than one report noted that both Kurt and Kristen were twenty-seven when they fatally overdosed—the same age as Jim Morrison, Janis Joplin and Jimi Hendrix when they met their own drug-related deaths a quarter century earlier.

But there was another intriguing coincidence. The fact that the two deaths involved someone close to Courtney wasn't lost on those who were just beginning to have their doubts about the official verdict in Kurt's death.

* * *

It is a muggy August night in 2003, and we are sitting at the bohemian Higher Ground Café in Buffalo. Janet Pfaff has agreed to discuss her daughter's death publicly for the first time since Kristen was taken from her nine years ago. She has brought along some Kristen memorabilia: journals, photos and a platinum record presented to her posthumously by Geffen Records, commemorating one million units sold of Hole's album *Live Through This*. Accompanying Janet is Kristen's twenty-eight-year-old brother, Jason.

"I'll never forget how I found out Kristen died," Janet says, her voice choking. "I had just come back from the grocery store, and my brother's car was in the driveway, very unusual for the middle of the afternoon. My brother, Don, came out of the house and told me the news. I kind of fell to the ground. He told me it was an accidental overdose. I just couldn't believe it. She had gone into rehab and got involved in religion. She stopped using drugs the day Kurt died. I talked to her every day. She said she was happier than ever being off drugs. That's why I was so shocked that police said she died of a drug overdose. I just didn't think it was possible because she hadn't used drugs for so long."

Janet recalls how Geffen Records relayed a message that the members of Hole would like to attend the funeral. She rejected the request outright. "I don't know what's going on in that Seattle scene," she told *People* in her only public statement about her daughter's death at the time. "But something's wrong, terribly wrong."

Geffen president Ed Rosenblatt issued a public statement of sympathy in which he mistakenly implied that Kristen was still a member of Hole at the time of her death: "This is all the more tragic because she had gone through a drug rehabilitation program this past winter. She was in the process of moving back to Minneapolis to be with old friends until the Hole tour resumed." Courtney issued her own statement, announcing that Kristen's death would not force the cancellation of Hole's upcoming tour: "I'm deeply anguished over Kristen's death. We are obviously shaken by the tragedies affecting the band in the last months, but have decided to continue on."

That week, against the family's explicit instructions, a member of the band did show up at the funeral—Eric Erlandson—who, to the shock of the family and assembled mourners, draped himself over Kristen's coffin just before it was lowered into the ground. He was immediately escorted out by security staff. An hour later, he showed up at the Pfaff house, looking strung out. They refused to let him in.

"He looked like he had done a lot of drugs," Janet recalls. "I didn't want a circus, and that's exactly what he created when he threw himself on her coffin."

Norm Pfaff had flown to Seattle immediately upon hearing of his daughter's death; when he arrived, he met with Courtney and the other members of Hole. He later described this meeting to the *Seattle Weekly*: "There was no sign of the type of remorse you would look for in a person who'd lost someone they cared about. It could have been that Kristen died or somebody missed a bus."

Meanwhile, Courtney had posted a message on an AOL Internet newsgroup about the recent tragedies in her life: "I'm begging you, pray for [Kurt] and Kristen . . . they hear it I know. . . . My friend has been robbed of her stellar life. My baby has no dad. . . . Please pray for Kristen's mom."

But prayers weren't going to do it for the Pfaff family. They were already beginning to harbor suspicions about Kristen's death. When Janet learned more about Kristen's time in Seattle, and particularly of Courtney's virulent jealousy over Kristen's relationship with Kurt, she called Seattle police to report her misgivings, only to be rebuffed. "They told me they couldn't investigate every heroin death in Seattle because in those days people were OD'ing every day, and they just didn't have the manpower to investigate all the drug deaths that were taking place," she recalls.

Indeed, Seattle police received the family's fears with barely concealed weariness. When a few days after Kristen's death the *Seattle Times* asked whether police were looking into the circumstances of Pfaff's overdose or attempting to locate the source of the heroin, Captain Dan Bryant of the Narcotics Division told the paper, "Unless we had someone who knew her and was willing to testify and work with us, we really have nowhere to go. We won't treat this case differently than any other case just because it's someone with notoriety. We did attempt to locate the source of drugs in the Cobain case but were unable to come up with any meaningful evidence. That may well be true in this case, too."

Soon afterward, the Seattle police returned a number of Kristen's belongings confiscated from her apartment the day her body was found. Among these items was Kristen's private journal, some of its pages inexplicably torn out. "I don't know who removed those pages," Janet says, "but I have my suspicions." She has brought the journal along but won't show us its contents. "They're very personal," she explains. "I'm still a grieving mother. It's been so difficult for me and my family to cope with our loss. Maybe when I feel the time is right, I'll release parts of her journal for the sake of her fans. Her death was very hard on them, too. I received messages of condolence from all over the world." She does, however, consent to show us the very last words Kristen had entered before her death: "I'll write it on my sleeve—I know how to live."

"That does not sound like someone who wanted to die," Janet says. "We had made plans to go back to Europe together so Kristen could show me all the great places she saw when she was on her last tour with Janitor Joe a couple of weeks before she died. That's one of the reasons I'm suspicious. She had been off drugs for so long. Why would she all of a sudden start doing drugs again the night she was leaving Seattle?"

Janet says she dismissed the idea of a conspiracy at first: "Originally, I had some doubts of my own about whether Kristen really died of an accidental overdose. I wondered if she might have been murdered. But emotionally, I just wasn't equipped to deal with that possibility, so I kind of let it go. At the time, the Seattle police convinced me that there wasn't any reason to investigate because they told me there weren't any signs of foul play."

But the missing journal pages rekindled her doubts, and when she learned that Nikolas Hartshorne had conducted the autopsy, it was no longer possible to ignore them. "It concerns me and my family greatly that Dr. Hartshorne did the autopsy," says Janet. "I've heard all about his close friendship with Courtney. It's a conflict of interest. It scares me. I don't want to accuse anybody of anything, but I have my concerns."

Meanwhile, Tom Grant was having doubts of his own: "It seems that everyone who tries to get away from Courtney does not live to tell about it. Kurt wanted a divorce, and he dies. Kristen wanted to get away from Courtney, and she dies. Their deaths both involved lethal amounts of heroin."

Over the years, Grant had never gone into very much detail about what he knew about Kristen's death, but he had always hinted that there was more to the story than what he had so far publicly revealed. Finally, after some convincing, he takes out a tape from a conversation he had with Courtney about Kristen's death on October 1, 1994.

On the tape, Courtney is discussing Kristen's drug use: "When Kristen did drugs for several months, she had always done cocaine with her heroin. This is according to Patty [Schemel, Hole's drummer]. I never did drugs with Kristen. I didn't even know about the problem until she [entered rehab]. I knew that she had done drugs a few times before she came to town. I knew that she partied. I don't think it's called partying. I think it's called totally self-destructive. I know what it is. It's fucking trying to kill yourself, or numb yourself. Partying? Please! Patty did drugs with her, but she never did cocaine with heroin. She only did heroin."

Courtney proceeds to talk about what she knows about the events on the night of Kristen's death. She reveals that Eric had visited the apartment that night on his way to a date with Drew Barrymore and found Paul Erickson there. Kristen was already sleeping in the bathtub, she says, when Eric arrived. "Eric's like, 'I heard her snoring, I heard her breathing. I thought if they were breathing, they were OK.' "

At this point in the conversation, Grant says, "Eric's the one who heard her snoring?"

"Yeah, it never gets attributed in the press, but I know exactly what happened that night," she replies.

Grant asks where Kristen's friend Paul Erickson was when Eric was listening at the door.

"He was in the apartment. It was a one-room apartment.... Eric said, 'I'm going to go on a date. If she's not out in twenty minutes, call my machine. I'll check it.' And then Paul goes to sleep. He wakes up at 9:30, and she's dead. Paul went to sleep at 9:00 P.M. I'm sorry, but people in rock bands don't go to sleep that early."

Then, bizarrely, Courtney begins to talk about Nikolas Hartshorne, who had conducted Kristen's autopsy: "I'm going to say one thing. Nikolas, my rock-and-roll medical examiner, he did say one weird thing. He goes, 'God, she's pretty.' This is a dead person he's talking about! 'God, she's pretty.' "

Two months later, Courtney was asked about Kristen's death during an interview with David Fricke of *Rolling Stone*. In this interview, published December 15, 1994, she claims that she was actually at Kristen's apartment the morning the body was found: "I had to go over there and get Eric away from the body," she tells Fricke. "Kristen was his lover for a really long time. He'd already broken down bathroom door after bathroom door for her. He'd kicked in drug dealers' doors."

When we press him, Grant is hesitant to talk about the significance of the fact that both Courtney and Eric were present in the apartment on June 16 while Kristen lay there dead, and the fact that pages were subsequently found missing from Kristen's journal. "I can't discuss that at this time," he says.

Shortly after Grant originally went public with his theory about Kurt's death, he had been contacted by Kristen's brother, Jason, who had deep concerns about his sister's overdose and suspected that Courtney was somehow involved. Nine years later, Jason says those suspicions are stronger than ever. After he heard about Grant's theory, he explains, everything began to add up: "There's too many coincidences here. First, Kurt dies, then Kristen. Both had fallen out with Courtney. Courtney is not the type of person you want to be enemies with. She has an explosive personality."

We ask him how Courtney could have possibly played a hand in his sister's death. Does he think Eric—Courtney's ex-boyfriend—was acting in league with her, as many conspiracy theorists have suggested over the years? But Jason, himself a former heroin addict who now works as a drug counselor in Buffalo, says he doubts that Eric knowingly killed his sister. "Maybe the heroin was a final going-away gift from Courtney to Kristen, and she asked Eric to deliver it that night," he speculates. "It could have been a dose of dirty (overly pure) heroin. The fact that Kristen was clean for so long combined with a dose of dirty heroin would have been enough to kill her." Jason thinks Eric's over-the-top emotional reaction to Kristen's death may have had something to do with the guilt he felt for unknowingly playing a part in the tragedy. But he admits it is all speculation.

Kim Young, a Seattle musician who knew both Kristen and Courtney, finds the conspiracy theories a little far-fetched: "As much as I liked Kristen, I think it's ridiculous to insinuate Courtney might have been involved. Give me a break. Kurt died a few months earlier, and Courtney was trying to promote her new record. I just don't think she's the type of person to do something like that. As crazy as Courtney is, why would she have wanted Kristen dead? I can understand why Kurt was better off dead to her, because he wanted a divorce. But do you think she would go out and kill Kristen just because she was leaving Hole? I don't think so. She could have got any bass player on the planet to join Hole."

Yet from her vista outside the scene, Janet Pfaff is more suspicious than ever. She is cautious about what she will say on the record because she says she doesn't want Courtney's "army of lawyers" descending on her. Her explanation is as elemental as fear itself: "She scares me. I really don't want to have anything to do with her, so I'm better off not saying anything. She's a person who I really do not want in my life. I want no connection to her."

* * *

When Kristen Pfaff was found dead in her bathtub on June 16, 1994, the news soon overshadowed another local tragedy that had been dominating the headlines of Seattle newspapers for more than a week. On June 4, an off-duty Seattle police officer named Antonio Terry was shot and killed in the middle of the night while driving home from work in an unmarked car. What made Terry's death unusual was the fact that he was the first police officer killed in the state of Washington since 1987.

The name rang a bell for Tom Grant, but it was only when he obtained the Cobain police report that he paid closer attention. There, on the missing person's report filed April 4 by Courtney in Kurt's mother's name, was a mention of Antonio Terry:

> Mr. Cobain ran away from California facility and flew back to Seattle. He also bought a shotgun and may be suicidal. Mr. Cobain may be at location for narcotics. Detective Terry SPD/Narcotics has further info.

"Courtney was always talking to me about her friend Detective Terry in narcotics and how she had scored 'brownie points' with him," Grant recalls. "When I was driving up to Carnation with her and Kat Bjelland after Kurt died, I went into a 7-Eleven to get a drink, and when I got back to the car, she was speaking to someone on my cell phone. I asked her who she called and she said, 'My friend Detective Terry.' I didn't give it much thought until I saw his name on the missing person's report and realized he was the same cop who was killed a week before Kristen."

Grant plays a tape of a conversation he had with Courtney on April 3. On it, she is talking about her pleas to the police to bust Caitlin Moore, whom she suspects is having an affair with Kurt. She tells Grant that she had once told a detective named Terry that she would "go in with a wire" to help entrap Caitlin. During another taped conversation, Courtney reveals to Grant that she is intimately familiar with the detective's case investigations, claiming that "Terry was onto a really big crack ring that was also a big heroin ring" and that Terry told her that the heroin had come from Woodburn, Oregon.

Terry was initially reported shot by two men after stopping to help a stranded motorist on an interstate ramp. Eric Smiley and Quentin Ervin were charged with Terry's murder. Both insisted in their statements that they didn't know Terry was a police officer and had shot him in self-defense when he took out a gun.

But when the case went to court eighteen months later, some curious details were made public for the first time. Witnesses testified that Detective Terry had not stopped to help a stranded motorist as was first reported, but had been deliberately flagged down by Smiley and Ervin as he turned onto the exit. As he stepped from the car, they shot him. Terry managed to shoot one of the suspects, get back in the car, drive to Seattle's South Precinct and make a statement about the incident before bleeding to death. In it, he described hearing one of the shooters say, "He's a cop," despite the fact that he was in civilian clothes and an unmarked car. Clearly, the two were lying in wait to ambush Terry as he turned off his regular exit to go home.

But that wasn't the only anomaly revealed at trial. Defense attorneys claimed that Terry's personnel records had been altered after his death to bolster the prosecutors' contention that the detective was on duty when he was shot. Terry's original checkout time of 1:15 A.M. was changed to 1:45 A.M. so that it would look as if he were still on duty when he was murdered at 1:30 A.M. The Washington State Patrol crime laboratory analyzed Terry's checkout sheet and concluded that it had been altered in six places. In Washington State, killing an on-duty police officer is an aggravating factor that automatically calls for life imprisonment upon conviction. Sergeant Donald Cameron—at that time still perceived as a beacon of integrity—happened to be the lead homicide detective in the Terry case. The SPD never determined who was responsible, and no officer was ever disciplined for the offense.

Grant says that, because of the unlikely combination of circumstances, he doubts that Antonio Terry's death is connected to the Cobain case but doesn't rule out the possibility entirely. "There certainly are a lot of strange coincidences," he says.

Although no evidence linking Courtney to Terry's murder has ever been presented, an intriguing fact was unearthed by *Newsweek* correspondent Melissa Rossi: at the time of his death, Terry happened to be investigating the source of the heroin found in Kurt's bloodstream when he died.

While working on her Courtney Love biography, *Queen of Noise*, two years later, Rossi told Courtney what she had learned about Terry's involvement in the Cobain investigation. And, although there was no suggestion of a connection between this investigation and Terry's subsequent murder, Courtney, with no explanation, told Rossi that she "felt responsible" for Detective Terry's death. She has never elaborated. However, we have learned that Courtney quietly paid a significant amount of money to Terry's widow in 1994.

11

During the course of our investigation into Kurt Cobain's world, we had encountered a fair amount of darkness, from the kids in his birthplace who dreamed only of getting wasted, to the serial overdoses in his last hometown. We had learned ugly things about Courtney, rock and roll, and love gone bad. But nothing was to prepare us for our meeting with a smirking rocker who all but boasted of having killed Cobain.

The bizarre series of events that led to this encounter began in 1996 while we were still researching our first book. There was a report out of Los Angeles that a musician named Eldon Hoke claimed Courtney Love had offered him $50,000 to kill her husband. We immediately flew to Los Angeles to meet with Hoke and check out his story.

He did not make a good first impression. Disheveled, drunk and somewhat pathetic, he looked more like a street person than a hired killer, and our first instinct told us we had made the trip for nothing. Still, we listened to his story because Hoke's background was intriguing.

In 1977, while attending Seattle's Roosevelt High School, Eldon Hoke had formed a band called the Mentors with two school friends, Eric Carlson and Steve Broy. In the beginning, the band played a primitive version of heavy metal influenced by the punk ideals emerging out of the American music underground at the time. Before long, they had raunched up their act considerably. Hoke, the band's singer/drummer, took on the stage name "El Duce," and the Mentors became notorious for their offensive, sexually explicit lyrics and obscene onstage antics, which included go-go dancers and sex toys. Members of the band sported black executioner hoods onstage. Among the Mentors' repertoire were such ditties as "Donkey Dick," "When You're Horny You're Horny" and "All Women Are Insane." Their timing couldn't have been better. Their young audience, appalled by the prevailing politically correct sensibility, hailed the Mentors, and a new genre of music—porn metal—was born.

The band had a huge cult following in the Pacific Northwest and soon signed their first record deal with Mystic Records. In Aberdeen, a teenage Krist Novoselic even played bass under the stage name "Phil Atio" in a Mentors cover band started by members of the Melvins. In the early eighties, Hoke and the Mentors relocated to Los Angeles, where they soon became a fixture on the '80s L.A. underground music scene, notorious for their wild on- and off-stage debauchery. Their fame reached its zenith in 1985 when, at a Senate hearing on obscenity in rock and roll, Tipper Gore named the Mentors as its very worst exponents and recited the lyrics to the band's song "Golden Showers": "Bend up and smell my anal vapors," Mrs. Gore memorably read out loud to the staid assembly of U.S. Senators. "Your face will be my toilet paper."

It was in Los Angeles during the late '80s that Eldon Hoke and Courtney Love crossed paths for the first time. Around 1987, Mentors guitarist Eric Carlson (a.k.a. Sickie Wifebeater) began to date Carolyn Rue, the drummer for an L.A. band called the Omelettes. Two years later, Courtney recruited Rue to play drums for her new band Hole.

Mentors bassist Steve Broy (a.k.a. Dr. Heathen Scum) recalls the scene: "Carolyn had already broken up with Sickie, and I hadn't seen her for a while. I think they had an acrimonious breakup. Then I ran into her at some club, and I remember her telling me that she had just joined this band called Hole and she was quite excited about it. We were talking, and she said she needed a roommate, so we moved in together. That's when El would have known Courtney, during that period when Carolyn lived with me. He already knew Carolyn very well from when she was dating Sickie. We used to tour a lot in the old days with Courtney's old boyfriend Rozz Rezabek's band, but I don't know if El ever met her back then."

By this time, Hoke was better known in the L.A. music scene for his alcoholic binges and drunken antics than for his music. As El Duce's drinking started affecting the band's live performances, Mentors bookings began to drop off significantly. By 1993, Hoke had taken to hanging out at the Rock Shop, a West Hollywood music store, where he did odd jobs and waited around for Mentors fans to drift in and offer to buy him a drink. It was there one evening around New Year's Eve 1993 that Hoke claims Courtney Love asked him to kill Kurt Cobain.

It was at the Rock Shop that we first met Hoke in February 1996. Reeking of alcohol, the burly musician told us of Courtney's queenlike arrival at the dingy establishment: "She got out of a limo, came walking up to where I was standing and said, 'El, my old man's been a real asshole lately. I need you to blow his fucking head off.' "

Hoke asked her if she was serious.

"I'm as serious as a heart attack," Courtney allegedly replied. "I'll give you fifty thousand dollars to do it. I'll fly you up to Seattle and tell you what to do."

They talked for about fifteen minutes, Hoke said, while Courtney outlined her plan to have him stage the killing to look like a suicide.

"She said she'd even give me a blow job if I did it. I said, 'Forget the blow job, just give me the money.' She asked me where she could reach me, and I told her I take my messages at the Rock Shop. We went inside and got her a business card, and I said, 'You can reach me here.' "

As we talked, a short, dark-haired man was standing behind the counter serving customers. Hoke pointed to him and said, "That's Sep. He was there that day." The man was Karush Sepedjian, manager of the Rock Shop. He said he remembered Courtney's visit as if it were yesterday: "I remember Courtney pulls up in this limo," he recalls. "She starts talking to El in front of the store, and my counter is right near the door so I could hear part of the conversation. She said to him, 'Look, can you handle doing this, can you get this done? What do you want for it?' They were talking about Kurt Cobain. Then they come into the store, and El whispers to me that she just offered him fifty thousand dollars to get rid of her old man. He was pretty excited. 'Courtney tells me she'll be calling me soon,' and she left."

Sepedjian—who claims he was friends with Courtney when she lived in Los Angeles years earlier—said that when the two didn't hear from Courtney again, they decided her request had been a joke. Then, one day in late March 1994, Sepedjian received a call: "Courtney phoned looking for El. At the time, he was out on tour with his band. I told her I didn't know where to reach him. She was all frantic. She says, 'I need to talk to him. He's got a job to do.' I told her I had no idea, and she starts screaming at me. I told her I've got a business to run, and I hung up."

As he spoke, we eyed the yellowing concert posters, the hash pipes and the general sleaziness of our surroundings. Somewhere, surely, there had to be a better source than these two guys, we thought. Later, after Hoke had left, we made the trek to the Rock Shop once again to question the marginally less weird Sepedjian alone. Why, we asked him, did he think Courtney would have approached somebody like Hoke to kill her husband? Why not a professional hit man?

"Everybody thinks he's crazy," he replied. "He's also got a reputation that he'll do anything for a buck."

Witness or no witness, it was difficult for us to take anything Hoke said seriously. We had even resolved not to use his bizarre claim in our book. Then we received a call from Santina Leuci, the producer of *Hard Copy*, which was then America's best-known tabloid TV show. She wanted us to appear with Tom Grant and Eldon Hoke in a segment about the Cobain murder theory. Grant refused outright, saying he did not participate in tabloid television. For our part, we feared that appearing with Hoke might jeopardize the credibility of our case. But when Leuci told us the show's attorneys had agreed to clear Hoke's appearance only if he passed a credible polygraph exam, we decided to accept her invitation—provided Hoke passed the lie detector test.

Hard Copy spared no expense. At their attorneys' insistence, they hired America's leading polygraph examiner, Dr. Edward Gelb, who is known as a pioneer in the field and at the time was the instructor for the FBI's advanced polygraph course. Shortly before O. J. Simpson was arrested for allegedly killing his wife, Simpson's attorney F. Lee Bailey had Gelb administer a polygraph on his client. Simpson reportedly failed the test quite badly, although Bailey would later claim he stopped the test midway through "because of Simpson's emotional state."

After administering Hoke's polygraph on March 6, 1996, Gelb concluded that his story was "completely truthful." To the question, "Did Courtney Love ask you to kill Kurt Cobain?" Hoke's positive response showed a 99.91 percent certainty that he was telling the truth. According to Dr. Gelb, that score falls into the category "beyond possibility of deception." When the question was repeated, Hoke's response scored exactly the same.

We asked Gelb about the common belief that psychopaths and

sociopaths can beat a polygraph. "That's a myth," he replied, explaining that a recent British Columbia study had shown the polygraph was actually *more* accurate when testing such people. Gelb said that many of the misconceptions about the polygraph stemmed from its earliest days, when the technology was much less sophisticated. Today, when conducted by a qualified examiner, the test is so accurate that its results are now being accepted in many court jurisdictions throughout the United States.

The results of Hoke's polygraph exam were too compelling to ignore. On March 6, 1996, one of Hoke's friends took it upon himself to call the Seattle Police Department and report the test's findings. For once, it seems, the SPD paid attention. We received a call a few days later from a source in the Seattle Police Department telling us that the Cobain case had been reopened for the first time in two years. Hoke's claim had caused a "flurry of activity," our source said, adding that if the story could be proven, it might be enough to have Courtney charged with conspiracy to commit murder—the usual charge for attempting to hire a hit man. Curiously enough, Sergeant Cameron denied the Cobain case had been reopened when a reporter asked him about it the same week.

Years later, an updated set of police reports we obtained under Washington State's Freedom of Information laws revealed that the Cobain file had indeed been reopened when word of Hoke's polygraph test came out—but only under barely concealed duress. A heavily blacked-out March 7 memo from Sergeant Cameron to his superior, Lieutenant Al Gerdes, mentions Tom Grant, who "currently has some type of dog and pony show touring the country with the bottom line being Courtney killed, or had killed, her loving husband Kurt Cobain." Cameron, citing Hoke's polygraph results, goes on to note that a detective named Ila is going to "follow up on this information and I believe we will also have to look into it." He concludes by advising Lieutenant Gerdes to "please make yourself familiar with all aspects of this investigation."

But after that there is nothing. Nowhere in the file is there any indication that the SPD followed up on Hoke's claim. In fact, when Hoke's friend first phoned the SPD about the polygraph test, he was brushed off with an instruction to relay the information to the Los Angeles Police Department. The SPD seems then to have sat on their hands waiting for the LAPD to investigate. Hoke said he contacted police in Seattle and Los Angeles offering to provide a statement but never heard back from either force.

We had approached the Eldon Hoke issue with the idea that he and Sepedjian had concocted the story for some sort of monetary gain, or for Hoke to reattain the kind of fame he had once enjoyed as the target of Tipper Gore's antiobscenity crusade. Yet Hoke had never asked for money to tell his story, even when *Hard Copy*—a program with a reputation for paying sources—called for an interview. Tom Grant was skeptical himself: "At first, I thought maybe Courtney put them up to it to set me up. I would start talking about these guys as proof and then they would come out and say they made the whole story up. I would then be discredited and have no more credibility." But after Hoke passed his polygraph, neither we nor Grant knew what to make of it.

"I called up the examiner, Dr. Gelb, and asked him if he thought there was a possibility that Hoke had somehow fooled the polygraph," Grant recalls. "After all, these things aren't a hundred percent foolproof. He told me, 'Not *this* guy.' "

Even if Hoke's story is true, it would not prove that Courtney killed her husband, but it would certainly prove intent. Still, Hoke himself did not commit the crime. His story left a gaping void.

By this point, our investigation had taken us to a dark place where rock-and-roll intersects crime. We had interviewed a bizarre cast of characters that included junkies, hit men in waiting, musicians who dressed as executioners and an assortment of other lowlifes. We had met sources in drug dens, back alleys, county jails and some of America's sleaziest bars. We were pursuing an alleged murderer. Our friends and family constantly asked if we were afraid. If we got too close to fingering the person who murdered Kurt, couldn't we be a potential target? they asked.

We pooh-poohed the suggestion. No one would target us, we countered, because it would attract too much suspicion. Never once, as we pursued our story, did we believe we were in any danger. And then the story of Eldon Hoke took an unexpected twist.

*　*　*

A few months after our first encounter with Hoke, we received a phone call from the British filmmaker Nick Broomfield, who said he was thinking of doing a documentary for the BBC about the Cobain murder theory and wished to hire us as consultants. At the time, Broomfield—dubbed "Britain's Michael Moore" for his in-your-face interviewing technique—was one of the world's leading documentary filmmakers, known for controversial films on topics as diverse as neo-Nazi politicians, Margaret Thatcher and female serial killers.

In March 1997, Broomfield flew us to Seattle for a week of filming, during which we shared some of our own findings and named some of the characters we had interviewed for our forthcoming book. Among them was Eldon Hoke, whom Broomfield was determined to interview when he headed to California.

A month later, we learned that Eldon Hoke's mangled body had been found on a train track in the dingy working-class city of Riverside, California. Nick Broomfield had interviewed him only a week before his death and had just heard the news himself. "What's going on? Should I be afraid?" Broomfield asked us. "Do you think Courtney had anything to do with it?" At that point, we weren't sure what to answer, knowing nothing of the circumstances of Hoke's death.

But two months later, we received a call from yet another veteran L.A. punk musician. Brent Alden (a.k.a. Brent Aldo), former leader of the band False Alarm, told us that two nights before Hoke was killed (in fact, it was the night before), the Mentors had played a gig at Al's Bar in downtown Los Angeles. Alden, who was writing a book about the L.A. punk scene, had interviewed Hoke before the show and found him unaccountably agitated: "Duce was acting very freaked out. He had heard that he might be in danger, and he asked me if I knew where he could get a fake driver's license. I asked him why and he said, 'People get buried in cornfields, people get lost in swamps.' I asked him what he was talking about. He said he had recently been told who killed Kurt Cobain, and he was superparanoid. I knew all about the thing where he said he was offered $50,000, but he said this was different."

Alden then told us that Hoke had actually revealed to him the name of Kurt's killer and that he planned to reveal it in his forthcoming book. We asked him if he was afraid that by divulging the information, he might share Hoke's fate.

"The information is locked in a safety-deposit box and will be made public if anything happens to me," he said.

In our first book, we call Alden "Drew Gallagher" because he asked to remain anonymous. We found his claim that Hoke told him the name of the killer dubious, and we said so. But six months after we spoke to him, an abrupt two-second slip of the tongue in Broomfield's newly released documentary brought Alden's claims into focus for us once again.

It occurs in an interview with Hoke taped on April 11, 1997, at the Riverside, California "Mentors Ranch"—a small compound owned by the band's bassist, Steve Broy. Broomfield had been escorted there by a man named Lomas, better known as the pimp for Divine Brown, the prostitute who set off a notorious Hollywood scandal in 1995 when Hugh Grant was arrested while availing himself of her services. Although Broomfield is notorious for paying his subjects, Hoke had refused money, asking only that the director buy him a drink. When Broomfield arrives at the ranch and asks Hoke about Courtney's offer, it results in the following filmed exchange:

HOKE "She offered me fifty grand to whack Kurt Cobain. When she offered me money, goddamn, I wish I would have taken it, man. But I know who whacked him."

BROOMFIELD "How were you going to whack him? Did she tell you how to do it?"

HOKE "Yup, blow his fucking head off."

BROOMFIELD "But where were you going to find him to do it?"

HOKE "Well, she mapped it out, up there in Bellevue, right outside Seattle. I know right where their house is, I know what garden to pop him in, I just didn't think she was serious."

BROOMFIELD "But did she tell you how to do it?"

HOKE "Yeah, blow his fucking head off, and make it look like a suicide."

At this point in the conversation, Hoke—clearly intoxicated—appears to reveal something he shouldn't have:

HOKE "But I told Allen, I mean, my friend [laughs nervously]—I'll let the FBI catch *him*—that's just the way it's done, end of story. Hey, fifty grand does a lot of talking."

Hoke makes no other mention of his friend "Allen," who, he appears to imply, had actually done the killing. Eight days after the interview, Hoke was dead—run over by a train about a mile from where the Broomfield interview took place.

By the time Broomfield's film was released, our book was already at the printer and it was too late to follow up on Hoke's disclosure or investigate the circumstances of his death. We assumed we were finished with this case forever. Four years later, however, we came into possession of a tape that would plunge us right back into the Cobain investigation and force us to reevaluate everything we thought we knew about the case.

We had never put much stock in Brent Alden's claim to know the name of Kurt Cobain's killer. By 2002, his book had still not appeared, and we assumed he had made up the story. Then, through an L.A. music source, we happened to obtain a copy of the actual interview that Alden had conducted with Hoke at Al's Bar in Los Angeles on April 18, 1997. On it, Hoke can be heard telling Alden of Courtney's $50,000 offer, when he suddenly blurts out something else:

HOKE "You see, I actually know the actual killer who killed Kurt Cobain."
ALDEN "Who is?"
HOKE "His name's Allen Wrench."

Could this be the same "Allen" that Hoke had let slip during his interview with Broomfield? We had never even heard of Allen Wrench, but a quick Internet search uncovered the website of a California band called Kill Allen Wrench (a.k.a. "Punk Rock's Most Important Band.") The site is surprisingly elaborate for a minor rock band. It comes complete with pages of band lore, lyrics, downloadable songs, animated skeletons and an exhaustive gallery of frequently updated free porn. The band, it declares, is about "all four rock essentials: Satanic Worship, Alcoholism, Spousal Abuse, and Self Destructive Drug Use!" In transcribed interviews and texts, there is much talk of groupies and sluts who will do "anything" for these "punk rock legends." One member bemoans in an interview what "a load of crap punk rock has become" because some punks have had the temerity to complain that porn is bad. The songs include no fewer than two about El Duce (a.k.a. Eldon

Hoke)—one describing how the Mentors' leader has been reduced to panhandling and "fucking chicks that are ugly and mean," and the other, replete with references to train tracks and trains, describing him as "feeling no pain." Papering the site are concert photos of Allen Wrench himself in devil's horns, pentagrams and slatherings of red glop. It appeared we had found our man.

It took us several weeks to arrange an interview, but in December 2002, the band's publicist, "Jimmy Soprano," informed us that Wrench was willing to talk. He arranged a telephone interview.

Wrench started off cautiously in that first phone conversation. As part of the Riverside music scene, he said, he had known Eldon Hoke for years and "Duce" was one of his best friends. When we asked him why Hoke would have claimed that he killed Kurt Cobain, Wrench replied, "I have no idea." He then told us that he was the last person to see Hoke alive: "I drove him to the liquor store that night, but I dropped him off in front of the store and then I went to pick up this chick. I never saw him again. Later, I heard that he got run over by a train a few minutes after I dropped him off."

Hoke rats out Wrench; Hoke winds up dead. The last person to see Hoke alive is the man he's just named as Kurt's killer. Isn't this scenario somewhat suspicious? we asked.

"Look, if I were to admit to you that I killed Cobain, I'd end up in prison, and I'm not going to risk that," Wrench replied. "That's why they'll never find the guy who really killed Kennedy. Nobody would be stupid enough to come forward and admit to the crime. They'd end up either dead or in prison. It's still entirely possible the [Cobain] case could be reopened. It used to be that homicide had a statute of limitations in the U.S., but now it doesn't anymore. If I said, 'Hey, I whacked Cobain,' a hundred years from now, when I'm 135 years old, I can still be put in jail for fucking whacking Cobain."

We said we understood his reluctance. But off the record, would he tell us the real story? "Nobody will ever know how he died," he responded. "That's the fun of it." We persisted: there must be some reason why Hoke named him as Kurt's killer. He paused and then said abruptly, "OK, off the record, I whacked him, as long as it's off the record."

Whoa! It was a telephone interview, so we couldn't study his face for signs of irony. Was he being flippant or facetious? Probably, but we needed to meet him in person to size him up and gauge his personality and credibility. It didn't take long for the opportunity to present itself. He offered to show us the "scene of the crime."

*   *   *

It's March 2003, and we are having a beer with Allen Wrench at a Riverside steakhouse called the Spunky Steer, a place Wrench has chosen for its proximity to the train tracks where Hoke had met his end. In the three months since we last spoke, we had dug a little into Wrench's background and discovered that he was a master of Brazilian jujitsu and had won the U.S. national judo championship (blue belt division) in 1997. The irony was not lost on us. Kurt had had a horror of jocks all his life. Was it possible that the last face the sensitive poet had seen on this earth was that of this martial arts fanatic? Whatever the case, we were reluctant to meet this man on our own, so we took along some protection in the form of an actor friend and martial arts master named Dan DiJulio, who was best known for playing Dan Aykroyd in the ABC-TV movie *The Gilda Radner Story*.

We had always assumed that the name Allen Wrench was made up because it is also the name of a common household tool. But in our preliminary background check, we discovered that this was in fact his real name, that he had been born Richard Allen Wrench on August 4, 1967, six months after Kurt himself was born. Beyond that, we knew little. In our telephone conversation, he claimed that he had been arrested "a few times" for assault, drunk and disorderly conduct, and various other offenses. But on our own, we found little more menacing in his police record than disturbing the peace and driving without a license.

The man before us at the Spunky Steer was a tall, powerfully built individual, dressed in the rock T-shirt, shorts and sneakers of the neater sort of California punk. Clean-cut, slightly balding at the temples and with an aura of grinding strength, he could have easily passed for a U.S. marine. Soon we discovered that he was also very articulate and highly intelligent. In short, he no more fit our stereotype of a hired killer than Eldon Hoke himself had when we met him seven years earlier. By the time Wrench finished telling his story, however, we weren't so sure.

Wrench first met Eldon Hoke in 1992, when Mentors bassist Steve Broy (a.k.a. Dr. Heathen Scum) graduated from college and moved to Riverside to start a job as an engineer: "I was a musician myself, and so Heathen Scum and Duce and I would hang out and jam together at the Mentors Ranch, which was the name of the house that Dr. Scum bought in Riverside," Wrench says. "It wasn't really a ranch, but there was some land and some animals there, so we called it that. Anyways, we all became pretty good friends. Duce was basically homeless, so when he didn't have anything going on in L.A., he would come up to Riverside and crash at the ranch."

Wrench's eponymously named band didn't form until two years after Hoke's death. Before that, he said, he spent most of his time practicing his martial arts: "That's my weapon of choice. I have a collection of guns, combat arms, stuff like that. But I prefer to use my hands." Since the band was formed in 1999, they have produced three albums on Wrench's own label, Devil Vision Records, but his music, he says, doesn't pay the rent: "We press about 2,500 copies of each album, but we end up giving most of those away."

Odd jobs here and there, along with the odd gig, get him through the month.

What's with the satanic imagery? we ask.

"That's just satire in the great tradition of El Duce himself," he explains. "We're not satanists or anything like that. We just like to stir things up with our music."

We decide to cut to the chase. Was Kurt Cobain's death a murder or suicide?

"Suicide all the way."

Why?

"Because I'm not going to incriminate myself. You see, the perfect assassinations always look like suicides. A good assassin would be like a military sniper. They know the game, they're not fucked-up by ego. They're cold and calculating. Look at Robert Blake: he was a dumbass. Look at Phil Spector. If you're going to be in that game, I think you have to have a little bit of intelligence. Some people buy into what they think it takes to kill somebody, which I don't think is that big a deal or difficult to do. They're just not smart about it; they're not realistic about what will happen when somebody ends up dead."

Did you ever meet Courtney?

"I never met Courtney. [Laughs] Why don't you ask her if she ever met me? That's a better question. I think Courtney Love is the victim of some bad publicity on this one. I don't think she's going to have any problems because the great thing is that the story sounds so far-fetched that it sounds totally unbelievable. My thing about Courtney Love is that I think she's being wrongly accused. I don't have any problem with her whatsoever and I don't think she has a problem with me. But you know, to you or me fifty thousand dollars isn't a lot of money, but to a guy like El Duce, who thinks that if you have five dollars you're rich, it would be a pretty appealing offer. But I don't think he could ever do it. As far as hitting up

Duce to knock somebody off, I don't think anybody would think that he would do it. But logically, he knows a lot of people in the kind of guttery underground of L.A. He would probably know someone. So that would probably be the inclination, that would probably be the strategy if Courtney actually indeed approached him. . . . Duce wasn't a professional hit man. I don't think he would have the intestinal fortitude to pull that off. [Laughs]"

Again, we ask Wrench why Hoke would have named him as Kurt's killer if he wasn't involved. We also want to know exactly when he found out that he had been named.

"That was somewhat problematic. I found out about Duce naming me from a guy named Lomas [Divine Brown's pimp], who's an infamous crackhead. He called me up. When I found out that Duce named me in the documentary, it kind of concerned me a bit, so I went over and talked to him about it. After I found out I was named in the *Kurt and Courtney* movie—I mean, what a horrible thing to say—I said, 'Hey, Duce, what the hell's up?' I wasn't very happy about Duce naming me as Cobain's killer. I wasn't too pleased with that. We had little arguments back and forth. He apologizes. He didn't mean to do it, things like that."

Why did he say he named you?

"He didn't tell me anything in particular. He just said it was accidental."

If it's not true, why would he say it?

"Well, you could argue the fact that he wasn't even talking about me because he doesn't mention my last name, he just says, 'Allen.' It could be any Allen."

What happened next?

"Well, Duce being a total out-of-control alcoholic, he asked me for a ride to the liquor store. I drop him off at the liquor store around eight P.M. and then I took off. I never saw him again. Then I heard that he wandered into the path of a train."

Wrench had referred to Hoke's death as a suicide several times in the course of the conversation. We ask him whether he thinks Hoke was suicidal.

"He seemed fairly distraught when I dropped him off," Wrench says. He bursts into a sudden maniacal laugh.

What was it that had made him so distraught?

"I think it was naming me in the *Kurt and Courtney* movie. I was fairly pissed off."

Were things OK between you by the time you dropped him off at the liquor store? Had you forgiven him?

"After I got home and read the newspapers the next day, it was OK," he says, laughing. "Problem solved."

From the first, Wrench had engaged in this kind of creepy denial-cum-admission—a coy wink-and-a-nod display where everything was verbalized except the "I did it." For some reason, he seemed to *want* us to believe that he had killed Kurt Cobain and Eldon Hoke. We still weren't buying it. On the phone, he had admitted to us off the record that he was involved in Cobain's death. Later, when we asked him on the record why he had told us this, he said he had been simply playing with our heads. Ultimately, we decided his near admission of responsibility in their deaths seemed just the type of prank this grand Guignolesque rocker would pull.

What was behind his bravado? To test his opportunism, we ask him how much money he wants to appear in our documentary. "I'm not motivated by money; you can buy me a case of Pabst," he replies. When he gets up to go to the bathroom, we consult with our "bodyguard." It seems we had all come to the same conclusion: Wrench was probably acting this way to gain notoriety for his band.

When he returns to the table, Wrench offers to take us outside and show us the exact location where Hoke had "bought it." The restaurant is in a little strip mall situated in an industrial section of Riverside, just off the highway. As we exit the Spunky Steer, he points left to a small row of stores about fifty yards west, on the other side of the mall exit: "That's where the liquor store used to be. That's where I dropped Duce off that night."

He then points to the tracks directly across a small field from the restaurant: "Say there was something underhanded going on here. Say there's an investigating officer who suspects he was murdered. He would say, 'Fuck, look at this parking lot. There would be a million witnesses.' But if you come with me, I'll show you something. Let's walk up here." He leads us about thirty-five yards east, past some trees onto the field next to the tracks. "Here's a nice industrial area. With the noise of cars passing by on the highway, you wouldn't hear any signs of a struggle." We arrive at a section of the tracks. "That's the spot. This is where El Duce committed suicide. You see, if you're up there at the intersection waiting for the light to change, you can't see us. On the other side, it's all industrial. A nice little spot."

He resumes where he left off inside, hinting strongly that Hoke's death resulted from foul play: "You see, if it had happened at the lights up there at the crossing, there might have been witnesses to see what happened. But over here at night, nobody could have seen it. The thing about train wrecks is that they kind of make it difficult for a forensic investigation. It's not like you have a body to examine. They can find no signs of a struggle. A lot of times when you're hit by a train, they have to take a trash bag to gather the pieces because there's nothing left of the fucking body. Then they call the fire department to hose off the train because there's nothing left but fucking juice. Let's say you have this alcoholic bum who gets hit by a train, who's sleeping by the tracks drunk and just stumbles in front of it. Who's going to ask questions? An investigator who's investigating the death, they look at the blood alcohol level; there's nothing left of the body, but they can take a blood sample from the tracks and still measure his blood alcohol level. An accident investigator would look at this, and everything would point to an accident."

We are standing at least eighty-five yards from the liquor store where Wrench claims he dropped Hoke off that night. Between the store and this spot, there is an intersection and railroad crossing. If Hoke had been heading home from the liquor store, it stands to reason that he would have crossed the tracks at the intersection. We ask Wrench why he would have wandered an additional fifty-five yards past where, once over the tracks, he would have had to cross a busy highway.

He has a ready explanation: "You have to remember that as a homeless person you're not going to have the same mind-set, where you say, 'Hey, I have to get home because my fucking wife or girlfriend is waiting for me.' The homeless lifestyle isn't really— actually, Duce wasn't really homeless; I think of him more as a hobo, kind of traveling, checking out the world. Here's what people don't understand. I've walked out of clubs a hundred times with Duce and we can't find our car and he's like, 'Oh cool, let's get a cardboard box and sleep right here.' That was his mentality. That's the beauty of it. Nobody will ever know if his death was an accident, suicide or murder."

Wrench's insinuations are starting to sound like the boastings of a severely attention-starved child. Whatever shock value they once achieved has now palled. We tell him straight-out that we don't believe he killed Kurt Cobain or Eldon Hoke, but that we suspect he enjoys the fact that people think he did. He grins and says nothing.

The interview finished, we accompany him to his car. There, in the parking lot behind the Spunky Steer, is a white, late-model luxury Lexus. The three of us look at the car, stunned at the incongruous sight. Other than the fact that the Lexus sells for almost $60,000, it also happens to be Courtney Love's favorite model of car—the automobile she demanded Kurt buy her in March 1994. Wrench climbs in, waves good-bye, and drives away, taking our certainties about the case with him.

* * *

Eldon Hoke began his last day on this planet the way he began any other day: by getting drunk. The night before, the Mentors had played a gig at Al's Bar in Los Angeles. "Duce had been more or less sober for four days before the gig," Mentors bassist Steve Broy recalls. "He would go into a kind of maintenance level before he performed, so that he'd be able to function onstage. He was an alcoholic, so he had to maintain a minimum level of booze in his system, but he was pretty straight. Then, as we were setting up our equipment before the show, somebody offers him a drink, and that was it, he just started drinking. He was superhammered that night to the point where the gig was a complete disaster. We got home at four or five in the morning. I crashed and then around eight A.M., I get woken up by Duce playing loud music. "

After Broy told him to turn it down, Hoke went out to look for more alcohol. He returned an hour later with a twelve-pack of 32-ounce King Cobras, which he drank throughout the day.

Broy replays the chain of events that led to his friend's death: "What happened was that I was asleep in the other room. I woke up in the afternoon, and Duce was gone. Allen [Wrench] came by and said there was a street fair going on in Riverside that day, so we went to the street fair and came back around five or six P.M., and Duce was there. He was starting a barbecue in the backyard, and he was superloaded. I was just so tired, I didn't have the time to deal with this superdrunk guy. So I just went in and hit the sack immediately, leaving them outside. When I woke up an hour later or whatever, I saw them pulling out in Allen's truck. Then I woke up the next morning, and Duce wasn't there. So I assumed he was over at Allen's because lots of times that's what would happen. He'd go over there and hang out at Allen's house. So around noon, the coroner came over to notify me as to what had happened, that he had been hit on the train tracks the evening before. I was kind of confused because I had it in my head that he had gone over to

Allen's house, and I said, Hmmm, there's no train tracks over there. I didn't realize that what had happened is that Allen had dropped him off at the store."

Does he believe that Wrench might have had something to do with Hoke's death?

"No way," he says. "He better not have. Duce was my friend. I think it was probably an accident." Although still a member of the Mentors, Broy now plays bass in Kill Allen Wrench and considers himself Wrench's friend. We ask whether he thinks Wrench could have killed Kurt Cobain.

"That's another question," he says. "I don't really want to comment on that."

We ask him what Hoke had told him about Courtney's $50,000 offer. Did he believe the story?

"Naw. Why would anybody approach somebody like Duce and ask him to kill their husband? You just had to look at him to realize that he's not your man. He was always drunk."

Was he equally pathetic in the '80s when Courtney was acquainted with him?

"That's a good point," he replies. "He definitely deteriorated in the last few years of his life. When she knew him, he was a lot more together. Maybe Courtney didn't realize how bad he had become. I don't know what to believe. He definitely hobnobbed with a lot of celebrities. Once he came back to the house and said, 'You'll never believe who I met and who I was hanging out with all night.' I said, 'Who?' He says, 'Tom Petty.' I wouldn't say he was a chronic liar or anything like that, but he could tell a tall tale here and there, so I wasn't buying that story for a second. Then a few days later, he starts elaborating on the story and says, 'We're good friends,' and I said, 'Yeah, right.' Then I found out it was completely true. Tom Petty comes over, and sure enough they're friends."

We do some sniffing around Riverside and find a man named

Chris Potter, who claims to know Allen Wrench from the local bar scene. He says he has heard "rumors" of Wrench's involvement in Cobain's death.

"Who the hell knows if it's true or not?" says Potter. "A few years ago, he starts driving around in this Corvette and waving around a lot of money. Then, all of a sudden, he has all this recording equipment, and he's driving around in a Lexus and a truck. He never used to have a dime to his name. I don't know where he got the money to buy that stuff. It's not from his music, I'll tell you that much."

Indeed, not long after Hoke's death, Wrench started a band, outfitted his house with $100,000 in sophisticated analog recording equipment—which can probably be bought used for about $25,000—and recorded his band's debut CD, *My Bitch Is a Junky*.

By the time we returned to Canada, we were more confused than ever. Though we still found the story of Wrench's involvement far-fetched, there had been enough coincidences in the case to sway even the most skeptical observer. Most puzzling of all was the new wealth Wrench seemed to have suddenly acquired. Where did he get it? We decide to call him up and ask.

The tone of his response was by now familiar, as was his demonic laugh: "I can make fifty grand go a long way," he declares.

12

It is February 2002, and Courtney has consented to appear on her friend Carrie Fisher's TV talk show, *Conversations from the Edge*, to talk about her life and career. Midway through the taping, they have already touched on a wide range of subjects—Courtney's childhood, her parents, her daughter, her films. But one topic has been conspicuously avoided, and now Fisher is determined to raise it: "So, how did you meet Kurt? We have never talked about that."

Courtney's answer is revealing. "Let's not. I wish I'd never married him," she replies.

Indeed, in the years since her husband's death, Courtney had skillfully emerged from Kurt's shadow and established a distinct persona of her own, carving out a successful music and film career while shedding—at least temporarily—much of the bad-girl image that Americans had come to love and loathe. The transformation from thrift-shop rags to Versace and from junkie grunge musician to movie star was accomplished so seamlessly that it's easy to see why she once described herself as a "chameleon press whore." In late 1994, while still receiving favorable national attention as the tragic widow of a rock icon, she can be heard gloating to Tom Grant on tape about how the national media are "falling at my footsteps wanting to interview me. I have the power," Courtney exults.

By 1995, she had become, as Barbara Walters called her, "one of the ten most fascinating people" in America. Her mainstream acceptance had involved lying about her drug use on Walters's show, but no one could deny that she had pulled off the heady transformation into a celebrity that all America could hail.

The transformation didn't happen overnight. In November 1994, Courtney was spotted wearing a floor-length slip, running barefoot after a woman on L.A.'s Sunset Boulevard and yelling, "I'm gonna kill you!" The woman was indie singer Mary Lou Lord, one of Kurt's ex-girlfriends, who had shown up at an after-hours party Courtney was attending. Courtney had shoved her, told her to "get your ass out of here" and then taken up the chase. When asked about the incident later, Courtney told *Spin* magazine, "There are five people in this world that, if I ever run into, I will fucking kill and she is definitely one of them." Two years earlier, while Kurt was alive, Courtney had phoned Lord and threatened, "I'm gonna cut your head off and shove it up your ass—and Kurt's gonna throw you in the oven." Reportedly, Courtney's wrath had been prompted by a profile of Lord in the *Boston Phoenix*, which mentioned in passing that she had once dated Kurt. After it appeared, the newspaper received two faxed letters from Kurt calling Lord a "creepy girl" and claiming that he couldn't even remember her name or her face. According to the paper's former editor, Brett Milano, the letters were signed by Kurt but written in Courtney's handwriting.

"I wouldn't say that Courtney's insanely jealous," recalls Lord of the incident. "She's just insane. I have no idea if she killed Kurt, but I think she's capable of something like that. There was a time that I was truly afraid that she was going to kill me."

In January 1995, Courtney was arrested after an air rage incident on a Qantas airplane during Hole's tour of Australia and New Zealand. After a flight attendant asked her to calm down, an appar-

ently drunk Courtney was heard yelling, "I'm allowed to do whatever the fuck I want! Do you know who I am?"

A few months later, on the first date of the 1995 Lollapalooza
tour, Hole had just finished their set when Courtney spotted Bikini
Kill's Kathleen Hanna heading backstage with the members of
Sonic Youth. Hanna had been a good friend of Kurt's in Olympia,
and it had long been rumored that they had had an affair. As Sonic
Youth took the stage, Courtney marched up to Hanna and punched
her in the face. When assault charges were filed, Courtney claimed
that Hanna had asked her, "Where's the baby? In a closet with an
IV?" but witnesses denied that Hanna had provoked her in any way.
Courtney then claimed that Hanna was "Kurt's worst enemy in the
world" and that she had done only what he would have wanted.
Like Lord, Hanna's only sin seems to have been her indulgence in a
long-gone romantic episode with Kurt. Courtney later pleaded
guilty in a Washington State courtroom to assault and was handed
a one-year suspended sentence, ordered to refrain from violent acts
and forced to take anger management classes. Outside the courtroom, she told reporters, "The judge said I can't punch her in
Grant County, but I can clock her again in Seattle."

Yet incidents like these barely found their way into the mainstream media, thanks to a carefully orchestrated campaign by
Courtney's PR agency, PMK, headed by the queen of celebrity
publicists, Pat Kingsley, who boasted a roster of clients including
Tom Cruise, Al Pacino, Jodie Foster and Tom Hanks. Before long,
any reporter who wished to interview Courtney or her band was
first required to sign a twelve-page agreement not to ask about the
murder theories, Courtney's drug use and a number of other con-
tentious issues from her past. Courtney once briefly stormed off
the set of the *Today* show, on which she was appearing to promote
her movie *The People vs. Larry Flynt*, when the interviewer asked
about her past drug use. "Where are you going with this?" snapped

Courtney. "I'm not going to talk about this on the *Today* show, I'm just not. It's not a demographic that I feel like talking about this."

But to attribute Courtney's success solely to her genius for media manipulation would be a mistake. Many consider Hole's *Live Through This*—named album of the year in *Rolling Stone's* 1994 readers' poll—a masterpiece. Her tour de force performance in *The People vs. Larry Flynt* earned her a Golden Globe nomination. To her vehement denials, Courtney bashers insisted that it was Kurt who had written the distinctive musical bridges on *Live Through This*, and recently surfaced evidence from unreleased studio recordings would seem to prove he did play a significant role in the recording. The charges became more pointed when Billy Corgan claimed to have written a good portion of the songs on her next album, *Celebrity Skin*, and publicly complained when Courtney attempted to take credit. As for her brilliant performance as Althea Flynt, skeptics pointed out that she was simply portraying an out-of-control junkie—hardly an acting stretch for Courtney. Nevertheless, the lyrics on both albums—which were indisputably written by Courtney—demonstrate genuine talent, and she more than holds her own in the films she has starred in post–*Larry Flynt*.

But, while mainstream America appeared to be enjoying a love affair with the new Courtney, her old peers had a decidedly different opinion. Seattle's original grunge band, Mudhoney, recorded a song, "Into Yer Schtik," clearly directed at her. It contained the lyrics "Why don't you blow your brains out too?" In his 1995 song "I'll Stick Around," off the first album Dave Grohl recorded with his new band, Foo Fighters, he sings, "How could it be / I'm the only one who sees your rehearsed insanity / I've been around all the pawns you've gagged and bound."

Her profile has been lower of late, thanks to a string of forgettable movies and the relative commercial failure of *Celebrity Skin*. But in 2001, Courtney resurfaced as the target of a very bitter, and very public, legal feud with the surviving members of Nirvana over Kurt's musical legacy. In June, Courtney sued Grohl and Novoselic to block the release of a proposed box set of unreleased Nirvana music, which was to come out on the tenth anniversary of the release of *Nevermind*. The lawsuit was designed to release her from the partnership she entered into with Krist and Dave following Kurt's death. Six months later, they countersued, claiming in Washington Superior Court that Courtney's legal action was "really about securing more money to support Love's prima donna lifestyle. In her professional dealings, Love is irrational, mercurial, self-centered, unmanageable, inconsistent and unpredictable. . . . In truth, her actions are only about the revitalization of her career motivated solely by her blind self-interest. . . . She is using Nirvana's music as a bargaining chip to increase leverage for her personal gain, without any regard for the Nirvana legacy. Our music is just a pawn in her endless legal battles and her obsessive need for publicity and attention." Four months later, Dave and Krist—claiming Courtney was "incapacitated"—filed a court motion asking that she be forced to undergo a mental examination.

The soap opera intensified when Kurt's mother issued a statement supporting Courtney and characterizing Grohl and Novoselic as "liars and crooks." "I am shocked and disgusted at the behavior of Krist Novoselic, David Grohl and their 'managers' and lawyers," Wendy wrote. "I know that Nirvana was never a partnership of any sort. I know that in the last year of his life, my son despised his bandmates and told me many times he no longer wanted to play with them or have anything to do with them. . . . Krist Novoselic and Dave Grohl never wrote a Nirvana song in their lives. For them to have formed an equal partnership is ridiculous beyond comprehension."

Few believed Wendy had written the words in the statement. According to Leland Cobain, Courtney bought Wendy a very expensive house a few years ago and provided her with a generous allowance. "I don't know what she has on Courtney, but it must be something for her to give Wendy all that money," says Leland. "I know that Kurt wouldn't have wanted that. His mother didn't want anything to do with him until he became famous."

Whatever goodwill once existed between Courtney and Wendy, however, appears to have finally dissipated after a widely publicized incident in Los Angeles in fall 2003 in which Courtney, apparently under the influence of drugs, was arrested by Beverly Hills police after she tried to kick in the door of her manager and ex-boyfriend James Barber while he was inside his house in bed with Courtney's former assistant. After her release on bail, she was arrested again hours later, this time on felony drug charges, when paramedics were summoned to her home, where Courtney had reportedly overdosed on the drug Oxycontin, a synthetic form of morphine commonly referred to as "hillbilly heroin." When it was reported that the overdose had taken place in the presence of Frances Bean, the L.A. County Department of Children and Family Services marched into Frances's school and took the eleven-year-old girl into protective custody, charging Courtney with "abandonment" of her child. The move set off a bitter custody battle between Courtney and Wendy, during which the two came to blows outside an L.A. courthouse. "Wendy went nuts," Courtney told the New York *Daily News*, "so I slapped her like a four-year-old."

Dave and Krist eventually settled their lawsuit with Courtney out of court, but the legal battles and her own dwindling commercial fortunes have stretched her financial resources thin. Since half of Kurt's royalties are held for Frances Bean in escrow, Courtney was obliged to look a little farther afield for a source of funds. In early 2002, she sold Kurt's unpublished diaries to Riverhead books for a reported advance of $4.5 million. A few months later, his more than twenty notebooks, full of private writings, doodles, drawings and song lyrics, were released in the form of a coffee-table book called *Journals* and became an immediate worldwide bestseller.

The publication of *Journals*, however, was not universally celebrated. One reviewer called it an act of "obscene grave robbery," while another urged a boycott because "every unsold copy gives publishers yet another reason why something as necrophilic as this should not be done again."

Ironically, *Journals* itself contains a hint at how Kurt might have felt about its publication. In one 1992 entry, he wrote:

> Within the months between October 1991 through December 92, I have had four notebooks filled with two years worth of poetry and personal writing stolen. . . . The most violating thing I've felt this year is not the media exaggerations or the catty gossip, but the rape of my personal thoughts. Ripped out of pages from my stay in hospitals and airplane rides, hotel stays, etc. I feel compelled to say "Fuck you Fuck you to those of you who have absolutely no regard for me as a person. You have raped me harder than you'll ever know."

*   *   *

As the tenth anniversary of Kurt's death approaches, the doubts over how he died show no signs of receding. If anything, they are stronger than ever. Kurt died just as the Internet was starting to take hold, and there are now countless websites and online forums devoted exclusively to the murder theory. Neither has Hollywood ignored it. In October 2002, NBC's *Law & Order*, known for presenting cases "ripped from the headlines," broadcast an episode clearly based on the Cobain murder theory. It portrays an ambitious but widely hated female rocker whose rock star husband had apparently committed suicide sometime before. When her own father accuses her of killing her husband and a diligent P.I. works to have the case reopened, her husband's death is found to be a murder.

Tom Grant is encouraged by such mainstream acceptance of the murder theory. Although he no longer works full-time as a private investigator, this "grunge world Inspector Javert," as one newspaper called him, continues to devote considerable time and energy to the Cobain case. He has vowed to pursue his investigation for another ten years if necessary, until "justice is done."

It is the copycat suicides that push Grant the hardest. Learning of the double suicide of two French schoolgirls in 1997 has been particularly difficult, he says. Aged only twelve and thirteen, the girls, Valentine and Aurelie, left a note saying they were "in love with Kurt" before shooting themselves in the head with a rifle. At the time of Kurt's death, they would have been only nine and ten years old. "They probably didn't even know who Kurt was at that age," says Grant. "As the father of three grown daughters, this waste of precious life is especially disturbing to me. Nirvana is gaining new fans every day. Kids continue to kill themselves because they *think* that's what Kurt did." A number of new copycat suicides have been reported in recent years, and some crisis clinics reported a sharp increase in teen depression after the release of the *Journals* in 2002.

In the face of the allegations against her, Courtney has maintained an unbroken silence. Shortly before the publication of our first book, a private investigator in Courtney's employ named Jack Palladino showed up in Ian Halperin's backyard and asked to see the manuscript. Palladino's impressive roster of clients included Patty Hearst, Snoop Dogg, and Bill Clinton's 1992 presidential campaign, for which he had been hired to "contain the bimbo eruptions." Over lunch, Palladino told Halperin, "You're a musician and I have a lot of contacts in the music industry. I can help you out if you help me out." He was carrying a thick file containing a complete dossier on our personal and professional lives. Halperin told Palladino our price for a glimpse of the manuscript: an interview with Courtney Love to get her side of the story. These were serious allegations that had been leveled against her, and it had always troubled us that we could not obtain Courtney's version of the events surrounding Kurt's death. "That will never happen," Palladino declared. We promised him we would not write about Eldon Hoke's allegations if he could provide any evidence proving that Courtney Love wasn't in Los Angeles at the time of the alleged $50,000 offer. He never got back to us. Later, a week before our publication date, Palladino showed up at the publisher's office demanding to see the manuscript. He was refused and quickly escorted out of the building.

Frances Bean turns twelve in 2004 and attends an exclusive private school in Los Angeles. Courtney told *US Weekly* that she didn't explain Kurt's suicide to her daughter until she was seven. Frances's passion, she revealed, is horses: "She's an amazing rider. Her trainer thinks she can go to the Olympics."

Michael "Cali" Dewitt was working for a time at Geffen Records, but, still plagued by drug problems, he appears now to have dropped out of sight.

Kurt's bandmates have never publicly commented on the murder theories. In a 1998 interview with Howard Stern, Dave Grohl was asked about the theories, but he refused to comment. Our own sources, however, tell us that neither he nor Krist give Grant's theory much credence. Hank Harrison claims to have an e-mail Krist sent him in 1994 declaring that "Kurt died like Trotsky," referring to the Russian revolutionary who was murdered in Mexico in 1940 by a Stalinist agent. "I understood what he meant," Harrison says.

It is unclear whether Rosemary Carroll, now senior partner in a new law firm in New York, continues to officially represent Courtney in any capacity. In 1995, shortly after Tom Grant publicly revealed Carroll's doubts about the suicide, Courtney revoked her status as Frances Bean's godmother and replaced her with Drew Barrymore.

Dylan Carlson still lives in Seattle, where he continues to play with his band, Earth. He does not believe Kurt was murdered.

Allen Wrench has refused our request to submit to a polygraph.

Caitlin Moore left Seattle and dropped out of sight shortly after Kurt's death.

Hank Harrison is currently seeking a publisher for his biography of Kurt.

* * *

When we failed to name Courtney as Kurt's killer in our first book, some murder theorists thought it was because we feared a lawsuit. The fact is that we just could not find a smoking gun directly linking Courtney Love to the crime. Courtney has never sued Tom Grant or anybody else for publicly accusing her of murder. Nor has she ever sued a single media outlet for airing the allegations. It is unlikely she will ever do so. Grant believes the knowledge that she would have to testify under oath prevents her from taking legal action. He says he would welcome a lawsuit. For our part, if we located the evidence to prove that she had her husband killed, no legal threat could prevent us from making it public.

Now, as we listen to the hours of Grant's recordings documenting the events of April 1994, Courtney does not come off well. Over the course of our listening, she alternately schemes, admits to lies and elaborate ruses, makes inexplicable requests and discusses the ins and outs of bending this or that truth to her needs. She appears to be frantically trying to locate her husband but always keeps a calculating eye on how the circumstances might affect her record sales. She is a weepy, one-woman antidrug crusade one moment and audibly strung out on drugs the next; alternately cloyingly solicitous when speaking of her missing husband and vowing furiously to wring every last dime from him; arrogant at times and then jarringly pious. Yet we did not hear a single iota of evidence on these tapes directly implicating her in Kurt's death or Kristen's overdose.

According to credible medical and law enforcement experts, the forensic evidence in the case is clearly strong enough to at least change the verdict from "suicide" to "undetermined." This would be the first step toward reopening the investigation, one that seems to have been characterized by indifference from the start. There is no question, moreover, that the circumstantial evidence is damning. Why did Courtney file two separate false police reports, and why did she apparently wait more than two hours before calling an ambulance after Kurt overdosed in Rome? These actions are suspicious, to say the least. It seems clear that at the time of his death, Kurt was determined to start a new life without Courtney. We may never know for whom he bought that second airplane ticket, whether it was for a new love, as Courtney believed, or not. But it is clear Kurt wanted out, literally and legally. Their prenuptial agreement, which ensured she would not have access to his millions if he divorced her, certainly provides a motive for the crime. At the very least, Courtney needs to answer some questions—questions that were never asked at the time of Kurt's death.

The sheer volume of people who believe Courtney had her husband killed, however, does not make it true. Perhaps she is simply the victim of several unfortunate coincidences. Yet only one person has the power to clear her name, and that person is Courtney Love.

* * *

In early 1995, Courtney made a reproachful phone call to Tom Grant while touring New Zealand with her band. It came just after

Grant had accused her of involvement in her husband's death on the nationally syndicated Tom Leykis radio show. For Grant, the truth lay in the medical examiner's report, available exclusively to Kurt's widow. Only the actual report could deny the controversial toxicological evidence that had already been leaked to the media. In addition, the photos it contained could rule out the possibility of murder. Providing this report, Grant tells Courtney on the phone, would end his doubts.

"Here's what can bring this to a real quick end and solve all your problems—if I had a copy of the coroner's report and if Cali comes down for a polygraph," Grant tells her. "It's as simple as that. You just have to make a phone call and it's done."

"So, let me get this straight," Courtney responds. "You want me to call up Nikolas [Hartshorne] and get the coroner's report? Am I entitled to that?"

"Of course," Grant replies. "It's yours. You just have to ask for it."

"OK. I'll be back on the sixteenth, and I'll get it from Nikolas," she assures him. "I will give it to you from my hand to your hand. I promise. You're going to owe me a big fucking apology when this is over."

"You'll get it," he responds. "Believe me."

Grant never heard from her again.

For the sake of Kurt, and for the sake of the many fans who may still be tempted to follow what they believe was his path, it's time for Courtney Love to keep her promise.

To **BoddAH** [promised]

Speaking from the tongue of an experienced simpleton who obviously would rather be an emasculated, infantile complainee. This note should be pretty easy to understand. All the warnings from the punk rock 101 courses over the years, since my first introduction to the, shall we say, ethics involved with independence and the embracement of your community has proven to be very true. I haven't felt the excitement of listening to as well as creating music along with reading and writing for too many years now. I feel guilty beyond words about these things. For example when we're backstage and the lights go out and the manic roar of the crowd begins it doesn't affect me the way in which it did for Freddie Mercury who seemed to love, relish in the love and adoration from the crowd, which is something I totally admire and envy. The fact is, I can't fool you, any one of you. It simply isn't fair to you or me. The worst crime I can think of would be to rip people off by faking it and pretending as if I'm having 100% fun. Sometimes I feel as if I should have a punch in time clock before I walk out on stage. I've tried everything within my power to appreciate it (and I do, God, believe me I do, but it's not enough). I appreciate the fact that I and we have affected and entertained a lot of people. I must be one of those narcissists who only appreciate things when they're gone. I'm too sensitive. I need to be slightly numb in order to regain the enthusiasm I once had as a child. On our last 3 tours I've had a much better appreciation for all the people I've known personally and as fans of our music, but I still can't get over the frustration, the guilt and empathy I have for everyone. There's good in all of us and I think I simply love people too much, so much that it makes me feel too fucking sad. The sad little, sensitive, unappreciative, pisces, Jesus man! Why don't you just enjoy it? I don't know! I have a goddess of a wife who sweats ambition and empathy and a daughter who reminds me too much of what I used to be. Full of love and joy, kissing every person she meets because everyone is good and will do her no harm. And that terrifies me to the point to where I can barely function. I can't stand the thought of Frances becoming the miserable, self destructive, death rocker that I've become. I have it good, very good, and I'm grateful, but since the age of seven I've become hateful towards all humans in general, only because it seems so easy for people to get along and have empathy. Empathy! Only because I love and feel sorry for people too much I guess. Thank you all from the pit of my burning nauseous stomach for your letters and concern during the past years. I'm too much of an erratic, moody, baby! I don't have the passion anymore and so remember, it's better to burn out than to fade away.

Peace, love, Empathy. Kurt Cobain

Frances and Courtney, I'll be at your altar.

Please keep going Courtney,

for Frances
for her life which will be so much happier
without me. I LOVE YOU I LOVE YOU!

A NOTE ABOUT SOURCES

This book draws upon a wide variety of primary sources, including hundreds of personal interviews with friends and acquaintances of Kurt and Courtney, conducted between 1994 and 2003; Seattle Police Department records acquired under State of Washington Freedom of Information laws; State of California police records; and Tom Grant's personal case tapes and files.

Roger Lewis's essay, "Dead Men Don't Pull Triggers," and Lewis's extensive medical and forensic research—much of which we expanded on in this book—were a rich source of information for chapter four, as was the forensic data provided to us by Colorado deputy coroner Denise Marshall.

The book *Cobain* by the editors of *Rolling Stone* was a valuable source of interviews with Kurt and Courtney over the years.

We are particularly indebted to Charles Cross's biography, *Heavier Than Heaven*. Because his book had the tacit authorization of Courtney Love, Cross was able to interview some of the key players who refused to talk with us, and we drew on a number of his interviews in our own research.

ACKNOWLEDGMENTS

During the nine years we have pursued this case, we have been assisted by a wide array of individuals determined to help us get to the truth. Among these are many who, understandably, asked that their names not be used, including members of the Seattle Police Department, friends of Kurt and Courtney, and others committed to justice for Kurt Cobain and Kristen Pfaff.

We are especially grateful to our agent, Luke Janklow, for believing in us from the get-go and for his confidence that a second book about this case would not be redundant. It was a pleasure working with our editor, Luke Dempsey, at Atria/Simon & Schuster, who made the editing experience an extremely positive one and whose patience, perspective and insight were invaluable.

Special thanks to Jacquie Charlton and Phyllis Bailey for reading and proofing the manuscript in progress, and for editing and offering sage advice as we went along.

And sincere thanks to the following: Leland Cobain, Alice Wheeler, Gillian Gaar, Roger Lewis, Lori Clermont, Dan Sears, Norm Pfaff, Dave Reed, Ethel Reed, Janet and Jason Pfaff, Dan DiJulio, Calvin Johnson, Shawn Scallen, CKCU-FM, Arlene Bynon, Todd Shapiro, Stuart Nulman, Michael Landsberg, Jeff Marek, Bob Mackowycz, Susan Rabiner, Marco Collins, Vernon

288 Geberth, Joel and Dione Teitelbaum, Jaime Roskies, Edward Gelb, Jackie Collins, Alicia Brooks, Pat Dwyer, Willow James, Felicia Sinusa, Michael Lewin, Rizia Moreira, Brenda and Marvin Luxenberg, Brian Rishwain, Kathy Hewitt, Humble and Fred, Mary Lou Lord, Maury Povich, Nick Broomfield, Max Jarrell, Experience Music Project, Jean-Pierre Ouesset, Neil Bakshi, Rachel Hauraney, Allan Katz, Fiona York, Joyce MacPhee, Lee Charlton, University of Toronto medical and law libraries, Aberdeen Public Library, Aberdeen Historical Society, Ted Nugent, Morag York, Hank Harrison, Anna Woolverston of Sub Pop, Ariel Lemercier, Steve Shein, Barbara Davidson, Brenda Plant, Denise Sheppard, Joachim Breuer, Duff Wilson and Diedtra Henderson of the *Seattle Times*, John Oakley, Peter Cleary, Megan Bochner, Karen Golden, Charlotte Golden, Mark Connelly, Dylan Carlson, Peter Anthony Holder, Greg Harris, Jane Hawtin, Mike Merritt, MTV, Scott Maier, Susan Varga, Nick Regush, Audi Gozlan, Julius Grey, MOJO radio, the Seattle Public Library, Jimmy Soprano, David Nanasi, Lamont Shillinger, Clover Sky Walker Halperin, 1077 The End, Jennifer Walker, Santina Leuci, Diane Dimond, the Crocodile, Margaret van Nooten, Warren Mason, Victor Shiffman, Alastair Sutherland, Slim Moon, James Moreland, Daniel Harris, Heather Robb, Neil Kushner, George Stellos, Heather Grewar, France Desilets, Robert Fleming, Howard Stern, Hilary Richrod, Ian Maclean, CHOM-FM, Julien Feldman, Charles Peterson, Daniel Sanger, Esmond Choueke, Noah Lukeman, Denise Marshall, Rochelle Marshall, Paul Erickson, Nonny Rankin, Rozz Rezabek-Wright, Donnie Collier, Patrick Sanfacon, Jeremy Wallace, Mel Wallace, *The Rocket*, our entire families, and finally to Max Wallace's late grandmother, Anne Bailey, and Ian Halperin's late mother, Miriam Halperin, who instilled in us a strong commitment to justice.

INDEX

Printed in the United States
By Bookmasters